The Incorporated Self

Interdisciplinary Perspectives on Embodiment

Edited by
MICHAEL O'DONOVAN-ANDERSON

ROWMAN & LITTLEFIELD PUBLISHERS, INC.
Lanham • Boulder • New York • London

ROWMAN & LITTLEFIELD PUBLISHERS, INC.

Published in the United States of America
by Rowman & Littlefield Publishers, Inc.
4720 Boston Way, Lanham, Maryland 20706

3 Henrietta Street
London WC2E 8LU, England

British Cataloging in Publication Information Available

Library of Congress Cataloging-in-Publication Data

The incorporated self : interdisciplinary perspectives on embodiment /
[edited by] Michael O'Donovan-Anderson.
p.   cm.
Includes bibliographical references and index.
1. Dualism. 2. Mind and body. 3. Body, Human (Philosophy).
4. Descartes, René, 1596–1650. I. O'Donovan-Anderson, Michael.
B812.I53   1996   128—dc20   96–16151   CIP

ISBN 0–8476–8281–1 (cloth : alk. paper)
ISBN 0–8476–8282–x (pbk. : alk. paper)

Printed in the United States of America

♾™ The paper used in this publication meets the minimum requirements of American
National Standard for Information Sciences—Permanence of Paper for Printed Library
Materials, ANSI Z39.48–1984.

Contents

Acknowledgments

Many of the essays contained herein were originally presented at the "Theories and/of Embodiment" conference held at Stonehill College, in North Easton, Massachusetts in April 1995. Thanks are due to Richard Capobianco, Fr. James Feeley, Dean Louis Manzo, and Richard Velkley (among many others) for their moral and financial support. Most of the conference funding came from the Dean's Office, the Aquinas Fund, the Honors Program, and the Department of Philosophy; the conference would not have been possible without this support.

Michelle Harris and Dorothy Bradley, my editors at Rowman and Littlefield, have been helpful and patient as this long labor lengthened. A huge debt of gratitude is owed Julia Legas, without whose expert help with typesetting and indexing this book would never have gone to press. And, as always, I must thank Maeve O'Donovan-Anderson, without whom none of this would be possible.

Chapter 1 is a reprint of pages 300-313 (chapter 11) of *The Roots of Thinking*, by Maxine Sheets-Johnstone (Philadelphia: Temple University Press, 1990). Reprinted with permission of the publisher.

Chapter 6 is a reprint, revised by the author, of "Hamlet's Entrails" from *Strands Afar Remote*, edited by Avram Oz (Cranbury, NJ: Associated University Press, 1996). Reprinted with permission of the publisher.

Introduction

In Search of Real Bodies
Theories and/of Embodiment

Michael O'Donovan-Anderson

Perhaps it is the sly, protovillainous expression of Descartes's most famous portrait—just the sort of look we (Americans) expect from a European intellectual courtesan: a bit disdainful, a bit amused, and most certainly intellectually detached from the immediacy of his surroundings—which makes it so easy to saddle him with responsibility for the duality of mind and body which continues to haunt the theoretical humanities. In reality, of course, no such simple attribution is possible; Plato at least must share some credit for his discussion of the immateriality of the soul, and certainly Christian metaphysics in general deserves recognition for the tendency towards a devaluation of the body and concomitant identification of the self with spirit.[1] Descartes's own arguments for the separation of soul and body are part of a long legacy of dualistic thinking and should always be read against his insistence that although conceptually, and therefore ontologically, distinct, soul and body are nevertheless an empirical unity. But although we inherit this ontological separatism only *through* Descartes, it is fair to say that we inherit *from* his peculiar clarity a picture of the epistemic position of the self which powerfully serves that ontological claim: our only epistemic contact with the world is to be had through the senses.

Insofar as questions of the nature and reliability of our knowledge have long occupied center stage, not just in philosophy but also in the disciplines for which philosophy plays an important role, these two Cartesian tenets have placed the body at the center of the theoretical humanities. For what better way to encapsulate the nature of the knowing, feeling, moving self than as an "embodied mind"? Descartes's famous ontological realization that he is a thinking thing is conditioned and tempered by the epistemological admission that all he had accepted as most true had come to him through the senses. The mind is in contact with the world only in virtue of the body, which transforms the causal impacts of material reality into the interpretable data of sense. Yet it is precisely the body's intrusion between knowledge and reality which philosophical reason abhors, for it credits the mind with the certainty of access to eternal truths and charges the body with momentary and unreliable flux; the body is a source of betrayal, a cause of the senses' deception.[2]

The body is for Cartesian philosophy both necessary and unacceptable, and this ambivalence tends to drive mind and body apart in a way Descartes did not intend. For without the theological underpinnings of Descartes's entire system, it begins to look as if objectivity requires us to sift from the data of sense the contribution of the body, to divide, that is, the data from the sense. Although all knowledge originates in sensation, we are called upon to repudiate that origin as personal, unreliable, subjective; as a result the "knowing" self becomes more ghostly, while the physical body's attachment to mind becomes more tenuous. If the physical body, captured in the form of sensation, is not permitted to ground the possibility of knowledge, to provide the originary locus and fundamental content of that knowledge, then that which mediates between the sensation-causing world and the information-processing mind begins to be defined in abstraction from the body; for the body itself is a source of sensation, is part of the sensibly known world, and must, therefore, be mediated in its contact with the mind by that in which the sensation is caused (and by which the unreliable physicality of sense can be removed). In order to account for the mediation, and ensure the objective validity of information about the body itself, we need to posit as mediator something which has no sensible effect of its own; this something stands between, driving apart, mind and body, transforming the body into mere known. Descartes's epistemic commitments reinforce and exacerbate his ontological stance.

Curiously, although these two Cartesian tenets clearly support each other in this way, the sustained rebellion against ontological dualism has generally been waged under the banner of epistemic sensualism. The efforts to reunite (or more properly speaking unseparate) body and mind (or body and self) have quite often involved embracing the Cartesian notion that our senses are surface receptors of object-surfaces, leading directly to an epistemic shallowness whereby knowledge is limited to and/or grounded in the obvious. This by no means implies a history of complacence in the face of skepticism, but our collective refusal of that doctrine has not generally meant finding a way around it (as has been the strategy employed against dualism) but rather finding a way through it, moving forward to certainty with the epistemic premises of skepticism intact. Thus idealism effects the unseparation of mind and body by reducing *esse* to *percipi*, and thereby, the body to a mental phenomenon.[3] Likewise materialism, as a condition of its own unseparation, takes bodily surface irritations to exhaust our epistemic repertoire and through a cleverly deterministic physical biology roots in this premise its explanation of our successful negotiation of reality.[4] In both cases we trade knowledge for certainty, disregarding reality and thought in turn.

The case is not much different even for thinkers more interesting than such caricatures allow. Derridean textualism (and its many variations) is a case in point. Having accepted our epistemic limitation to the visible,[5] and yet recognizing our capacity to discern meaning in the apparent world, one can see the theoretical promise in understanding the world in terms of text, that paradigmatic instance of visible significance. The attraction is, of course, much increased after the "linguistic turn" in philosophy. According to textualism, the world, and especially the ever significant body, can be understood as essentially, quite literally, legible: the body is not merely, as Maxine Sheets-Johnstone puts it, a "semantic template" (and as such readable) but is in its essence a text.

What is interesting about this approach, what has proven both exciting and frustrating for the cultural theorists who appropriate this epistemic-cum-metaphysical stance, is its casting of the body not simply as readable, but as *written*; since the body as written has not the resources to validate the writing (*il n'y a rien au dehors du texte*), we are compelled to ask who dictates the plot and logic of the body's story. Here the problems which this valorization of the visible creates for the invisible come to the fore: for precisely what has disappeared from this account is the subject (who is *not* obvious)[6] and with it the authority to determine the roles in which the body is cast as (a) self. The more we insist on obviousness as the only sign of existence or importance, the more unreal (apparent, ghostly, phenomenal) become the things so exhibited.

To extend this metaphysic is to submerge a great deal, to repress the evidence of that which exists beyond the veil of sense, below the text; it is to deny that we are writing on, writing *over*, the already significant. But as we know, the repressed eternally returns, and the body has a way of bleeding through even the thickest of conceptual overlays.[7] It is important that this return always takes the form of the irrational, that which is illegible or, often, visible only as its opposite within enforced interpretive constraints. Thus does the hysteria of the Victorian Woman, which appears as confirmation and validation of the mantle of illogic and illegibility which she wears as social role in place of (to prevent) self-determination, in fact serve as the foremost sign of her psychosomatic articulacy. Likewise the emotions, which are expressed only by an embodied self,[8] nevertheless appear as the body's illogical subversion of the self and will.[9]

It is the nature of these appearances which makes possible the valorization of illogic as a strategy of resistance and freedom.[10] For insofar as the text is constituted by *logos*, then the self which remains submerged by that text can be recovered only as illogic, anti-*logos*. But to take the step, perhaps as a small rebellion, of identifying the self with the illogical submerged is just to make the materialist mistake of jettisoning thought[11] for the sake of unity.

This book is meant to herald a new way of thinking about these issues. Together, the essays gathered here aim to recover the notion of a fully embodied self by challenging *both* Cartesian tenets.[12] The hope is thereby to avoid the dualism of Descartes's ontology *and* the reductionism which results from his epistemology.

Maxine Sheets-Johnstone is perhaps most forceful of all the thinkers gathered here in calling for a philosophy of real bodies, a philosophy which understands thought to suffuse the whole of the living body, manifesting itself in actions far beyond speech production. Relying heavily on Darwin's observational biology, it is her explicit aim to give the body its due by insisting on the intelligence of behavior and the continuity of "animal" and "human" in all aspects of our lives. The body is, to paraphrase Evan Thompson's contribution, a mindful entity. Even the unlikely field of cognitive science, until recently apparently unconcerned with the mind's embodiment, has begun to recognize the validity of such insights. Thompson details the emerging focus within cognitive science on "situated action" (as opposed to concept manipulation or information processing) as a model for and sign of mindedness. According to this approach perception is not reception but action, and cognition is an emergent property of this activity, and not an epiphenomenon of behavior miraculously present only in humans. The self which knows, thinks, and does is quintessentially an embodied self, and the mind is not merely attached to this body, located at and limited to some single command center, but is present throughout the body in lived experience. Thus is thought fully present in activities beyond the linguistic, and language, we must presume, once understood as the incorporeal yet worldly repository of mind, must be more bodily than heretofore imagined. In this spirit (perhaps more appropriately, in this vein) Colin Sample informs us that language is not just semiotic, but mimetic; meaning is carried not only in virtue of the consensus of a given community, but also by the body's capacity, through gesture, posture, and movements more subtle still, to communicate mimetically, carrying in the physicality of movement a protoconceptual significance which in some sense resembles and grounds the conceptual. In aesthetic language in particular, the body's ability to grasp onomatopoetic, physiognomic, and other expressive underpinnings of the conceptual (negation is a pushing away; sadness is blue; a low, slow, and heavy musical line; the downward "aww" rather than the bright, uplifted "hey!") is essential to the possibility of full and complete communication. As Sample writes, "Verbal communication is not merely the exchange of propositional contents. It is also a meticulous dance . . . envelop[ing] verbal utterances in a felt context of emotion [and] physiognomic significance . . . expressed by the bodies of the interaction partners."

Our bodies, this is to say, are far more important than has generally been reflected in the canon. Indeed, Steven Meuse points out that it is a condition of self-awareness to have a grasp of ourselves as a bodily presence in the world, to know where we are and where we are not. The ur-self takes itself to extend and encompass the entire cosmos, but it is just this expansiveness which prevents consciousness from being self-consciousness. The formation of a workable ego thus requires the amputation of those parts of the psyche which extend beyond the limits of the body; the ego is in fact a body-ego. This basic thesis is elaborated and expanded by Meuse through a study of an interesting converse phenomenon: the amputation of a bodily limb which leaves behind its psychic, or "phantom," counterpart through and with which some amputees seem still to experience and confront the world. Meuse intriguingly suggests that the rash of phantom-limb reports and "appearances" in the late nineteenth century can be attributed to a socio-historical context in which our collective body image (and/as the body politic) was threatened with amputations.

We should not be surprised to find such a correspondence or affinity between the individual and social body. As Ed Casey carefully details, the human body is always everywhere both biological and psychical, empirical and cultural. The body, Casey writes, "carries culture and brings it to bear by performing it outright," an insight expanded and developed in Loren Noveck's work. Noveck sets up four scenarios which examine from different perspectives the demands placed upon the body by the roles into which it is cast by the life it leads. Insofar as all life is a stage, performance theory offers us an especially apt tool for analyzing and uncovering the potentials and pitfalls of freedom and subjectivity in the face of social demand. Casey's analysis complements Noveck's by insisting that the notion of a self-contained socially saturated self connected to a culturally free empirical body is not viable; the opposition of nature and culture is an artifact of the opposition of body and mind which we hope here to overcome. We cannot without conceptual if not literal damage divorce the "real" body from some acculturated body-in-society, and neither can we take the subject, revealed here as a socially saturated body-ego, to be transcendentally free. But what is freedom if not transcendental? Noveck suggests that the notion of performance itself possesses the resources to think free agency into the subject; she calls for a real freedom, a situated freedom, to accompany the real body.

But to recognize that real bodies are acculturated bodies is not to assert their reality apart from the empirical or the adiscursive. Bodies exist both within, and sometimes in spite of, the cultural categories woven in, through, with, and around them by language. As is made apparent in these essays time and again, the purely textual body is the unreal body. Michele Janette is at particular pains to counter the textualist tendency in literary theory. For how shall we understand that text by, through, and within which the body-subject is identified when it is not the theoretical, analogical "text" of the hermeneutic encounter, written, as it were, in the epistemic air between known and knower, but is instead carved from flesh, available not as interpretive matrix but as scar-healed wounds which both shape and symbolize the self? The body-texts of Janette's essay are literally inscribed on the backs of two women in different social but similar hermeneutic situations; the text is thoroughly owned by and part of the women, and yet its placement on their backs makes it impossible for the women to read themselves. Interpretation of the text requires the introduction of another reader. Thus the tension between self-definition and an externally imposed identity so central to Noveck's paper is played out here again on the bodies of the characters Janette investigates, and her analysis indicates that real bodies are at once more stable, and also more ambiguous, than the "text" of their identity suggests.

David Hillman inverts Janette's inquiry in interesting and complementary ways, for Prince Hamlet is concerned with the meaning not of surface shape, but of the interior of the body, the significance of innards. Further, the focus of

Hillman's essay is on the eros of the *reader*, rather than on the position of the read, on asexual ingression of the body *of* the other, instead of on visual, tactile, and sexually charged transgression *from* the other. For Hamlet, to know the other's mind is essentially to know his innards; gut feelings and innermost thoughts are played out in the viscera to which Hamlet desires access. Interestingly, Hillman shows how closely this desire to know is linked to the desire to be known (as is always the case with eros); the (desire for the) revelation of the other, it seems, always involves the (desire for the) revelation of the self, an insight which problematizes any reduction of the act of interpretation to the phallic, visual penetration of the other in which the reader remains closed, unseen, invisible. The hermeneutic encounter may instead imply a mutual vulnerability; thus was Janette's woman warrior able to decapitate (castrate) the baron even as he "feminized" her with his intrusive gaze.

The concern with the status of the knower and the accessibility of the known takes different form in "Science and Things." There I argue that the canonical epistemology of science, according to which the information gathered by the senses is given form and significance by the conceptualizing mind, fails to account for actual scientific practice and for science's epistemic success. This essay is meant to be a direct confrontation with the epistemic tenet of Cartesianism, and I insist therefore that the body possesses a nonsensual receptivity to the structure of the world, an epistemic openness intimately bound up with the active, moving body. Following Thompson, we might usefully understand our perception-organizing/interpreting concepts or theories, not in terms of mental constructs working on sensual material to produce contentful representations, but rather in terms of comportmental potentials and practices whose epistemic value and activity cannot be so easily located in a "mind" considered separately from the body; this brings the body more fully into the epistemic picture than "perception" allows. The knowing self is not just the sensing mind, but the living, moving, intruding, fully embodied interactive self, a self which can access the world by means other than the epistemic text of interpreted sensation. This opens the possibility of an epistemology which allows the world to provide epistemic friction, revealing that skepticism, in those very areas of scientific knowledge where it seems most plausible, can be subverted by insisting that the knowing, thinking, interpreting self is more fully and thoroughly embodied than Cartesianism admits.

It is my hope that this collection will reveal not just that the thinking self is embodied, but that the embodied self is mindful; not only that a subject is far more corporeal than we generally have had the courage to admit, but that a body is a far more rich, complicated, and interesting thing to be than we have seen fit to acknowledge. It is in this thorough-going revisionism, the vision of the full, complicated reality of the incorporated self, that the strength of this volume lies. I can only hope that the theoretical challenge it represents will one day be embodied in the corpus of the theoretical humanities.

Notes

1 Of course, Plato's soul-as-harmony requires the existence of physical parts, and likewise certain strains of Christian metaphysics insist on the necessity of the body to resurrection.

2 The science of mechanics would do much to temper this image of the unreliability of the physical, thus making possible the philosophical promise of materialistic determinism.

3 This tendency to treat perception as a largely "mental" phenomenon follows easily from the above noted tendencies to distance knowledge from its bodily origin. Here the knowing self (the perceiving self) is not really a body at all, or is a sort of ghost in a machine.

The further reduction of body to instances of perception has been the source of some consternation among feminist thinkers, for in a cultural context which denies subjectivity to female bodies, the woman exists only for the other (or narcissistically for herself-as-other) as the object of the gaze.

4 E.g., "Awareness ceased to be demanded when we gave up trying to justify our knowledge of the external world by rational reconstruction. What to count as observation can now be settled in terms of the stimulation of sensory reception, let consciousness fall where it may." W.V.O. Quine, "Epistemology Naturalized," in *Ontological Relativity and Other Essays* (New York: Columbia University Press, 1969), p. 69.

See also Joseph Margolis's commentary on this and other features of recent analytic philosophy in "A Biopsy of Recent Analytic Philosophy" *The Philosophical Forum* 16, no. 3 (spring 1995): 161-88, esp. p. 164.

5 Literally, of course, we have five senses, but sensible knowledge has so much been taken as knowledge of surfaces that vision has seemed an appropriate metaphor for all of them (and the senses, as well as knowledge itself, have often been reconceptualized along visual lines). See, e.g., *Modernity and the Hegemony of Vision*, ed. David Michael Levin (Berkeley: University of California Press, 1993).

6 Although it is, of course, the object of certain strains of neo-behaviorism (I am thinking in particular of Daniel Dennett and Wittgenstein in certain moods), where they wish to preserve the subject at all, to do so by *making* subjectivity obvious.

It should be noted that I am not setting up an argument for an epistemically inacessible subject; rather I wish to argue for an account of access which goes beyond perception.

7 I find this notion that the body will always bleed through its conceptual coverings in Foucault, much to the dismay of those who take him to be a prime representative of cultural constructivism.

8 See, e.g. Albert A. Johnstone, "The Bodily Nature of the Self or What Descartes Should Have Conceded Princess Elizabeth of Bohemia," in *Giving the Body its Due*, ed. Maxine Sheets-Johnstone (Albany: SUNY Press, 1992).

9 When in fact the emotions are necessary to agency precisely because they are not "rational." See, e.g., Ron Katwan's work on Schopenhauer.

10 For a thorough, although critical, review of this way of thinking, see Calvin O. Schrag, *The Resources of Rationality* (Bloomington: Indiana University Press, 1992).

11 Or, more specifically, what *appears* as thought given the preenforced dualism, for thought is in fact the embodied unity of structure and content which the anti-logocentric and logocentric theorist equally fail to capture.

12   This is to say, the essays were gathered with their service to this end in mind; they were not necessarily written for this use. In this sense I am making the authors speak in one voice without being able to claim that this voice always speaks for the authors.

Part I

The Nature of the Natural Body

1
Darwinian Bodies
Against Institutionalized Metaphysical Dualism

Maxine Sheets-Johnstone

> From the point of view of how the whole thing actually worked, we knew how part of it worked. . . . We didn't even inquire, didn't even see how the rest was going on. All these other things were happening and we didn't see it.
>
> —Barbara McClintock

> Anderson [a theoretical physicist] ends his discussion with the remark that when he was asked to write something about his personal scientific philosophy he discovered for the first time that he had one! Moreover he found that one of the central tenets was entirely different than what he would have expected, namely that the whole can be greater than, and very different from, the sum of its parts.
>
> —W. H. Thorpe

Unnatural Species

The choice of "the mental" by the philosopher, or its relegation to philosophers, and the choice of "the physical" by the scientist establish a division of the animate that is mirrored neither by a Darwinian scheme of the world, a Darwinian methodology, nor by everyday living reality. However restrictively or generously their genetic programming is conceived, all creatures, humans and nonhumans, undeniably move about in purposeful ways. They make life-enhancing choices, at minimum not only about what and what not to eat (including the choice of a new food item) and when to eat (e.g., when it is safe to do so as well as when they feel hungry); they make choices as well in the very act of procuring food. Movements in hunting, for instance, are coincident with choices to pursue a certain animal as prey, to continue or discontinue a chase, to change tactics, and so on.[1] In no such behavior is there empirical evidence of a mental as opposed to a physical or a physical as opposed to a mental. There is only a creature using its native wits to outsmart its prey or outmaneuver its predator. Hunting creatures clearly live their lives as animate wholes.

If there were a law of nature to which to appeal in such a matter, surely it would decree first that academically propagated creatures are unnatural species; and second, that in order to render creaturehood properly, it is necessary to regard living forms as organic wholes, even if one is studying only partial aspects of a form. Such a law of nature is in fact exactly what the eminent biologist J. S. Haldane was at pains to formulate in his fundamental axiom of biology: What life scientists properly study is "the life of organisms," "manifestations of persistent wholes,"[2] what in concrete, empirical terms can be identified as *Darwinian bodies*. A full justification and elaboration of the term *Darwinian bodies* will be found below. It suffices to note at this point that in his exposition of evolutionary theory, Darwin started with physical attributes and behavior, but remained an organic wholist. He did *not* fail to recognize and acknowledge the whole animal, the living creature. It is precisely because he was an organic wholist that he did not conceive bodies to evolve in the absence of minds (mental powers), nor conceive mental powers to be vouchsafed to humans alone. When his organic wholism is preempted on the one hand by a biology of the body, or an anthropology of behavior, and on the other hand by a philosophy of mind, then the life of living organisms fades from view and Darwinian bodies fall through the crack.

Failure to think in persistent wholes or to tie one's thinking to intact living organisms results in queer statements revealing queer conceptions of the nature of creaturely life vis-à-vis the role of scientific analysis. A psychologist recently wrote: "It may seem strange that a conference on [brain] lateralization should have to concern itself with the essential unity of the individual but that is our fate, and this is a question which we cannot avoid facing."[3] A physical anthropologist recently pointed out in a college textbook that "many of the functions of primates can be classified as *behavior*; that is, besides biochemical and physiological functions of cells or organs there are many actions of the whole animal."[4] Such statements both begrudge and distort what is first and foremost in a living individual: its persistent wholeness. They ignore the fact that what evolves are not piecemeal parts but intact organisms: animate forms.

By and large, present-day philosophers do not so much begrudge the essential unity of the individual as omit fundamental aspects of it because of the skewedness of their subdisciplinary focus. Disquisitions on minds seldom touch on bodies, and if they do, it is commonly the body as a visual object or the source of visual perceptions. In contrast, when Aristotle wrote about the soul, he underscored the necessity of finding the most adequate definitions for each of its forms and, in the process of doing so, had much to say about the body, in particular about the biological primacy of touch among all the senses.[5]

Now it might be though naive to call attention to what are now traditional academic divisions. Most academics realize there is more to being human than what their particular discipline defines or particular approach reveals, even if that realization is not often buttressed by personal interdisciplinary breadth or efforts. If this generalization is true, then the problem is not academic divisions per se. They are a problem only when disciplinary choice is not simply an expression of personal interest, but is conceived in more lofty terms: as the hub of all human understandings, or even coincident with some universal axiology. The problem is with the partial beings that academic divisions tend to generate. With the proliferation of these partial beings, the Darwinian body continually loses ground and is ultimately lost sight of altogether.

But there is a secondary problem as well, namely, the point from which typical academic investigations begin. There are at least two reasons for this problem. To avoid repetition, both will be discussed in terms of "the mental" only. Corollary omissions, preconceptions, and conceptual/linguistic ensnarements beset studies of "the physical."

Present-day philosophers almost uniformly start with "the mental" and omit a concomitant, not to say complementary, philosophy of the body. When they do, "the physical" seems predictably foredoomed. It is reduced either to the status of a handmaiden or to a brain, the latter most often conceived as in a vat on some distant astronomical object or involved in complicated cerebral exchange programs.[6] The latter situations actually owe their reflective existence to science; that is, philosophers are merely taking science seriously. If the brain is the physical seat of "the mental" as present-day science teaches, then the possibility of detaching the mental, on the one hand, and the possibility of changing corporeal drivers, on the other, become logical possibilities engaging the attention of philosophers. More specifically, the possibilities make the reality of the perceived world, on the one hand, and the criteria for personal identity, on the other, problematic. But they also make the living body problematic. The living body seldom makes an appearance in these scenarios: squeezed out by pressing concerns with brains, the living body has become so much superfluous pulp.

The lack of a complementary philosophy of the body aside, no sooner is "the mental" disengaged for study than a worrisome problem arises. How is "the mental" connected to "the physical"? How, *in terms of everyday life*, do the two interact to form a union? In view of the metaphysical ease with which people normally lead their day-to-day lives, it is ironic that a separation into parts rather than an essential unity is so readily conceived and accepted as metaphysically sound. The latter is the difficult problem, not the former, just as it was for Descartes, who is credited with the original conceptual separation.[7] There is a further irony in the fact that many second-generation existential and even phenomenological philosophers who deal with the still unresolved problem (a legacy left them, many times in compounded form, by seminal first-generation existential philosophers such as Heidegger) commonly solve it by way of *embodiment*. The solution is ironic since instead of discounting the ready-made division and starting with a fresh analysis of the experiential dimensions of existence, as is consistent not only with an existential approach but with the phenomenological tradition from which existential philosophy derives, the point of departure is actually Cartesian: the self is conceived as packaged in the flesh. The solution is in fact nothing more than a grammatical union. The body "embodies"—presumably as the mind "inspirits." Richard Zaner, for example, first declares that there are two kinds of matter, "bodily life and psychical life. . . which stubbornly refuse being taken as *merely* material." He then defines the first of these as "the living body *embodying*" and the second as "the subject (self/mind)" (italics added).[8] Where the original conceptual separation between the mental and the physical is mended by a grammatical union, an empirical frame of reference is lost from view. Nothing in experience is shown to tether the grammatical constructs of an *embodying* body and an *embodied* subject. In consequence, the conceptual gap between "the mental" and "the physical" remains unclosed.

Embodiment in such instances appears to be a matter of having one's metaphysical cake and eating it too, but with a forked tongue—not to malicious but to inadvertent effect. In other words, while broaching the long overdue investigation, even celebration, of the centrality of "the lived body" (in German, the *leib* as opposed to the *körper*), many existential philosophers simultaneously cling to the traditional Cartesian metaphysics that refuses to acknowledge the centrality.[9] The duplicity is covered over by the grammatical-raised-to-the-power-of-the-metaphysical concept of embodiment that, at the same time it hoists the body to newfound prominence, keeps it in its usual place with regard to a self, mind, or subject. Moreover without language it is doubtful the concept of embodiment would even arise; it is an abstract lexical offshoot of a flesh and bone body. "*Processes* of embodiment" (italics added),[10] for example, or "the Self's *incarnate* potential" (italics in original)[11] are empirically empty attempts at reification, both of an "embodying body" and of a self the latter purportedly embodies. The empirical deficiency is forcefully if negatively highlighted by eighteenth-century empiricist philosopher David Hume's conclusions about "the self"; all Hume could find when he looked for a self was "a flux of impressions."[12] Could this flux be what the living body embodies? It scarcely seems hardy enough stuff to interest an embodying body. What, then, is the *self* or *mind* that is embodied? What is this *act* or *fact* of embodiment? Statements about "our lived experience of being embodied"[13] need to be cashed in (as Husserl would say)[14] for evidence that *shows* embodiment to be an experienced fact. Unless and until such experience(s) can be described, the metaphysical (and logical) disjunction between, on the one hand, an incarnate subjectivity—or lived body—and, on the other, a Cartesian metaphysics, will remain—and with it the problem of how "the mental" and "the physical" are in fact united.

On Darwinian Bodies

Because "the mental" can be conceived as estranged from, and even thoroughly independent of, "the physical" (not as a brain in a vat but as a pure spirit or "thinking substance"), and in consequence, because the Darwinian body can easily fall through the crack, it is most reasonable to begin an investigation of the roots of human thinking from the perspective of a Darwinian body, that is, with intact living creatures in the throes, pleasures, industries, and curiosities of their everyday lives. The reasonableness of the approach is augmented on at least two counts. To start with a Darwinian body is to follow the path of evolution itself in the sense that the efflorescence of thinking in terrestrial creatures is chronologically keyed to the evolution of primates of which, so far as we know, hominids are the most recently evolved lineage. (To start with the Darwinian body also follows the hypothesized path of the evolution of evolution. Where the latter is itself understood as a process that evolves, the present-day world is conceived as being at a particular stage [metacultural] in the biohistorical process. Within this perspective, the Darwinian body, originally a product at the stage of natural selection, is viewed not as displaced in subsequent evolutionary stages but as having undergone transformation at the hands of further selective mechanisms, namely, cultural and metacultural selection.)[15]

Second, to start with a Darwinian body is of course to proceed as Darwin did, that is, with neither academic allegiances nor strictures. Darwin's observations and descriptions were clearly not restricted by certain disciplinary perspectives, methodologies, and concepts, but were grounded in perspicacious and painstaking perceptions of creatures in the process of their everyday lives. Darwin described the bodily form, the actions, the emotions, and the mental qualities of living creatures. True, he observed only bodies, but he gave them their living due. A body that is given its living due is given as much as its bodily comportments and behaviors allow. A detailed example from Darwin will illustrate just how generous a just allowance was and should be.

In his second major work on evolution, *The Descent of Man, and Selection in Relation to Sex*, Darwin showed how the principles of selection apply equally to humans—that humans are not special creations, but have affinities in every respect to "the lower animals."[16] In his first chapter, he presents evidence showing that structural aspects of the human body are homologous to structural aspects of nonhuman bodies, that embryonic development is similar in both cases, and that humans, like "the lower animals," have rudimentary organs. In effect, in this first chapter, Darwin is recapitulating in human terms much of the corporeal evidence substantiating evolutionary theory that he presented in *The Origin of Species*, his first work on evolution. But Darwin obviously does not think he has made his full case. "The descent of man" involves much more than an evolution of physical features correlative to those of nonhuman animals. In the second and third chapters, Darwin presents evidence showing that *human mental powers are on a continuum with nonhuman mental powers*. In the first of these chapters, he points out affinities with respect to the power of attention, memory, imagination, and reason. He is clearly untroubled by brain size with respect to the attribution of these "mental powers." He is concerned only with overt animate behavior. In this respect he gives a pragmatic, even Wittgensteinian, assessment of mental powers. Just as the meaning of a word is given in its use according to Wittgenstein, so the mental powers of an animal are given in *their* use. The criteria for affirming power of attention, deliberation, and so on, are in effect palpably present; they are there in the flesh.

Darwin goes on to affirm that the verbal language of humans is similar to the language of nonhuman animals in several important respects, and to question whether with "self-consciousness, mental individuality, abstraction, and general ideas,"[17] the difference is, as elsewhere, *in degree rather than in kind.* In each case he presents evidence for believing that just such a difference obtains. Thus just as there are differences in degree and not differences in kind between humans and nonhumans with respect to the evolution of physical features, so with respect to the evolution of mental powers.

It should be pointed out that Darwin intended his study of emotional expression in humans and nonhumans to be part of *The Descent of Man, and Selection in Relation to Sex,* but owing to the latter's already extended length, the material on emotions was published separately. Accordingly, *The Expression of the Emotions in Man and Animals* constitutes the third of Darwin's three major works on evolution. In this book, Darwin again presents evidence for the same thesis: humans and "the lower animals" are all creatures of evolution *in every respect,* in this instance, sharing the same emotional etiology, similar patterns of emotional behavior, and similar means of emotional expression.[18]

What is remarkable in Darwin's presentation throughout both *The Descent of Man* and *The Expression of the Emotions* is his tacit insistence upon the *observability* of "mental characters:" "The lower animals, like man, *manifestly* feel pleasure and pain, happiness and misery" (italics added).[19] Moreover not only are these *observed* features not subjective gloss, they are not reasoned conjectures: "*The fact* that the lower animals are excited by the same emotions as ourselves is so well established, that it will not be necessary to weary the reader by many details. Terror acts in the same manner on them as on us, causing the muscles to tremble, the heart to palpitate, the sphincters to be relaxed, and the hair to stand on end" (italics added).[20]

From such statements it is clear that, *though analytically divisible ex post facto,* Darwin conceives the mental and the physical to be experientially and behaviorally intertwined, and as much in the act of reasoning as in the feeling of terror. In reviewing the capacity of nonhuman animals to reason, for example, Darwin follows the statement "Few persons any longer dispute that animals possess some power of reasoning" with the observation that "animals may constantly be seen to pause, deliberate, and resolve."[21] The putative jump (typically fancied by twentieth-century Western observers) from a so-called *physical* pause to a so-called *mental* deliberation and resolve is nowhere to be found. In effect, for the Darwinian observer, to live means not merely to survive in the struggle for existence, to have the more viable morphological, physiological, and/or behavioral variation—the longer canines, the higher threshold for pain, or the swifter run, for example—but to live out in the fullest corporeal sense the struggle itself: to be not merely *un corps,* but *un corps engagé.* Behavior in Darwinian terms is thus not reducible to a series of inputs and outcomes. It is not equivalent to twentieth-century laboratory proceedings and results even though it may be shown to follow certain behavioral patterns described in those proceedings and results. It is, in the most basic and incontrovertible sense, a corporeal slate upon which much is written and written legibly. In sum, while Darwin clearly subscribes to a classificatory separation of mental and physical qualities—undoubtedly an unquestioned Cartesian legacy— he does *not* subscribe to their essential division. His meticulous and detailed analyses within those classifications notwithstanding, what he observes and what he is bent on rendering are "persistent wholes," "the lives of organisms," "the essential unity of individuals."

It is furthermore clear from a theoretical point of view that what Darwin is saying by his insistence on the observability of the mental is that the same rule of analogical *apperception* applies to nonhuman bodies as to human ones.[22] That analogical apperception is the rule among humans hardly needs documentation. When humans perceive one another's behavior, they at the same time read in certain attitudes, dispositions, rationales, and the like, and certain feelings, such that the perception of other bodies is always filled in (*ap-perceived*)—by motivational ascriptions, for example. What is specifically read in—what is *analogically* apperceived—is empirically rooted in the cognitive and felt dimensions of one's own prior bodily experiences of attention, deliberation, reason, feeling, and so on. In effect, other human bodies are perceived not as empty shells of doings; observed living bodies are given their living due.

Analogical apperception is not only a built-in factual presupposition of a Darwinian metaphysics and biology; it is a built-in fact of corporeal life. It has its origin in the *biological disposition to use one's own body as a semantic template*, in the specific context under discussion, to understand the behavior of other creatures on the basis of one's own corporeal experiences. Moreover it is in the long run a necessary biological fact of life. Whatever the degree of genetic programming toward that end, correct readings of the cognitive and felt dimensions of the behavior of others are as critical to the evolutionary success of a creature as are typically morphological characters, all the more so for predominantly social creatures. Their biological necessity to a harmonious social order is often written between the lines in studies of primate social behavior, in Harry Harlow's deprivation and nondeprivation experiments with monkeys, for example, and Jane van Lawick-Goodall's observations of chimpanzees in the wild.[23] The principle is furthermore directly documented in primatologist Stuart Altmann's coinage and use of the term *comsign* to designate signals understood by all individuals of a particular species or social group on the basis of behaviors common to all members of the species or group.[24] Comsigns are in essence the result of analogical thinking based on a commonality of animate form and of tactile-kinesthetic experience. They are at the same time, and in a broad evolutionary sense, the result of the biological disposition to use one's body as a semantic template. Accounts of social behavior (including the Tanzsprache of honeybees) found in the paleoanthropological case studies presented in *The Roots of Thinking*[25] show that living bodies are consistently given their living due by creatures in nonhuman and human societies alike. Thoughts and feelings are indeed *manifestly* present in bodily comportments and behaviors. "The mental" is not hidden but is palpably observable in the flesh.

In sum, Darwin's metaphysical passage from homologous bodily structures to homologous mental ones is smooth and untroubled because it is undergirded by the biological principle of analogical apperception. The question should nonetheless be raised as to whether Darwin is giving too much credit. Is the practice of analogical apperception by humans misplaced in the case of their observations of nonhuman animals? Is Darwin violating C. L. Morgan's famous canon: "We should not . . . explain any instance of animal behavior as the outcome of higher mental processes, if it can fairly be interpreted as the outcome of mental processes which stand lower in the order of mental development"?[26]

Analogical Apperception and Biological Reductionism

The twentieth-century philosopher Thomas Nagel has long been concerned with conciliating the objective and subjective, to the point of securing a place for the subjective in the annals of behavior. He insists that an objective account is insufficient since "the subjectivity of consciousness is an irreducible feature of reality—without which we couldn't do physics or anything else—and it must occupy as fundamental a place in any credible world view as matter, energy, space, time, and numbers."[27] There are similar rumblings of disquietude from scientists as well, particularly those sympathetic to a Whiteheadian metaphysics—for example, the physicist David Bohm[28] and biologist James A. Marcum[29]—or to the tenets of hermeneutical analysis, for example, the biologist Gunther Stent.[30] Such philosophers and scientists are fundamentally in accord with Darwin: description at a merely physical level is not a complete description. Their joint answer to Morgan's canon might be formulated in the most basic way as follows: In no case may we interpret an action as the outcome of a lower psychic faculty if such an interpretation voids the integrity of the body in question. For Darwinian observers there is no metaphysical or methodological problem in identifying the integrity of a particular body, since the mental is neither an epiphenomenon of behavioral evolution nor a thing evolving apart on its own. It is there in the living flesh of the creature before them. The viewpoint is mirrored in a tantalizing statement made by Merleau-Ponty: "It is no mere coincidence that the rational being is also the one who holds himself upright or has a thumb which can be brought opposite to the fingers; the same manner of existing is evident in both aspects."[31] Merleau-Ponty never actually brought this evidence to light. He never showed just how rationality and uprightness, or rationality and an opposable thumb, constitute "the same manner of existing," in part because, as indicated earlier,[32] he started with the wrong body and in part because the conjunction of rationality, uprightness, and an opposable thumb points in an incisively Darwinian direction. The conjunction invites a bona fide existential *and* evolutionary perspective, one in which traditionally omitted evolutionary dimensions are acknowledged as part and parcel of an *existential* history and in which traditionally omitted existential dimensions—Nagel's "subjectivity"—are acknowledged as part and parcel of an *evolutionary* history.

The latter acknowledgment is not only tenable; it is crucial. Too low a bow to the "purely objective" tends to end in a collapse. The reduction of *tactility* to *cutaneous stimulation* is a pertinent case in point. Biologist Samuel Barnett's attempt to behaviorize Darwin's descriptive label of a photograph of a cat rubbing itself against someone's leg actually ends in selfdefeat.[33] In lieu of Darwin's "affectionate frame of mind," Barnett would substitute "cutaneous stimulation." Clearly the latter label does not shed any new and penetrating light on the feline situation. Indeed, the word *rubbing* and the phrase "affectionate state of mind" are both more concrete and precise designations of the phenomenon than *cutaneous stimulation* since anything a cat does can be labeled "cutaneous stimulation"—even standing on a patch of grass or lying by a fire. In the most precise empirical sense, cutaneous stimulation is an ever-present aspect of every creature's life: no animate being is ever out of touch with *something*. Aristotle recognized this fundamental meaning of tactility when he upheld the primacy of touch among all the other senses by showing it to be "the essential mark of life." "Without touch," Aristotle concluded, "it is impossible for an animal to be."[34] Two-thousand-year-old truths about the primacy of touch would be hard won in a world of cutaneous stimulation.

The question, then, is not whether the practice of analogical apperception is misplaced with respect to nonhuman animals, in effect, whether analogical apperception is to be trusted as a methodological assumption. Darwin's implicit allegiance to analogical apperception was not the result of a reflective act. It was not a choice among possible construals of animal behavior but a spontaneously and implicitly extended principle of everyday creaturely life. The question in turn is twofold: What is the evidence for analogical apperception and what are its biological roots? The paleoanthropological case studies in Part II of *The Roots of Thinking*[35] both document its pervasive practice in nonhuman animal societies and show overwhelming evidence of analogical thinking in the evolution of hominids. In effect, the gathering of evidence in those chapters shows both the significance of analogical apperception to human evolution and how analogical apperception is rooted in corporeal life.

It should finally be noted that Darwin has never actually been shown wrong in his view of the observability of "the mental" in human and nonhuman behavior. He has only been accused of wrongdoing, either directly as by Barnett or by a tacit boycott of his writings on mental powers in *The Descent of Man* and a relative dismissal of his writings on the expression of emotions. Neither has he ever been shown wrong in his view that mental powers and emotions have *evolved*. The evidence he presents for mental continuities has nowhere been seriously considered and methodically rebutted. It has only been sifted out in what amounts to a highly, one might even say egregiously, selective reading of Darwin. Here, then, are added reasons a biology of mind—and a philosophy of the body—is called for: not only to open the possibility of a progressively complete human self-understanding, but to examine and elaborate a basic tenet of Darwinian evolutionary theory. If evolution is the guiding thread of life on earth, then Darwin's thesis that nonhuman animals think is directly pertinent to an understanding of our hominid kinfolk. Ancestral hominids whose discoveries and practices are integral to our humanness were *non*human. If they did not think, how is it that we do? By divine intervention? By chance genetic mutation? Given the comprehensive evidence for organic evolution, the most likely answer is that thinking evolved hand in hand with doing (which means necessarily that experience evolved hand in hand with behavior) and that it was neither a merely chance nor in any way a separate evolutionary biological development. The integrity of the body is sustained in this Darwinian view. How otherwise explain decisions made by present-day chimpanzees as to which twig is best for termite fishing, for example, or decisions made by our long-ago ancestors as to which stone would be best for flaking, and where and how it would be best to flake it in order to make it into a serviceable tool? If the roots of human thinking are to be uncovered, then the viewpoint of a Darwinian observer must be taken seriously to the extent of examining it and of taking *everything* corporeal—not just behavior but experience—as grist for the evolutionary mill.

Notes

This essay is a reprint of Chapter 11 of Maxine Sheets-Johnstone's *The Roots of Thinking* (Philadelphia: Temple University Press, 1990). It carried the title: "The Thesis and its Opposition: Institutionalized Metaphysical Dualism." Opposition to the book's thesis—that thinking is modeled on the body—is examined in two consecutive chapters, the first focusing on cultural relativism, and the second on institutionalized metaphysical dualism.

1   For a detailed analysis of such choices and behaviors, see Maxine Sheets-Johnstone, "Hunting and the Evolution of Human Intelligence: An Alternative View," *The Midwest Quarterly* 28 no. 1 (1986): 9-35; for a related perspective on the subject, see Maxine Sheets-Johnstone, "Thinking in Movement," *Journal of Aesthetics and Art Criticism* 39 (1981): 399-407.

2   J. S. Haldane, *The Philosophical Basis of Biology* (New York: Doubleday, Doran and Co., 1931), pp. 26 and 13 respectively.

3   Stuart J. Diamond, "Introductory Remarks," in *Evolution and Lateralization of the Brain*, ed. Stuart J. Diamond and David A. Blizard, *Annals of the New York Academy of Science* 299 (1977): 2.

4   Gabriel Ward Lasker, *Physical Anthropology* (New York: Holt, Rinehart, and Winston, 1973), p. 177.

5   Aristotle, *De anima*, trans. J. A. Smith, in *The Basic Works of Aristotle*, ed. R. McKeon (New York: Random House, 1968).

6   See, for example, Derek Parfit, *Reasons and Persons* (Oxford: Oxford University Press, 1986).

7   See the correspondence between Princess Elizabeth of Bohemia and Descartes during May and June 1643 in *Descartes: Correspondence*, vols. 4-8, ed. Charles Adam and Gerard Milhaud (Paris: Presses Universitaires de France, 1960).

8   Richard M. Zaner, *The Context of Self* (Athens: Ohio University Press, 1981), p. 3.

9   See also specifically the same shortcoming in the writings of many anthropologists in *The Anthropology of the Body*, ed. John Blacking (London: Academic Press, 1977). Through the essays he has gathered together, Blacking attempts to forge a *full-scale* anthropology of the body, but until theoretical and methodological issues are clearly conceived and resolved, the prospects of achieving that goal shrivel quickly to zero.

10   Zaner, *The Context of Self*, p. 29.

11   David Michael Levin, *The Body's Recollection of Being* (London: Routledge and Kegan Paul, 1985), p. 8.

12   David Hume, *A Treatise of Human Nature*, ed. L. A. Selby-Bigge (Oxford:

Clarendon Press, 1960).

13 Levin, *The Body's Recollection of Being*, p. 43.

14 Edmund Husserl, "The Origin of Geometry," trans. David Carr, in *Husserl: Shorter Works,* ed. Peter McCormick and Frederick Elliston (Notre Dame, Ind.: University of Notre Dame Press, 1981), p. 261.

15 For an in-depth discussion of this view, see the well-known evolutionary biologist John T. Robinson's "Human and Cultural Development," *Indiana Historical Society Lectures 1973-74* (Indianapolis: Indiana Historical Society, 1974).

16 Charles Darwin, *The Descent of Man, and Selection in Relation to Sex* (Princeton: Princeton University Press, 1981 [1871]).

17 Ibid., p. 62.

18 Charles Darwin, *The Expression of the Emotions in Man and Animals* (Chicago: University of Chicago Press, 1965 [1872]).

19 Darwin, *The Descent of Man*, p. 39.

20 Ibid.

21 Ibid., p. 46.

22 For a descriptive (phenomenological) analysis of analogical apperception, see Edmund Husserl, *Cartesian Meditations*, trans. Dorion Cairns (The Hague: Martinus Nijhoff, 1973), particularly the fifth meditation.

23 See, for example, Harry F. Harlow, "Development of the Second and Third Affectional Systems in Macaque Monkeys," in *Research Approaches to Psychiatric Problems*, ed. Thomas T. Tourlentes, Seymour L. Pollock, and Harold E. Himwick (New York: Grune and Stratton, 1962), pp. 209-29; Jane van Lawick-Goodall, *In the Shadow of Man* (New York: Dell, 1971).

24 Stuart A. Altmann, "The Structure of Primate Social Communication," in *Social Communication among Primates*, ed. Stuart A. Altmann (Chicago: University of Chicago Press, 1967), pp. 325-62.

25 See first endnote. Eight paleoanthropological case studies are presented in *The Roots of Thinking*, ranging from early hominid stone tool-making, counting, bipedality, corporeal representation, and primate sexuality to the origin of language, the conceptual origin of death, and the origin and significance of paleolithic cave art.

26 Conwy Lloyd Morgan, *The Animal Mind* (New York: Longmans Green and Co., 1930), p. 22.

27 Thomas Nagel, *The View From Nowhere* (London: Oxford University Press, 1986), pp. 7-8.

28 See, for example, David Bohm, "On Insight and Its Significance," in *Education and Values*, ed. Douglas Sloan (New York: Teachers College Press, 1979), pp. 13-17, and *Wholeness and the Implicate Order* (London: Routledge and Kegan Paul, 1980).

29 See, for example, James A. Marcum and Geert M. N. Verschuuren, "Hemostatic Regulation and Whitehead's Philosophy of Organism," *Acta biotheoretica* 35 (1986): 123-33.

30 See, for example, Gunther Stent, "Hermeneutics and the Analysis of Complex Biological Systems" (paper presented at the University of California at Davis, 14 November 1984).

31 Maurice Merleau-Ponty, *Phenomenology of Perception*, trans. Colin Smith (London: Routledge and Kegan Paul, 1962), p. 170.

32 The reference is to Chapter 10 of *The Roots of Thinking*. See the first endnote of this chapter and note 25.

33 See Samuel Anthony Barnett, "The 'Expression of the Emotions,'" in *A Century of Darwin*, ed. Samuel Anthony Barnett (Cambridge: Harvard University Press, 1959),

---

pp. 206-30.

3 4   Aristotle *De anima* 435b16-17.

3 5   *The Roots of Thinking* is the monograph from which this chapter is excerpted. See the first endnote of this chapter.

2
The Ghost of Embodiment
Is the Body a Natural or a Cultural Entity?

Edward S. Casey

> There is not a word, not a form of behavior which does not owe something
> to purely biological being—and which at the same time does not elude the
> simplicity of animal life, and cause forms of vital behavior to deviate from
> their pre-ordained direction, through a sort of leakage and through a genius
> for ambiguity which might serve to define man.
> —Maurice Merleau-Ponty,
> *Phenomenology of Perception*

> Then, like Hegel's cunning of Reason, the wisdom of the cultural process
> would consist in putting to the service of its own intentions natural systems
> which have their own reasons.
> —Marshall Sahlins,
> "Colors and Cultures"

Human embodiment was among the first victims of the Cartesian revolution in
philosophy. This embodiment—the lived fact of experiencing the world from and
in and with just *this* body, *my* body—was exorcized or, perhaps more exactly,
volatilized. Given the forced choice between *res extensa* and *res cogitans*, the
lived body (for which the Germans have invented a separate word: *Leib*) had no
place to go: still worse, no place of its own. But like any good ghost, it returns
to haunt its exorcists. Albeit an unwanted guest ("ghost" and "guest" are
cognates), such a body—everybody's body—stays on without warrant, spooking
self-assured philosophical and scientific discourse about "body" (which is to say,

again in German, *Körper,* "body-as-object"). Unwelcome as it has been, embodiment acts as the covert basis of human experience and of coherent connection among human beings: a basis and connection that occur not only in time but in space (and more particularly in place).

"The Ghost of Embodiment" refers to this factor of lastingness—of lingering across space and place and time and history. For embodiment lingers on the sidelines in periods of philosophical neglect (such as the Cartesian era from which we are only now beginning to emerge), just as it also endures in the face of massive cultural vicissitudes. I shall not dwell on the first form of remaining[1] as I am much more interested in exploring how the lived body subsists through the cultural inlays and overlays that have, in contemporary parlance, "written it," and not only subsists, but carries culture and brings it to bear by performing it outright.

In the current climate of cultural constructionism—when an overdue recognition has been accorded to the importance of accumulated history and acquired language and of ethnic and gender differences that are not given but constituted (and constituted not merely by individuals but by whole groups of human beings)—it is timely to ponder the fate of things that are too often considered to be imponderable. One of these "things" is the human body as it is lived by human persons. This body has been of central concern for phenomenologists such as Husserl and Merleau-Ponty in earlier parts of this century, and more recently for feminist theorists such as Irigaray and Butler. Whereas phenomenologists focus on *anyone's* lived body in its sensory and orientational powers, feminists have discerned the different ways this same body is lived by men and women. Butler, in particular, attempts to show how something as seemingly extradiscursive as the lived body remains a posit, if not an effect, of discourse about this body.[2] Its materiality may not be created by discourse (to hold this amounts to discursive idealism), but it is what it is for us because of the ways we talk and write about it. Moreover, Butler's emphasis on the performative aspects of gender identity strikes a clarion chord in a miasma of confusion and prejudice. She is surely right to bring into the light of day the manifold learned behaviors of "gender": to show how much of gender is enacted mimetically rather than being merely the supposedly "natural" "expression" of existing bodily structures, however anatomical or "innate" they are presumed to be. Butler has begun to spell out, in *Gender Trouble* and *Bodies that Matter,* the many ways that (to reverse the infamous Napoleonic-Freudian formula) "anatomy is *not* destiny": for example, by showing that "tacit normative criteria [in]form the matter of bodies."[3] This is important and valuable work—a work of reclamation as it were. Where Freud had declared that "where id was, there ego shall be,"[4] Butler would say that where the opaque matter of unexamined presupposition is, there the illumined body of cultural practice and social prohibition can be seen for what it is.

In the very face of Butler's convincing constructionism, I nevertheless want to ask whether there are modes of embodiment that resist being reclaimed so quickly or so well—that are not the ghostly creatures of "the prior delimitation of the extra-discursive,"[5] much less the residua of certain texts. Are there not aspects of bodily being that, if not undecipherable or uninscribable, are still not the mere positings of discursive or textual practices? One such aspect is found in the primate origins of human bodily behavior, especially as discussed by Maxine Sheets-Johnstone in *The Roots of Power*. Another is revealed in the assessment of the natural environment as it impinges on bodily conduct—as explored by ecologically sensitive contemporaries such as Gary Snyder or Wendell Berry. But I prefer to follow another path into the darkness—one that does not pit *ecos* or *bios* against *socius*—and thus prefer to avoid antagonism or reactionism. Could it be, I find myself wondering (and invite you to wonder with me), could it be that the body's ghostly essence lies in its very capacity to be at once thoroughly natural and thoroughly cultural—not unlike the Spinozan infinite attributes of Extension and Thought, which together characterize all things, despite their intrinsic differences? And I ask you to ponder, too, whether it is precisely because the body is such a dense matrix of nature and culture that it presents itself to us—indeed, must present itself—as obscure, as having a "genius for ambiguity" in Merleau-Ponty's altogether apt phrase: in short, as ghostlike, spectral.

Only if body were obdurate matter on the one hand or an epiphenomenon of spirit on the other, could we usefully apply the designations "nature" or "culture" to it in some exclusive way. But body is no such matter and no such epiphany of spirit. It is its own unique realm or type of being, one which lends itself to both natural and cultural modulations and always to both at once, in varying combinations and connections. Never a physical or metaphysical monolith (despite continual efforts to depict it as such), body, the human body, is metamorphic in its being—even if it tends to be sedimentary in its habits and igneous in its moods.

All too often, however, we fall prey to thinking of the body in extreme terms, sometimes regarding it as simply and solely "natural"—that is, biological, genetic, racial, somatotypic (i.e., "ectomorphic," "mesomorphic")—and sometimes considering it as a purely cultural creation: as the mere composite of certain gestures or movements that are socially conditioned or as the expression of certain interests and ideologies. I say that "we" fall prey to these extreme conceptions without referring to the further fact that this *we* is itself an amalgam of nature and culture, their conjoint creation. This is shown by the sheer fact that the same "we" tends to think of the relation between nature and culture as involving a forced choice between them, putting them into opposed and mutually exclusive positions to start with. But the choice and the opposition are themselves shaped by antecedent choices and oppositions that make this particular choice and opposition possible: consider only the way the folk psychology of a people deeply affects such matters. Furthermore, any such cultural precedents themselves reflect certain physical and physiological constraints such as the character of the human brain, limits of bodily strength, the structure of the hand, and so on. But the very ideas of "character," "limit," and "structure" are in turn culturally constituted.

What, then, are we to make of this conceptual regress in which we keep spiralling back in crisscrossing causal series, without any certainty that we can determine which series is the most formative? (Even the idea of "most formative" is culturally contingent.) Does the swirling vortex of natural and cultural forces mean that we should give up the very effort to sort out nature from culture, or even body from mind? Here we are tempted to claim that the very distinction of nature versus culture, or that of body versus mind, is itself a cultural artifact, a factitious invention of modernity.[6] Yet this claim begs an important question: just what induces a given modern thinker to make such distinctions in the first place? Might it not be the recognition of a discrepancy or otherness which that thinker cannot fully contain in accustomed cultural categories and is therefore tempted to attribute to "nature" or "body," which become names for a genuinely recalcitrant otherness that resists cultural assimilation—on the very admission of the culture itself? Either that admission is to be respected or, if it is not, the burden of proof falls on the skeptic who holds that even the culturally unassimilable is cultural in character.

One could also argue that the natural and the cultural are *always already* so completely assimilated with each other—so deeply coimplicated—that it would be futile to tease them apart: otherness is already sameness in some sufficiently generous sense.[7] Merleau-Ponty puts it this way:

> Everything is cultural in us (our *Lebenswelt* is "subjective") (our perception
> is cultural-historical) and everything is natural in us (even the cultural rests
> on the polymorphism of wild being).[8]

Yet it is one thing to hold that the natural and the cultural are thoroughly intertwined and quite another to maintain that, because of this interpenetration, there is no point in trying to distinguish them at all. In the interest of distinction and in the effort to retrieve the body from its ghostly exile, let us consider some quite particular instances of embodiment with respect to what is contributed by natural forces and as to which cultural conditions operate and how they do so. We shall proceed in three stages, each increasingly complex and elusive: first, by an analysis of the learning (or relearning) of bodily skills; then by a look at the acquisition and sedimentation of taste; finally by a consideration of hysterical symptoms.

The year 1936 marked the appearance of Marcel Mauss's seminal article, "Les techniques du corps." It was also the year in which Jacques Lacan first presented his ideas on the mirror phase, and the same year saw, by curious convergence, the publication of Anna Freud's *The Ego and the Mechanisms of Defense* and Sartre's *Transcendence of the Ego*. All four events went virtually unnoticed at the time, yet each can be said to be of capital importance for considering the status of the body in contemporary thought. For there is an intimate link between the formation of the ego and the body of the subject. Freud had said (twice!) in *The Ego and the Id* that the ego "is first and foremost a body-ego."[9] This is not to say that body and conscious ego form one continuous entity; in the same text of 1923 Freud proposed that large parts of the ego, those that are the products of repression, are unconscious. But it *is* to suggest that the imbrication between soma and psyche is very close indeed.[10] Lacan and Anna Freud went on to spell out the procedures by which the ego of the individual, the core of the psychic self, is formed. Both of them insisted on the importance of identification, in Anna Freud's case "identification with the aggressor"—which includes imitation of the aggressor's bodily gestures—while Lacan emphasized identification with the image of oneself in the mirror, that is, with one's already existing body as it perceives itself before itself.[11]

Mauss, for his part, insisted on the utter specificity of bodily techniques. Remarking on his inability to give up his entrenched practice of swallowing water and spitting it out as he swam—a common practice of swimmers of his generation—the French sociologist makes this remark:

> It was stupid, but I still make this gesture [of swallowing and spitting]: I cannot free myself of my technique. Here is thus a specific bodily technique, a gymnastic art perfected in our time. Yet *such specificity is the character of all [bodily] techniques.*[12]

Freud, Lacan, and Anna Freud all agree with Mauss that those bodily practices that have to do with personal (and more particularly with egological) identity are all specific in character. But what does it mean to say this? Is there no *general* technique of the body? And what does the specificity in question tell us about the incursion of culture into bodily practices?

Let us stay for a moment with Mauss's own preferred example of swimming. Recently, I have been swimming a fair amount—or, more exactly, relearning how to swim. I have had no instructor, but have been trying to get back into the sport on the basis of a small set of dimly grasped body memories, a few unformulated thoughts as to how I might swim more efficiently, as well as furtive and envious glances at fellow and sister swimmers who stream past me in the fast lane of my local pool. Buoying me up in the water, then, has been a loose assemblage of memories, thoughts and perceptions.

But what is actually happening when I relearn a basic bodily skill such as swimming? One way of viewing this is to say that I am reviving, and also reshaping, a tacit corporeal schema—where "schema" implies not just form or pattern but something much more dynamic: a basic way of doing something, a manner of proceeding, a mode of acting. A schema for bodily action, such as that for doing the crawl stroke, is intermediary between image and rule, thus between the specific and the general: between the condensed specificity of an image (which gives just one version of how to do the stroke) and the generality of the role (which remains abstract and normative: how anyone, anywhere, could in principle do this stroke). Nevertheless, as I make my flailing way, floundering if not yet foundering, I catch myself summoning up demi-images of "the right form" ("every technique, properly speaking, has its form," says Mauss)[13] as well as a sense of the right rule (as in the Kantian schematism for causality, it is a matter of "objective succession": first this arm goes out of the water and over the head, then the immersed head turns to the side to catch a breath, then the other arm swings over, with the legs kicking all the while). Thanks to the corporeal schema I possess, I effect a spontaneous alliance with image and rule alike: the image (however dim and merely recollective it may be) affords detail and, as it were, leads the way into the stroke itself, as if it were an initiatory amulet; the rule reassures me that this is the socially sanctioned right way to swim the crawl stroke, even if it is not the *ideal* way to do it. (Let us leave aside a host of further questions: Can the ideal form of swimming a given stroke ever be realized by any individual swimmer? Is there only one such ideal form for each stroke? Is this ideal sensuous or quasi-sensuous—as Kant proposes—or is it strictly abstract in a Platonic mode? Is not the body *as body* foredoomed to fall short of any such ideal; is this not why the body needs the guidance of rules, which it can at least "follow" in Wittgenstein's ample sense, even if it cannot embody the ideal stroke *überhaupt*?)

One thing is clear: neither the image nor the rule needs to be stated in so many words, that is, in anything like a text. I might, of course, consult a treatise on swimming the crawl stroke, one which includes both images and words. Helpful as such a treatise might be, however, I do not require it in relearning to swim—nor do I even need it in learning how to swim in the first place. Indeed, the insertion or insinuation of a text or textlike entity into the circumstance would be distinctly counterperformative, making me only more self-conscious of what I am trying deliberately but not desparately to do. Ultimately, the water I place myself in and the body placed there teach me more than any set of words I read or hear, for they inculcate the schema by the actual means of which I swim. The fact that this schema presents itself to me as an informal amalgamation of memories, perceptions, and thoughts, far from being a problem, represents a perfectly adequate instance of the kind of open-ended hybridization that is appropriate to the occasion. It is, we might say, general enough to be specific.

The crawl stroke schema itself, that which I embody as I swim this stroke, is socially transmitted—and thus socially determined. Mauss tells us that it was from observing the variety of swimming techniques across different generations in France that he first began to ponder the question of "bodily practices."[14] My own simple schematic pictorial rule of the crawl stroke is inherited from a shared history of teaching and learning this same stroke. The stroke is, in Mauss's striking formulations, "an efficacious traditional act," "the work (*l'ouvrage*) of collective practical reason."[15] But to be the *work* of a socialized reason, even a traditionalized reason, is not necessarily to be the *text* of such a reason. It is only to be its deliverance or outcome—its "accomplishment," as *l'ouvrage* can also be translated. From this collectively constituted source comes my individuated bodily practice, which realizes the source in so many motions; the schema of this practice transmits the general form of the stroke from the social mass of more or less competent swimmers to the given imperfect swimmer who, like myself, is learning or relearning the stroke in an idiosyncratic way, shaping it as *my* version of the stroke. Just as my body is between me and you—it is the mediatrix of every social scene—so the schema at stake in learning and relearning bodily skills exists between the generality of others and the specificity of myself, instigating in *me* the form which *they* have instituted, "e-ducating" me.[16] And I lead the form back out into publicity and visibility by per-forming it, forming it through bodily practice.

Educators or instructors, whether actually or only implicitly present, convey to me the schema that represents the condensation, the gist, the gesture of the technique. Indeed, it is precisely because the teacher is not able to be continually present that the schema plays such a critical role; it stands in for the absent teacher, much as a text stands in for its absent or dead author; but, unlike a text, the bodily schema is intrinsically indeterminate, oscillating as it does between image and rule. It is indeterminate because the body as lived and experienced is itself indeterminate: the body is "the general medium of my existence,"[17] and as such is easily overlooked—becoming a spectral presence, a wraith of my life. Not surprisingly, then, corporeal schemata have no final or definitive formulation. It is sufficient to assimilate, literally to incorporate, the bodily movements of an instructor (or, lacking this mentor, an exemplary image of myself as once performing the stroke) in order to learn, or to relearn, the technique in question.[18] These movements become my movements (or mine again), but only thanks to the intermediacy of the schema that allows the perceived or remembered performativity of the instructor to be deposited in the customary body of the fledgling performer.

The foregoing analysis allows us to infer that the indisputable social determination of conduct is not something simply superimposed from without, since the social moment (here, the moment of learning or relearning a basic skill possessed primarily by others) operates from within by way of schematic identification with the exemplary other. This identification is found in my body and nowhere else, and it stays in my body thanks to the schema in which it is embedded. By the same token, we cannot say that the biological basis of an action such as swimming is simply supplied from below, as if this basis were an unformed and unproblematic substratum, a brute given. The formation of bodily actions, their *in-formation*, is part of these actions from the beginning. Even the dog paddle is a *form* of swimming, a consistent and particular way of keeping one's head above water; it, too, is learned and internalized, even if it is never taught as an exemplary way to swim (hence, doubtless, its attribution to another species).[19]

It follows that in the intermediate realm constituted by the corporeal schemata of skilled actions, the natural and the cultural are always already conjoined. Nothing here is entirely natural;[20] nor is anything entirely cultural either. Or rather, everything is both at once, albeit differentially so. I swim *with* my biological body but *as* I am taught by others. I swim *by* or *through* the body that connects self and other as surely as its schemata link image and rule, the specific and the general, and also past and present. I swim rather than sink by virtue of the schema that, more or less successfully executed, keeps me afloat.

It is certainly not adequate to think of my lived body as a mere instrument, yet we must, by the same token, be able to think of the body in terms that allow for the learning of skills and other habitudes. Just as works of art may be conceived as "quasi-subjects"(in Dufrenne's term), so skilled bodies as culturally in-formed can be considered "quasi-technical." In other words, the body can be considered as if it were an organ for the acquisition and sedimentation of skillful actions. And I say "technical" rather than "mechnical," since it is a matter of technique in the Maussian sense, which requires a body that is at once: (a) able to learn particular skilled responses on the basis of certain minimal sensorimotor capacities and bodily motions (ultimately dependent on the central nervous system, the brain, and appropriate musculature); (b) socially absorptive and responsive, that is, sensitive to occasions of possible instruction as they arise in the immediate life of the learner; (c) "docile" enough (in Foucault's sense) to submit to the rigors of learning new skills in given institutional settings.

To endorse the body's quasi-technicality does not mean capitulating to the temptation to consider the lived body as an objective body. We can respect Merleau-Ponty's fierce resistance to this temptation, while remaining open to such less than completely objectifying designations as "apparatus" (Freud, Lyotard), "régime" (Foucault), "habitus" (Bourdieu), "cyborg" (Haraway), and so forth. Each of these epithets is exemplary of the body in its quasi-technicality. Not entirely unlike the Aristotelian notion of soul (*psyche*) as the "first actuality" of the body, its most formative *form*, each serves to normalize the lived body's biological propensities and involuntary actions. We are thus brought back to the intermediacy of the body as what Bergson calls a "place of meeting and transfer"[21] between biology and culture, the physical and the social. Precisely as such an interplace, the lived body lends itself to cultural enactments of the most varied sorts, all of which are themselves dependent on particular corporeal techniques for their own realization.

Pierre Bourdieu's book *Distinction: A Social Critique of the Judgment of Taste*, published in 1979 and inspired by Mauss's essay of 1936, delineates the social arrangements that bodily techniques afford and support in matters of taste. Bourdieu analyzes, for example, both class and gender differences in eating practices of the French working class, finding (among other things) that

> Fish tends to be regarded as an unsuitable food for [working class] men, not only because it is a light food, insufficiently "filling," which would only be cooked for health reasons, i.e., for invalids and children, but also because, like fruit (except bananas), it is one of the "fiddly" things which a man's hands cannot cope with and which make him childlike . . . but, above all, it is because fish has to be eaten in a way which totally contradicts the masculine way of eating, that is, with restraint, in small mouthfuls, chewed gently, with the front of the mouth, on the tips of the teeth (because of the bones). The whole masculine identity—what is called virility—is at stake in these two ways of eating, nibbling and picking, as befits a woman, or [eating] with whole-hearted male gulps and mouthfuls . . . .[22]

From this analysis—and others like it—Bourdieu concludes that "taste, a class culture turned into nature, that is, *embodied*, helps to shape the class body . . . . The body is the most indisputable materialization of class taste."[23] He tellingly invokes what he calls "the whole body schema." Such a schema, operating on and with existing "biological differences," is put into practice by "differences in bearing, [i.e.,] differences in gesture, posture and behavior which express a whole relationship to the social world."[24]

Bodily schemata of taste are specifications in turn of the *habitus* that is the true pivot between nature and culture: a pivot whose primary means of enactment is found in the quasi-technical body. Bourdieu defines *habitus* as "an acquired system of generative schemata" that enable it to be "the product of the work of inculcation and appropriation necessary in order for products of collective history, [that is,] objective structures such as those of language, economy, etc., to succeed in reproducing themselves more or less completely, in the form of durable dispositions, in the organisms."[25] As a system of schemata, the *habitus* is what enables the link between comparatively enduring bodily "dispositions" or quasi-technical aptitudes and continually changing surrounding "situations" to be forged and reforged in the inculcation of taste. A *habitus* is what draws dispositions and situations together in reliable and regular practices of taste.[26]

Thanks to this clue from Bourdieu, we can begin to appreciate the deep commonalities between skill and taste. Both involve an essential reference to an exemplary type (e.g., the model crawl stroke, the right way to eat as a French working-class man) as well as an image of this type (whether perceptual, memorial, or imaginative). But both also invoke a rule by which the image is rendered operative (a correct, if not ideal, sequence of coordinated movements, whether those of swimming the crawl or masticating meat). Taken together, the image and rule facilitate in the lived body a set of practices that represent the performance, the realization of the skill or taste in question. Further, both skill and taste require bodily schemata as the means by which images and rules are knit together. Without bodily schemata, the images would be merely static condensations and the rules abstract formulae. With them, images and rules configurate in a lived body that incarnates culture even as it transmutes nature.[27]

It is surely striking that we have now been led twice to the notion of schema: first in relation to the learning of a basic bodily skill such as swimming, then in regard to the question of taste as exhibited in eating practices. It is the lived body in its quasi-technicality that possesses and exercises schemata, those of basic skills as well as those of the subtleties of taste. In neither case do we have to do with the superimposition of cultural constructions on preexisting bodily givens but, rather, with a circumstance in which the (biologically) given and the (culturally) constructed meet in the crucible of the body. Of course, material conditions and cultural formations meet in many places: buildings, works of art, technology. But only in the meeting place of the living-moving body do they undergo such dynamic interaction. The dynamism, I have been suggesting, is due to the schema, which is at once self same and yet alterable. It is self same as involving a *habitus* that guarantees continuity of action, and it is alterable insofar as habitudes (unlike mere routines) are open to innovation: as Dewey, Merleau-Ponty, and Bordieu all insist.[28]

I do not mean to imply that bodily skills are on precisely the same plane as matters of taste. The latter presuppose the former and appropriate them for their own purposes. Taste is more encompassing than skill insofar as on its basis an entire life style may be generated.[29] Moreover, taste, unlike skill, *always* reflects class and gender differences, incorporating and reinforcing them (though also, at times, transforming them). Taste transmutes physical things (e.g., items of food and clothing) into signs and, still more importantly, makes social necessities into individually felt virtues. I come to "like" (or even to crave) that which, nevertheless, is a quite limited range of things made available to me as a member of a certain social class or as having a particular sexual identity: again, fish if I am French and female.[30] Indeed, there are no effective limits to the extent to which taste may shape our bodily practices. It is so pervasive of the person that it may influence the very choice of which basic skills are to be learned (in the first place). I may decide to learn how to swim not for purposes of sheer survival or just for pleasure but because my peers have encouraged me to do so—and to do so in a very particular, not to say peculiar, way: like swallowing and spitting while swimming.

Nature and culture meet, then, in the lived body. They meet, for example, in the insistent but subtle way that right- and left-handedness infiltrate and influence an entire metaphoricity and symbology of a given culture.[31] They meet as well in the manner in which basic color terms, at once remarkably congruent and yet discretely variant across different cultures, reflect both the physiological optics of vision and the peculiarities of naming in diverse natural languages. As Marshall Sahlins has put it: "It is not, then, that color terms have their meanings imposed by the constraints of human and physical nature; it is that they take on such constraints insofar as they are meaningful."[32] Only those constraints are "taken on" (i.e., assumed, assimilated, made use of) that bear significance or can be made to bear it. *Bodily* constraints in particular—the ways our sheer physicality delimits and determines us—are massively and not exceptionally meaning-bearing. It follows that such culturally specific phenomena as ritual and style represent ways of taking corporeal pregivens—for example, certain modular motions and shapes—and giving them a local habitation and a name: a place (and time) of enactment and a particular named role in the practices of that culture. The list of culturally specified ways of carrying corporeal constraints into the realm of meaning—carrying them, I would insist, on the backs of habitually structured schemata of the body—could continue indefinitely.

If I have been stressing skill and taste in particular, this is above all because, taken together, they reveal the range of the human body's capacity for exhibiting and enacting what Merleau-Ponty calls "incarnate meaning."[33] Skills inhabit one end of this spectrum, representing the places or moments when bodily capabilities and proclivities lend themselves to manipulation and training: when, as Foucault would say, the "intelligible body" becomes the "useful body."[34] What counts for the useful body (which is not even the whole of the quasi-technical body!) is learning and performance, the start and finish of one continuous process. Taste occupies the other end of the spectrum, where bodily determination as useful and skillful is submerged in matters of preference and value—matters so pervasive that, in the final analysis, nothing in a given culture is not, directly or indirectly, a matter of taste, including style and ritual as these eventuate in such concrete practices as dress, table manners, or blowing one's nose![35] What counts in taste is the slow and often nonreflective process of inculcation and staying within the rules. The inculcation implies whole ranges or types of action taken as showing sensible or sensitive taste; and the rule-bound behavior need not seek finesse (indeed, finesse in taste risks being considered merely precious, whereas finesse in a skill is altogether fitting).[36]

Taken to the limit, skill tends toward sheer repetition of the sort that is resistant to change of any sort: Mauss found that, despite his best intentions, he could not give up his early habit of swallowing a mouthful of water and spitting it out with each successive swimming stroke. The skillful body may get locked into a particular practice that, whatever its initial utility, can become anachronistic and counterproductive, or that can come to seem simply embarrasing. The same body is also conscriptable by a dominant state institution into the obedient postures of an all too docile body, that is, the body all too easily bent to the service of that institution, especially in characteristic modern forms of extensive supervalent control.[37] Taste in turn is easily co-opted by the preferences of the dominant class—dominant economically and politically as well as culturally—so as to become "correct" taste, that is, the decorum of a "civilized" elite who alone are held to have not just "good" or "acceptable" but "fine" taste.[38] The very genius of taste to operate in the midst of virtually any constraint and to make something socially commensurable and congenial out of it is here put into abeyance. Further, taste all too often entails a notion of normalization that in principle excludes the eccentric and literally ab-normal. In this case, taste becomes "proper taste," that is, what one *ought to do* in a given situation.[39]

But short of these extremes and despite their manifest differences, bodily enacted skills and tastes land one in a middle realm that, on the one hand, is only quasi-technical and not rigidly stylized and that, on the other, is a matter of receptive and spontaneous consensus and not of elitist exclusions. It is precisely this intermediate corporeal domain that is most fully enlivened and structured by habitudes and schemata—those mediating factors par excellence that, by their very action and interaction, constitute nature and culture as coeval, if not always equal, partners in the common enterprise of creating a genuinely incarnate meaning.[40]

Disparate as they are in so many ways, skill and taste both exhibit a certain voluntarism: I can choose to acquire new skills or reacquire old ones, and I can decide to change my taste—though this change may prove to be arduous indeed. But if the acquiring of skills is deliberate, that of taste is usually semideliberate; I tend to pick up tasteful behaviors merely by commingling with the apposite social milieu. On the other hand, there are some bodily practices that are strictly nondeliberate, that is, involuntary, insofar as they are not only not initially chosen (this much is true of most practices of taste) but are decidedly recalcitrant to subsequent modification. I have in mind psychopathological symptoms of the sort that dominate those who suffer from them—that literally control their movements beyond any conscious choice in the matter. The automatism of these movements remains, however, schematic and habitual, and they deserve discussion along with skill and taste as a third class of phenomena in which nature and culture are inextricably embroiled, yet with revealing differences from the cases previously considered.

Such a discussion is all the more called for inasmuch as my analysis thus far has involved an implicit double limitation: the *self*-restrictedness of skillful action, on the one hand, and the restrictedness *by others* of taste on the other. I myself decide as to how pervasive in my life a skill such as swimming will be, whereas others typically take the lead in taste: they literally show the way. But in the case of psychopathology it is not at all clear whether self or other is determinative of practical actions: indeed, it is not certain that this very distinction remains pertinent, given that the very meaning of *self* and *other* is in question in the more extreme forms of such suffering.[41]

I shall resrict myself here to an examination of hysteria, in which there is no such thing as explicit learning (though there is a certain kind of mimetic performance) and no such thing as gradual inculcation or playing by accepted rules (though there is a complex connivance with such rules). Hysterical symptoms are neither self-limited (they are notable precisely for their exuberant unpredictability) nor the mere internalization of the norms of a society or its elite. They are as seemingly unskilled as they are ostensibly in dubious taste. Yet they remain valid instances of taking on bodily constraints and making them into something still more, indeed much more, meaningful than vagrant bodily motions. Freud says of Dora, for instance, that meaning was "lent to, soldered as it were" to her symptoms in such a way as to become inseparable from them.[42] Despite the soldering, such symptoms were enigmatic both to Dora and to her immediate social milieu. Unlike skill and taste, which incorporate and display cultural and social interests and norms more or less transparently, hysterical symptoms are initially opaque even if ultimately quite significant, that is to say, *telling*.[43] They are "ghosts" of an embodiment unknown to itself in terms of first origin and final sense: they are shadows of this origin or sense fallen upon the hysteric's body and on the body politic with which this body is covertly continuous.

Hysterical symptoms make of this body a memory machine, a mnemonic (and demonic) device.[44] Hysterics, as Breuer and Freud already noted in their "Preliminary Communication" of 1893, "suffer mainly from reminiscences"[45]— memories in and on their bodies, which thereby serve as bearers of unconsciously retained memories. Hysterical symptoms are to be considered "mnemic symbols,"[46] and as such they are ghostly traces in the body, revenants of unabreacted experiences.

This story is well known and has itself become an integral part of late modern Western culture. I want to single out just two aspects that are especially pertinent to the problematic of this paper: the suppressed social significance of hysteria and the apparatus of conversion and somatic compliance. As to the social significance, we need only notice that, despite Freud's emphasis on the highly individuated trajectories of the neurosis and on its "idiopathic products,"[47] this emphasis in no way precludes the massive presence of social determinants in its actual psychogenesis. Nor does the density of the body,[48] its sheer biological heft, in any way bar such presence. On the contrary: just because the body is such a compact entity—as thick physically as it is opaque psychologically—it is a propitious scene for the transmutation of social structures into concrete symptoms. To be dense is to be capable of harboring diverse, covertly situated types of meaning, including those with cryptic social significance. In its very density, the hysteric's body is, as it were, an *idiosyncratic habitus*. It is a *habitus* as a set of predispositions to act in certain ways, yet is idiosyncratic in that the style of action is peculiar to a given hysteric's body and is not mimetic of more general, normative practices. The same body nevertheless represents a schematization of social structures, since hysterical symptoms harbor such structures by inversion, denial, projection, and other forms of repression. The idiopathy is a sociopathy.

Indeed, at both extremes of their history, hysterical symptoms are social in status on the Breuer-Freud model—at the beginning: in the form of specific prohibitions that prevent the abreaction or catharsis that would put to rest the wayward affect which is the energetic basis of the eventual symptom, and at the end in the specifically symbolic character of the symptoms themselves. Mnemic symbols of a hysterical sort are not natural givens; like dream images, they are formed by primary processes of condensation and displacement which themselves are designed to evade the censorship of the socialized self.[49] Hence, both in the (aborted) first reaction to a trauma and in the (eventual) symptomatic expression of it, sociality is powerfully determinative. For this very reason, hysterical symptoms are at once protests against the reigning social order and yet also collusions with it.[50]

This ambivalent relation to sociality—at once resistant and conniving—is itself made possible by the human body's "genius for ambiguity," its never being quite entirely what it gives itself out to be. And this ambiguity in turn is founded on the body's capacity for conversion and for compliance which are centrally at stake in hysteria. "Conversion" is the main mechanism of hysterical symptom formation:

> In hysteria, the incompatible idea is rendered innocuous by its sum of excitation being *transformed into something somatic*. For this I should like to propose the name of *conversion*.[51]

The affect aroused by the initial trauma, then, is converted into a corporeal state such as paralysis or anesthesia. But this state—in short, the symptom—requires a body part in which to be lodged. The liability of this part to be chosen and used in such a way is an effect of its "somatic compliance," a term first employed prominently by Freud in the Dora case. Such compliance means that a region of the body—such as Dora's throat in the case of her hysterical coughing—offers itself as "a privileged medium [or locus] for the symbolic expression of unconscious conflict."[52] For the compliant zone has a "capacity for conversion," indeed "a psychophysical aptitude for transposing very large sums of excitation [i.e., affects] into somatic innervation."[53] (Hysterical somatic compliance thus differs from the compliance of taste, in which the pertinent *habitus* openly—and not secretly—colludes with prevailing social norms, and from that of skill, in which a more or less dextrous body submits itself willingly to the discipline of learning the skill in order to attain consciously chosen goals.)

The closely related ideas of psychophysical conversion and somatic compliance—the latter is the organic condition of possibility for the former—suggest that the body is never taken over entirely by the social basis of its own symptoms. Undeniable and powerful as this social basis is, it requires a foothold (or handhold, or throathold, etc.) in the body if it is to be fully effective. To be determined, even overdetermined, by social structures is still to need somatic constraints against which to lean and upon which to rely. For the hysteric's symptoms to "enter into the conversation"[54]—as Freud puts it revealingly—they must find leverage in the patient's own body; indeed, they must find a home-place there. From that place they speak, reentering the social nexus from which they first arose (and from which they have become so deeply alienated).

Freud conceives such a body-place in two striking metaphors: on the one hand, it is "like the grain of sand around which an oyster forms its pearl," while, on the other, it is to be understood as "a pre-existing structure of organic connections, much as festoons of flowers are twined around a wire."[55] Notice that common to both metaphors is the adverb *around*, not *upon* or *over*. Just as symptoms twine around a somatically compliant part of the body, so we can say more generally that the cultural arises *around* the natural, the social around the somatic instead of *upon* or *over* it—as in too many models of strict stratification.[56] As with symptoms that become one with the patient's very flesh, so a society is tightly bound around (and doubtless *in*) the bodies of its subjects: so tightly as to be inseparable from these bodies (*socius*, the Latin etymon of *society*, means "companion"). The body remains in the center; it is the congenial or compliant other side of the social subject, its intimate *in*-side as it were. The bodily and the social are inseparable in practice even if they are distinguishable upon analysis—both psychoanalysis and socioanalysis—with the result that we cannot claim that one is finally dissolved into, much less *becomes,* the other. It is a question not of this *versus* that but of this *in* that.[57]

This logic of coimplication comes close to what Freud himself concludes in his discussion in the Dora case as to whether the symptoms of hysteria are of psychical or somatic origin:

> Like so many other questions to which we find investigators returning again and again without success, this question is not adequately framed. The alternatives stated in it do not cover the real essence of the matter. As far as I can see, every hysterical symptom involves the participation of *both* sides.[58]

The "both" is finally both body and mind, body and society, nature and culture. It is a matter of a mutual (but not necessarily symmetrical) participation in which each of the paired partners retains an undiminished and indissoluble force of its own.

The same is true of the normalized, nonneurotic practices of skill and taste. In all three cases, nature and culture require each other in their very extremity: culture calling for body (as a narrow place and thick entity in which to express, and sometimes to repress, its aims and demands), body calling for culture (as the indispensable scene of acknowledgment, whether in emotional abreaction, articulation in words, or other socially specific ways). Each is a limit for the other; yet each invades and pervades the other. *Les extrêmes se touchent.* They come into each other's presence in the massive, yet elusive, fact of their coimplication. Rather than being pristine opposites incapable of contamination, each exists to be con-taminated by the other.[59]

It becomes evident that it was wrong—wrong because artificial and factitious—to have posited nature and culture as separate poles to begin with: a bad nineteenth-century habit, for which there were equally bad nineteenth-century solutions. Yet the problem of how the natural and the cultural (including the social) relate to each other is still with us in the latter part of the twentieth century. My suggestion has been that they are not *re*joined from positions of initial separation but instead are continually *con*joined, never not intertwined to some discernible degree. They are coeval epicenters in the common field of habitual-schematic interaction, immersed in this field rather than standing out from it as exclusive poles. Even (and precisely) as extremes, nature and culture come to be what they are only from within the highly schematized, habitual middle realm co-inhabited by bodily skills, by collective tastes, and (however unstably) idiosyncratic symptoms.

I have suggested as well that the body is the agent, the pivot, the crux, of this same middle realm. In the body and through it—by its unique signature— culture coalesces and comes to term. It comes into its own there. Without embodiment, culture would be schematic in the perjorative sense of empty or sketchy. It would be a ghost of itself. By the same token, the body, were it not to bear and express culture, to implicate and explicate it, would be itself a ghost: an exsanguinated shadow of its fully encultured liveliness.

The body was bled out and abandoned by Descartes not just because he did not recognize its status as "lived," that is, diversely experiential and self-reflexive, but also (and perhaps more critically) because he did not concern himself with its cultural and social dimensions. But it will not do, either, to reduce the lived body in turn to an object or product of discourse, as has happened in post-structuralist thought. This, too, renders the body a spector of itself, a paper-thin textual entity: it is to refuse to recognize the body as at once insinuating and insinuated, permeating and permeated, when it comes to culture and the social.

It is time to return to the body both as a lived presence and as a cultural and social force in its own right. Only then can the ghost of embodiment, which has haunted so much of modern philosophical thought, be exorcised and embodiment itself restored. The body that will thereby come forth is not just a grain of sand or stretch of wire: Freud's images intimate something far too settled, far too much like a merely physical thing. The body alive, or re-enlivened, is part and parcel of the cultural and social nexus that not only surrounds it but, finally, *is it*. But it, in turn, *is this nexus*. Or we could say that each element twists around the other, not unlike a double helix. But I am running out of metaphors, and so I shall let matters stand just here, at this appropriately indeterminate ending-point—where the inconclusiveness of bodily being contests any account purporting to provide the last word on this delicate matter.

Notes

1 The remaining is already evident in Descartes himself. He admits to Queen Elizabeth that "everyone feels that he is a single person with both body and thought so related by nature that the thought can move the body and feel the things which happen to it" (letter of 28 June 1643 as translated by A. Kenny, *Descartes: Philosophical Letters* [Oxford: Clarendon Press, 1970], p. 142). Drew Leder has

demonstrated how Descartes's body-mind dualism "reifies the absences and divergences that always haunt our embodied being" (Drew Leder, *The Absent Body* [Chicago: University of Chicago Press, 1989], p. 108).

2 "To claim that discourse is formative is not to claim that it originates, causes, or exhaustively composes that which it concedes; rather, it is to claim that there is no reference to a pure body which is not at the same time a further formation of that body" (Judith Butler, *Bodies That Matter: On the Discursive Limits of "Sex"* [New York: Routledge, 1993], p. 10).

3 Ibid., p. 54. This strong claim, which makes the very constitution of bodily matter dependent on prior metaphysical and epistemological criteria, is in my view much more controversial than a claim also made (and embedded in a question) in the same paragraph: "a bodily schema is not simply an imposition on already formed bodies, but part of the formation of bodies." This latter statement comes close to the position which I wish to take myself in this essay.

4 Sigmund Freud, *The Ego and the Id*, vol. 19 of *Standard Edition of the Complete Psychological Works of Sigmund Freud* (London: Hogarth Press, 1971), p. 53. Future references to these volumes will be of the form: Freud, Standard Edition, vol:page.

5 *Bodies That Matter,* p. 11. I owe this reference and that on p. 10 to Kelly Oliver, in her unpublished paper, "Save the Mother: Psychoanalysis and Ethics," p. 11.

6 Merleau-Ponty attributes to "the Cartesian tradition" a "reflective attitude" that "simultaneously purifies the common notions of body and soul by defining the body as the sum of its parts with no interior, and the soul as a being wholly present to itself without distance." Maurice Merleau-Ponty, *Phenomenology of Perception,* trans. Colin Smith (New York: Humanities Press, 1962) p. 198.

7 I am distinguishing "sameness" from "identity," where the latter excludes difference altogether: as in "identity" theories of mind-as-(nothing but)-matter— notably in certain current neurological models of mind—or (in a more ninteenth century mode) of matter-as-(nothing but)-mind.

8 Maurice Merleau-Ponty, *The Visible and the Invisible,* trans. A. Lingis (Evanston: Northwestern University Press, 1968), p. 253.

9 Sigmund Freud, *The Ego and the Id*, p. 27. This statement is said to apply to the "conscious ego."

10 I say "psyche" in order to capture more adequately than does "mind" Freud's preferred term *Seele*, which is capacious enough to include unconscious as well as conscious aspects. See my unpublished paper, "Unconscious Mind and Pre-reflective Body," forthcoming in J. Morley and D. Olowski, *Merleau-Ponty: Desires and Imaginings* (New York: Humanities Press, 1996).

11 In this way Lacan detailed the hitherto unknown "specific action" postulated (but not specified) by Freud in his essay "On Narcissism" an action by which the ego is first formed. For Anna Freud's discussion of identification with the aggressor—which often includes specific bodily actaions of imitation—see *The Ego and the Mechanisms of Defense* (London: Hogarth, 1968), pp. 109-21.

12 Marcel Mauss, "Les techniques du corps," *Journal de Psychologie* 32 (1936); reprinted in M. Mauss, *Sociologie et anthropolgie* (Paris: Presses Universitaires de France, 1968), p. 367. My italics.

13 Ibid., p. 367.

14 Ibid., pp. 366-7, 382.

15 Ibid., p. 371 and p. 369 respectively. The full phrase of the second citation is "l'ouvrage de la raison pratique collective et individuelle." Durkheim adds "et individuelle" because what is learned socially must be *enacted* by individuals. On the

social determination of basic categories and forms of intuition, see Emile Durkheim, *The Elementary Forms of the Religious Life,* trans. J. W. Swain (London: Allen & Unwin, 1915), pp. 21-25.

16 I hyphenate "educate" and put it in quotation marks to indicate that it is a question of something more than imitation. As Mauss remarks, "In all the elements of the art of employing the human body the facts of *education* dominate. The notion of education can be superimposed on that of imitation" (Mauss, *"Les techniques du corps,"* p. 369; his italics).

17 Merleau-Ponty, *Phenomenology of Perception,* p. 146.

18 It is, once more, a question of identification, not now with my own mirror image or my aggressive rival but with the educative movements of the teacher or his or her surrogate. As Mauss says, "The individual borrows the series of movements of which he is composed from the act executed before him or with him by others"(*"Les techniques du corps,"* p. 369).

19 Although it may not be the object of any particular instruction, the dog paddle is not part of a preconstituted bodily repertoire—in the manner, say, of breathing or of one's diastolic and systolic heart movements. Mere flailing as it may appear to be, the dog paddle is nevertheless in-formed with the sagacity of swimming, albeit a sagacity in this case shared with members of another species.

20 "In sum, there does not perhaps exist a 'natural manner' with the adult"(Mauss, *"Les techniques du corps,"* p. 370).

21 Henri Bergson, *Matter and Memory,* trans. N. M. Paul and W. S. Palmer (New York: Anchor, 1959), p. 168.

22 Pierre Bourdieu, *Distinction: A Social Critique of the Judgment of Taste,* trans. R. Nice (Cambridge: Harvard University Press, 1984), pp. 190-91. I have substituted "at stake" for "involved." Bourdieu adds: "The practical philosophy of the male body a sort of power, big and strong, with enormous, imperative, brutal needs, which is asserted in very male posture, especially when eating, is also the principle of the division of foods between the sexes, a division which both sexes recognize in their practices and their language" (p. 192).

23 Ibid., p. 190. His italics. Bourdieu adds that taste is "an incorporated principel of classification which governs all forms of incorporation, choosing and modifying everything that the body ingests and digests and assimilates, physiologically and psychologically."

24 Ibid., p. 192. But Bourdieu also concludes, much less plausibly, that "the body [is] a social product which is the only tangible manifestation of the 'person'" (p. 192). This last step goes one step too far. It is one thing to hold (as Bourdieu also says) that "bodily properties are perceived *through* social systems of classification" (ibid., p. 193; my italics) and quite another to maintain that these systems—more precisely, the signs emitted by such systems—act to *constitute* the perceived body, which only "seem[s] grounded in nature" (ibid.). Only "seems grounded"? Why not *actually* so grounded: which is not incompatible with a social overdetermination by class and gender distinctions that nevertheless stop short of complete constitution. Or, more exactly, these distinctions do constitute the major ways in which the body is a signifying entity, a set of somatic signs, but *not* the body as presignifying— i.e., as material (biological and physical) and even as expressive (assuming that expressivity does not require a separate set of discrete signs for its conveyance). Thus I find the following statement of Bourdieu's at once redundant and problematic: "There are no merely 'physical' facial signs; the colour and thickness of lipstick, or expressions, as well as the shape of the face or the mouth are immediately read as

indices of a 'moral' physiognomy, socially characterized, i.e., of a 'vulgar' or 'distinguished' mind, naturally 'natural' or naturally 'cultivated'" (ibid., pp. 192-93). This is redundant insofar as the purely physical is not yet semiotic, and it is problematic insofar as the expressivity of a physiognomy need not be taken as an indicative sign, an index, of something else.

25   The first phrase cited in this sentence is from Pierre Bourdieu, *Outline of a Theory of Practice*, trans. R. Nice (Cambridge: Cambridge University Press, 1977), p. 95; the second citation is from ibid., p. 85. (I have changed "schemes" to "schemata"; and slightly altered the translation of the second quotation.) On p. 82, Bourdieu defines *habitus* as "a system of lasting, transposable dispositions which, integrating past experiences, functions at every moment as a *matrix of perceptions, appreciations, and actions* and makes possible the achievement of infinitely diversified tasks, thanks to analogical transfers of schemes permitting the solution of similarly shaped problems" (his italics). "Appreciations" clearly refers to taste.

26   "The dispositions and the situations which combine synchronically to constitute a determinate conjuncture are never wholly independent" (ibid., p. 83).

27   This is not to say that skill and taste are altogether alike. There are at least three critical differences. (1) In learning or relearning a skill, I need not be joining (or rejoining) a given group: when I decided to learn how to swim again, it was no part of my intention to become a member of a swimming team or even of the casual group of swimmers who gather on Wednesday nights at the Stony Brook gym: I would be just as content if I were able to swim in a private pool all by myself. The deliberate choice of relearning swimming is matched by the choice of whether I will make swimming a social activity. In contrast, the enactment of taste is forcibly social: there are no solo performances of taste. Even when done literally alone, the French working man perforce rejoins other members of his class of common fellow masticators. Where there can be truly idiosyncratic swimming, there can be no fully idiosyncratic eating. (2) In enacting a skill I not only undertake an agile action but in so doing I enter into something quite material, indeed elemental: e.g., water in the case of swimming, wood in that of carpentry. A skillful action entails its own characteristic material medium. In exhibiting taste, on the other hand, I do not undergo any such elemental immersion; instead, I enter into an entire social nexus that is neither material nor elemental—even if this has its own concreteness and density on its own terms. (3) Another major difference is found in the factor of *habitus*. A skill certainly requires habits qua settled routines: that is to say, specific corporeal bases for knowing how to perform a certain action with comparative facility. But habits do not *habitus* make: the latter (as the English equivalent "habitude" insinuates) entails elements of slow sedimentation over time, resulting in durable dispositions to act in particular prescribed ways (I can learn certain skills in a matter of minutes; I inculcate taste over periods of indefinite duration); of agreement by convention rather than agreement out of a concern for efficiency; of immanent style (the relation between taste and style is very close: both are deeply ingredient in the total life-form of their practitioners); and of knowledge that is more than know-how—a knowledge that is not so much learned as *absorbed* from the appropriate social milieu, "taken in" rather than merely "taken up," as with so many skills.

28   Cf. John Dewey, *Human Nature and Conduct* (New York: Henry Holt, 1922), pp. 66 ff., and Merleau-Ponty, *Phenomenology of Perception*, pp. 145-46.

29   "Taste, the propensity and capacity to appropriate (materially or symbolically) a given class of classified, classifying objects or practices, is the generative formula of life-style" (Bordieu, *Distinction*, p. 173). Cf. also ibid., p. 174: "Taste is the basis of

the mutual adjustment of all the features associated with a person."

30 "Taste is the practical operator of the transmutation of things into distinct and distinctive signs. . . . It continuously transforms necessities into strategies, constraints into preferences, and, without any mechanical determination, it generates the set of 'choices' constituting life-styles. . . . It is a virtue made of necessity which continuously transforms necessity into virtue by inducing 'choices' which corresond to the condition of which it is the product" (ibid., pp. 174-75).

31 On right- vs. left-handedness in human culture, see Robert Hertz's classical essay, "Death and the Right Hand," in *Right and Left: Essays on Dual Symbolic Classification*, ed. R. Needham (Chicago: University of Chicago Press, 1973), p. 3 ff.

32 Marshall Sahlins, "Colors and Cultures," in *Symbolic Anthropology: A Reader in the Study of Symbols and Meanings*, ed. J. L. Dolgin, D. S. Kemnitzer, & D. M. Schneider (New York: Columbia University Press, 1977), p. 167; in italics in the original.

33 "Incarnate meaning is the central phenomenon of which body and mind, sign and sense are abstract moments" (Merleau-Ponty,*Phenomenology of Perception*, p. 166).

34 Michel Foucault, *Discipline and Punish: The Birth of the Prison*, trans. A. Sheridan (New York: Pantheon, 1979), p. 136.

35 On rituals of the table, and blowing one's nose, see Norbert Elias, *The Civilizing Process: The History of Manners*, trans. E. Jephcott (New York: Urizen, 1978), chap. 2, sections IV, VI.

36 Concerning the comparative latitude (and yet outer limits) of social rules, e.g., for table manners, see the variant texts translated by Elias. Ibid., pp. 84-99.

37 On the docile body, see Foucault, *Discipline and Punish*, pt. 3, chap. 1..

38 On the evolution of the idea of "civilized" (vs. "cultural"), see Elias, *The Civilizing Process*, chap. 1, pt. 1.

39 If one does not act in proper taste—and this means *do it bodily*—one acts not so much in bad taste as without taste, tastelessly, inducing all the cultural opprobrium such aberrant action brings with it. Bourdieu remarks astutely that "nothing seems more ineffable, more incommunicable, more inimitable, and, therefore, more precious, than the values given body, *made* body by the transubstantiation achieved by the hidden persuasion of an implicit pedagogy, capable of instilling a whole cosmology, an ethic, a metaphysic, a political philosophy, through injunctions as insigificant as 'stand up straight' or 'don't hold your knife in your left hand'" (*Outline of a Theory of Practice*, p. 94; his italics).

40 "Incarnate meaning is the central phenomenon of which body and mind, sign and sense are abstract moments" (Merleau-Ponty, *Phenomenology of Perception*, p. 166).

41 This is not to suggest, however, that the neurotic engages in *anonymous* actions. On the contrary: they are highly personalized. It is *habitus* that is properly anonymous in status. See Christina Schües, "The Anonymous Powers of the Habitus," *The Newsletter of the Study Project in Phenomenology of the Body* 7, no. 1. (1994): pp. 12-25 as well as Elizabeth A. Behnke, "A Readers' Guide and Commentary" to the essay by Schües in ibid., pp. 25-37.

42 S. Freud, *Dora; An Analysis of a Case of Hysteria*, trans. J. Strachey (New York: Macmillan, 1963), p. 57. I shall refer to this henceforth as "the Dora case."

43 Jennifer Church of Vassar College points out that skills respect bodily anatomy in ways that hysterical symptoms do not. But I disagree with her observation that "hysteria uses the body for a task that is essentially non-bodily—i.e. to say what

would be 'better' said to language," (e-mail communication with author, 21 April, 1995). The hysteric's body, on my view, *already says* in corporeal terms what is meant to be communicated—and it does so both eloquently and efficiently, so long as it can come to be adequately interpreted (e.g., by psychoanalysis or more expressly by somato-analysis).

44 As Bourdieu observes in treating "the dialectic of objectification and embodiment": "If all societies and, significantly, all the 'totalitarian institutions,' in Goffman's phrase, that seek to produce a new man through a process of 'deculturation' and 'reculturation' set such store on the seemingly most insignificant details of dress, bearing, physical and verbal manners, the reason is that, treating the body as a memory, they entrust to it in abbreviated and practical, i.e., mnemonic, form the fundamental principles of the arbitrary content of the culture. The principles embodied in this way are placed beyond the grasp of consciousness, and hence cannot be touched by voluntary, deliberate transformation, [and] cannot even be made explicit" (*Outline of the Theory of Practice,* p. 94; Bourdieu underlines "dress," "bearing," and "manners").

45   J. Breuer and S. Freud, *Studies on Hysteria* (New York: Avon, 1966), p. 42; in italics in the original. Freud, *Standard Edition*, II:7.

46   On mnemic symbols, see Freud, *Standard Edition* II:16-17 (*Five Lectures on Psychoanalysis*) and *Standard Edition*, II: 297 (*Studies on Hysteria*).

47   Freud, *Standard Edition*, II:4 (*Studies on Hysteria*): "Our experiences have shown us, however, that the most various symptoms, which are ostensibly spontaneous and, as one might say, idiopathic products of hysteria, are just as strictly related to the precipitating trauma as the phenomena to which we have just alluded and which exhibit the connection quite clearly" (in italics in original).

48   The density is *not* that of consciousness. Freud's first use of "defile" is in reference to consciousness as a place of restricted movement of repressed memories: cf. Freud, *Standard Edition*, II:291 (*Studies on Hysteria*). He uses the phrase "narrow defile" at the beginning of chapter 3 of *The Interpretation of Dreams* to signify the moment of passing through the analysis of a specimen dream and just discovering the prospect of its meaning as a form of wish fulfillment.

49   The connection between the psychic trauma and the symptom consists in "what might be called a 'symbolic' relation between the precipitating cause and the pathological phenomenon—a relation such as healthy people form in dreams" (*Studies on Hysteria*, p. 39). Freud makes it clear in chapters 4-6 of *The Interpretation of Dreams* that both condensation and displacement (especially the latter) aim at producing a "distorted" manifest dream that evades the censorship of the official ego.

50   Concerning this point, Susan Bordo cites Catherine Clément—"the hysterics are pointing; they are pointing"—and then remarks that "the pathologies of female protest function, paradoxically, as if in collusion with the cultural conditions that produce them, reproducing rather than transforming precisely that which is being protested. . . . Female pathology reveals itself here as an extremely interesting social formation, through which one source of potential for resistance and rebellion is pressed into the service of maintaining the established order" (Susan R. Bordo, "The Body and the Reproduction of Femininity: A Feminist Appropriation of Foucault," in *Gender/Body/Knowledge: Feminist Reconstructions of Being and Knowing*, ed. A. M. Jaggar and S. R. Bordo [New Brunswick: Rutgers University Press, 1989], p. 22; the citation from Clément's *The Newly Born Woman* is from ibid., p. 20).

51   Freud, *Standard Edition*, III:49 (*The Neuro-Psychoses of Defense*), his italics ("sum of excitation" is also italicized). Freud adds: "The conversion may be either

total or partial. It proceeds along the line of the motor or sensory innervation which is related—whether intimately or more loosely—to the traumatic experience. By this means the ego succeeds in freeing itself from the contradiction [i.e., the incompatible idea]; but instead, it has burdened itself with a mnemic symbol, which finds a lodgment in consciousness, like a sort of parasite."

52 This is the definition of "somatic compliance" in J. Laplanche and J-B. Pontalis, *The Language of Psychoanalysis,* trans. D. Nicholson-Smith (New York: Norton, 1973), p. 423.

53 "The Neuro-Psychoses of Defense," *op.cit.*, p. 50.

54 For the idea of symptoms as "entering into the conversation," see Freud, *Standard Edition,* II:148, 296 (*Studies on Hysteria*).

55 Freud, *Standard Edition* II:113 (*Dora*).

56 Not that Freud is immune to the lure of stratificational models: in the Dora case as well, he says that "in *the lowest stratum* we must assume the presence of a real and organically determined irritation of the throat" (ibid., pp. 97-98; my italics). Compare here Merleau-Ponty's view: "It is impossible to superimpose on man a lower layer of behavior which one chooses to call 'natural,' followed by a manufactured cultural or spiritual world. Everything is both manufactured and natural in man" (*Phenomenology of Perception*, p. 189). This statement presages the later passage from *The Visible and the Invisible* which I have cited in the text above (cf. n. 48).

57 As Derrida is wont to put it, it is a matter of "neither/nor, that is, *simultaneously* either *or*" (Jacques Derrida, *Positions,* trans. A. Bass [Chicago: University of Chicago Press, 1981], p. 43; his italics).

58 Freud, *Dora*, p. 40; his italics. Freud continues: the symptom "cannot occur without the presence of a certain degree of *somatic compliance* offered by some normal or pathological process in or connected with one of the bodily organs. And it cannot occur more than once—and the capacity for repeating itself is one of the characteristics of a hysterical symptom—unless it has a psychical significance, a *meaning*" (ibid.; his italics).

59 Each exists, we might say, to leak into the other, to be "a being by promiscuity": "It is in the universal structure 'world'—encroachment of everything upon everything, *a being by promiscuity*—that is found the reservoir whence proceeds this new absolute life" (Merleau-Ponty, *The Visible and the Invisible,* working note of January 1960, p. 234; my italics).

Part II

The Embodied Self

3
Phantoms, Lost Limbs, and the Limits of the Body-Self

Stephen Meuse

The following notes of my own case have been declined on various pretexts by every medical journal to which I have offered them. There was, perhaps, some reason in this, because many of the medical facts which they record are not altogether new, and because the psychical deductions to which they have led me are not in themselves of medical interest. I ought to add that a great deal of what is here related is not of any scientific value whatsoever; but as one or two people on whose judgement I rely have advised me to print my narrative with all the personal details, rather than in the dry shape in which, as a psychological statement, I shall publish it elsewhere, I have yielded to their views. I suspect, however, that the very character of my record will, in the eyes of some of my readers, tend to lessen the value of the metaphysical discoveries which it sets forth.[1]

With these words, thirty-six-year-old Philadelphia physician Weir Mitchell opened one of the strangest short stories written in the nineteenth century, "The Case of George Dedlow." This was not Mitchell's first literary effort; he had been a contributor to medical journals on a regular basis since 1850, and had seen a handful of his poems published in magazines as early as 1846. But when in 1866 *The Atlantic Monthly* led off with this bizarre tale of soldiers and spirits, the public response astonished author and publisher alike. In a power-fully realistic narrative that anticipated the work of Stephen Crane, Mitchell described how a young medical student enlists in the Union army and sustains wounds that eventually necessitate the amputation of both arms and legs. After

one of his operations, having awakened from the effects of the chloroform—
Dedlow became aware of a cramp in his left leg:

> I tried to get at it to rub it with my single arm, but finding myself too weak,
> hailed an attendant. "Just rub my left calf," said I, "if you please."
> "Calf?" said he. "You ain't none. It's took off."
> "I know better," said I. "I have pain in both legs."
> "Wall, I never!" said he. "You ain't nary leg."
> As I did not believe him, he threw off the covers, and, to my horror, showed
> me that I had suffered amputation of both thighs, very high up.
> "That will do," said I faintly."[2]

The sensation of the enduring presence of a severed limb becomes the focal
point of Dedlow's narrative. While recuperating at what was called the Stump
Hospital in Philadelphia, the ex-medical student reflects on his own condition,
and observes with a clinician's eye the experiences of his fellow amputees:

> I amused myself at this time by noting in my mind all that I could learn from
> other limbless folk, and from myself, as to the peculiar feelings which were
> noticed in regard to lost members. I found that the great mass of men who
> had undergone amputations for many months felt the usual consciousness
> that they still had the lost limb.[3]

Presently, Dedlow ventures an hypothesis on the strange phenomenon. Our
knowledge, he surmises, is comprised of a numberless series of individual
impressions which are conveyed from the body's periphery to the brain by the
nervous system. When a limb is severed, the agitated nerve endings continue to
transmit messages to the brain, which refers these sensations "to the lost parts to
which these nerve threads belonged." Nerves are like the bell rope that may be
pulled from any part of its length but still causes a ring at the front door. Later,
as nerve endings heal, these transmissions diminish, eventually disappearing
along with the eerie sensation of possessing that which is not. In some cases,
however, these sensations persist in the form of uncomfortable sensations he
calls "neuralgia."

Although Dedlow goes on to describe variations experienced by amputees
with respect to this phenomenon, his most serious reflections center on the
question of his own identity. He had lost, by his own reckoning, four-fifths of
his body weight. He slept and ate little, and his heart rate had declined to forty-
five beats per minute.

> Still more remarkable, however, were the psychical changes which I now
> began to perceive. I found to my horror that at times I was less conscious of
> myself, of my own existence, than used to be the case. This sensation was
> so novel that at first it quite bewildered me. I felt like asking someone if I
> were really George Dedlow or not. . . . At times the conviction of my want
> of being myself was overwhelming and most painful. It was, as well as I can
> describe it, a deficiency in the egoistic sentiment of individuality. About
> one half of the sensitive surface of my skin was gone, and thus much of
> relation to the outer world destroyed. As a consequence, a large part of the

receptive central organs must be out of employ, and, like other idle things, degenerating rapidly. Moreover, all the great central ganglia, which give rise to movements in the limbs, were also eternally at rest. Thus one-half of me was absent or functionally dead. This set me to thinking how much a man might lose and yet live. I thus reached the conclusion that a man is not his brain, or any one part of it, but all his economy, and that to lose any part must lessen the sense of his own existence.[4]

Dedlow's consideration of his diminished body size, along with his strange neural sensations had put him in a metaphysical frame of mind. He considers the nature of personal identity, self-consciousness, and relation of mind to body. While musing on such matters, he is approached by a fellow patient, an adherent of Spiritualism, who invites him to a séance. At first reluctant, Dedlow agrees, and that night, within a "circle" led by the medium Sister Ephemera, he is briefly reunited with the spirits of his departed legs, who attach themselves to their former places, carry him for a few blissful moments across the floor, and then disappear, lowering the astonished (and converted) man gently to the carpet.

Mitchell apparently intended this story only for his own amusement and that of his friends. Its appearance surprised even the author who had no idea that it had been submitted for publication. Most surprising to all concerned were the letters that began to pour in from thousands of readers who thought the story true, and some who even wanted to establish a fund for the unfortunate Dedlow. Five years later, Mitchell published a second, less imaginative, account of limb-loss phenomena in another periodical, *Lippincott's*. In this article Mitchell, speaking in the third person, tried to play down his sensational Dedlow story calling it a mere *jeu d'esprit*, "He certainly never could have conceived it possible that his humorous sketch, with its absurd conclusion, would for a moment mislead anyone."[5] There reverberates however, in this second article, an echo of Mitchell's earlier work that falls strangely and suggestively upon the ear. Mitchell entitled the essay "Phantom Limbs."

What is the experience of the phantom limb and what is its history? Most persons suffering the amputation of a leg, arm, hand, or any external body part experience an enduring consciousness of the lost member which is vivid and frequently painful. Because of this, patients often find it impossible to believe that they have suffered amputation until they confirm the truth of it by sight. The most vivid experiences of phantoms coincide with those parts of the body which are most rich in sense receptors and which extend prominently into the environment, and it is relatively uncommon for phantom limbs to seem to be either complete or continuous. An individual, for example, who has lost a leg will usually sense the foot and toes most vividly, while the midportion of the limb seems non-existent. In some cases the hand or foot may be felt to emerge directly from the stump. Like its ghostly namesake, the phantom part is often unpredictable in its coming and going, at one moment or time of day vividly present, at another entirely withdrawn. It appears that changes in shape, position, and intensity of phantoms may be related to the emotional or psycho-logical state of the experient. Some amputees have reported that they are capable of moving and flexing their phantoms at will (even being able to pass them through the body or other solid objects), while others testify that theirs are unresponsive to command. In a few terrible cases, amputees assert that their absent limbs have remained permanently twisted in the grotesque postures they experienced while awaiting medical attention, as if the memory of their trauma were too awful to be forgotten. While many phantoms eventually seem to be absorbed into the stump, there are reports of men experiencing vivid phantoms fifty years and more after their amputations.

A case study that is extraordinary for both its classic features and an unusual variety of wonderful symptoms was presented by Allen Bailey and Frederick Moersch in 1941. I present it here in its entirety as it appears in their 1941 Canadian Medical Journal article:

> A man, aged sixty-two years, came to the clinic because of symptoms entirely unrelated to his absent limb. We chanced to ask him about it. Twenty-two years previously, while he had been at work, his entire arm had been drawn into the cogs of a machine and amputation had been necessary. Following amputation he had felt the absent limb, and for a month or two he had experienced the sensation of moving the hand of the absent limb freely, but when seen at the clinic he had to use terrific force to move it. He had never seen a physician concerning the phantom limb nor had he taken any treatment. He had simply learned to live with a phantom limb of which he was more conscious than of the one present. Even more interesting was the fact that for a week prior to the accident he had had a sliver under the nail of the index finger, which had been moderately painful and annoying. He stated emphatically that he later felt the sliver in his phantom limb as it had existed before the accident. This sensation had continued for about two years. As further evidence of the psychical processes involved, we wish to mention that he had ordered the amputated limb to be burned. While the hospital authorities had been burning the extremity he had felt the ashes gradually drop off the phantom limb.[6]

Amid the bevy of fascinating details that crowd this brief narrative is one that might easily escape notice. It is the fact that prior to this close questioning, the subject had evidently never confided his bizarre experiences to a doctor! This not uncommon reluctance to divulge the secret of the phantom limb may help explain how the phenomenon remained obscure for so long. Although amputation is known to be very ancient, references in literature to the consciousness of lost limbs are not frequent before the nineteenth century.[7] How could a phenomenon so extraordinary remain on the back shelf of medical research for centuries, then emerge so suddenly?

What first commands our attention is the fact that the experience of the painful amputated limb moved into the professional and public spotlight within the format of a tale of the supernatural, rather than in a scholarly monograph or field report as we would expect. Although Mitchell himself, as we have seen, considered it a lark, we have good reason to doubt that the choice of format was haphazard. It appears far more likely that "The Case of George Dedlow" forms a link with a tradition of ghost story composition that began in the seventeenth century, and which through the nineteenth century released fundamental tensions that had arisen as new scientific and materialistic trends gradually displaced older, more wholistic, views of human beings in the world.

In her book *Night Visitors: The Rise and Fall of the English Ghost Story*, Julia Briggs emphasizes that the success of the supernatural tale depends on a backdrop of rationalism and sober realism against which it can contrast a series of events which appear to defy reason.[8] Although the tradition of ghost storytelling has its roots in preliterate antiquity, it was this contrast of order, reason, and light with disorder, irrationality, and darkness which made the nineteenth century, and particularly the last half of the nineteenth century, "the high water mark of the form"—a golden age of the genre.[9]

Fitting in with other manifestations of the so-called gothic revival,

> the ghost story set about deliberately reviving the system of magical interaction between man and his universe that belonged to a past increasingly identified with the middle ages. The conviction with which authors wrote of traditional beliefs was often related to their knowledge or intuitive understanding of that lost animistic world-picture.[10]

Though the "inherent logic" of such a world picture has been discredited by science, and, in general, Western culture has been gradually disengaging itself from it, "the older concepts have not totally lost their power because most people occasionally think and react like savages; primitive magical laws still govern the outlook and beliefs of children, and are often re-instated in dreams, neuroses and madness."[11]

In *Totem and Taboo*, Freud analyzed the persistence of such thought. He gave the name animism to the "doctrine of souls, and, in its wider sense, the doctrine of spritual beings in general,"[12] and noted that a key element of its philosophy is "the omnipotence of thought" by which the line which science has drawn between the subjective and objective world is obliterated. Freud considered this "the spiritual expression of the natural state of man, so far as it is accessible to our observation."[13] While it is based on a certain dualism (spirit and matter), the interaction between the two is free and constant, and the universe constituted by their interaction is wholistic, and characterized by a telepathy in which distance is disregarded and the whole (body and spirit, animate and inanimate) comprises a fluid unit. Freud considered this view as a variety of neurosis, asserting that "the omnipotence of thoughts, the over-valuation of mental processes as compared with reality, is seen to have unrestricted play in the emotional life of neurotic patients and in everything that derives from it."[14] Moreover, Freud saw in the neurotic behavior of the individual who had failed to progress from childish modes of thought to adulthood a pervasive cultural tendency. If we accept Freud's analysis, we should not be surprised that during the period in question, from, let us say, the mid-seventeenth century to the early twentieth, a period during which the scientific worldview is making a strong bid for cultural hegemony, fundamental tensions created by resistence to its offensive will be evident. William Day has noted that "nineteenth century readers saw the source of anxiety and fear in the failure of religious, scientific and philosophical systems to create a sense of wholeness and unity in the self and in the world, which would have allowed individuals to define their own existence."[15] The emergence of the ghost story with its catalogue of anomalistic experience challenged the claims of science to provide a fully comprehensive account of human experience, particularly with reference to subjective states. During the nineteenth century, the ghost story is an ubiquitous and persistent critic of the movement of science toward a definition of man that is wholly materialistic, mechanistic and which asserts that he is doomed to die with his body.

Further, the ghost story deals with that most provocative and problematic phenomenon, that outpost on the frontier between subjective and objective reality: the apparition. Apparitions, varying from the vague sense of presence through the thirsty man's desert mirage, the visions of religious mystics, and the visual representations of persons known to have died, are persistent and well attested phenomena that enjoyed an upsurge of interest concurrent with the rise of scientific materialism. In several important ways, the experience that Mitchell introduced in "The Case of George Dedlow" pursues closely issues we have described as important in the emergence of ghost stories in general.

First, against the realistic backdrop of Civil War service, the grisly experience of amputation opens the door to the subject's heightened awareness of aspects of being to which he had heretofore been oblivious. The deprivation of his limbs forces the thoughtful Dedlow to confront vexing questions of self-identity and self-definition as he experiences a reordering of the borders between his body and the world. Old assumptions are challenged as Dedlow is faced with sensory experience which cannot be denied, but does not fit any previous corporeal or psychological paradigm.   Moreover, Dedlow experiences what seems to be a bona fide apparition of his own body; his severed legs, though absent (indeed buried), maintain a telepathic communication with the body of which they were formerly a part, thereby suggesting the real existence of a spirit body or soul. The connection that Mitchell sensed between the age-old tradition of the apparition or ghost and the experience of the lingering presence of an amputated limb not only prompted the fictional Dedlow story, but continued to inform the more formal discussion published in *Lippincott's* five years later, and is responsible for the "haunted" quality of the vocabulary that has persisted in the discourse of the phenomenon to this day. The most obvious example is, of course, the phrase "phantom limb," which was taken up immediately as the term used both by specialists and the general public to describe the experience, but in Mitchell's *Lippincott's* article he went even further, richly coloring his report with spectral metaphors. "A person in this condition," he noted,

> is haunted, as it were, by a constant or inconstant fractional phantom of so much of himself as has been lopped away—an unseen ghost of the lost part, and sometimes a presence made sorely inconvenient by the fact that while but faintly felt at times, it is at others acutely called to his attention by the pains or irritations which it appears to suffer from a blow on the stump or a change in the weather.   There is something almost tragical, something ghastly, in the notion of these thousands of spirit limbs haunting as many good soldiers, and every now and then tormenting them with the disappointments which arise when, the memory being offguard for a moment, the keen sense of the limb's presence betrays the man into some

effort, the failure of which of a sudden reminds him of his loss.[16]

A more detailed examination of the tradition of supernatural literature in the nineteenth century would further illuminate Mitchell's choice of format as he prepared to describe his experiences with amputees and their persistent sense of presence of their lost limbs. I propose that the proliferation of the popular ghost story in midcentury and Mitchell's sly exploitation of both the genre and the medium (the popular monthly magazine) were two key elements contributing to a surge of interest in the neglected subject.

It seems clear, however, that a third ingredient can be identified among these other important trends—a phenomenon which reached its peak during the moment when materialism seemed poised for victory. Like the ghost story, Spiritualism owed its life to a tension between the materialist and the animistic worldviews. Like science, it sought empirical proof for its beliefs; like religion, it focused on the soul or spirit and its survival of bodily death. By the mid-nineteenth century, Spiritualism had assumed a position of leadership with respect to the various forms of antimaterialist thought trends, both in the effect it produced on the direction of scientific inquiry and the sheer numbers of persons involved in some form of its practice. Not since the Great Awakening in the first half of the eighteenth century had America experienced something to compare with the fascination in the supernatural that gripped the nation in the 1850's. Although its ancestry is undeniably in a remote, occult past,[17] the proximate impetus for its popularity in the United States was the experience of a Hydeville, New York farm-family named Fox, who in 1848 reported that they had heard mysterious rappings which appeared to have an intelligent source. When one of the daughters suggested a simple code, communication was established with what was claimed to be a spirit. Further "questioning" resulted in the identification of the spirit as that of a pedlar, murdered by a former owner of the home. In fact, a body was unearthed in the basement of the house. Some neighbors were impressed with the spirit's ability to answer queries with plausible accuracy. When Margaretta Fox later visited her sister at Rochester, the rappings began to occur there also, and the phenomenon bloomed. The three Fox daughters became the first mediums, and their system of sitting around a table to invite contact with the spirit world soon became the hallmark of the séance.[18]

The rapidity with which this new movement spread was stunning. In 1855, The New England Spiritualist Association boasted nearly two million adherents nationally. Within ten years Spiritualism had made successful invasions of Britain, Germany, France, "and soon reached all parts of the civilized world."[19] At first, the phenomena produced by mediums was rather unimpressive. Table turning and rappings were the most common, little more than parlor magic, really. Automatic writing and trance speaking were also popular. It was not long, however, before mediums began to produce phenomena of a more spectacular nature. Called "materializations," these were the appearances in the séance environment of body parts: hands, arms, legs, heads, and eventually of entire bodies. Phantom bodies.

Since Spiritualism's first concern was the survival of bodily death, it naturally challenged the scientific community to offer an explanation for the many eyewitness accounts of apparitions which came both from its own ranks and from a growing popular literature. Spiritualism's focus on apparitions—those problematic creatures whose domain is the shadowy acreage between the subjective and the objective—sought a reconciliation of science and the occult just at the point where the conflict between them was most acute. Spiritualists were bound together by the conviction that apparitions, whether found in the abundant ghost lore of the prescientific period or the necromantic séances of their Victorian drawing rooms, were, in fact, the spirits of the dead. But, to the question of how spirits might make themselves seen and heard by mortal faculties, Spiritualists offered a scientifically plausible—if unproven—hypothesis. The doctrine of the ethereal body asserted that each individual, in addition to possessing a physical body, also possesses a duplicate body comprised of a "substance subtler than physical matter, which leaves the physical body upon death but continues to serve as a vehicle for the individual's memory and personality."[20] This body is thus at once a material and a spiritual body, which during life corresponds perfectly and completely in extension and location with the physical body, interpenetrating it and remaining invisible and unperceived during life but separating from it at death and enduring in a vaporous and changeable form.[21] Also called the psychic body, it was identified by Spiritualists as the source of all the supernatural phenomena they claimed to experience, and constituted firm empirical proof of life after death.[22] While Spiritualism before 1850 had focused on communication (clairvoyance and the reception of spirit messages by planchette or spirit-writing during trance states), after this date Spiritualism became primarily an exercise in manifesting the ethereal body, and these manifestations were often sensational. Gossamer hands appeared to float in space, while diaphanous arms embraced the sitters and fingers plucked the boutonnieres from gentlemen's lapels. British chemist Sir William Crookes, Royal Society member and convinced spiritualist,[23] described a hand he saw in a séance that

> is not always a mere form, but sometimes appears perfectly lifelike and graceful, the fingers moving and the flesh apparently as human as that of any in the room. At the wrist or arm, it becomes hazy and fades off into a luminous cloud.[24]

Under the mediumship of the American D. D. Home, three sitters watched as, in "the full light of the day . . . twenty pairs of hands formed and remained visible for about an hour."[25] At a séance conducted by the celebrated Davenport Brothers in London in 1868, a Seignor Damiani saw an arm materialize "of such enormous proportions that had it been composed of flesh and bone, it would, I verily believe, have turned the scale (being weighed) against the whole corporeal substance of the smaller Davenport."[26] The *Hartford Times* of 18 March 1853 described a séance conducted by Home during which the reporter watched as a silver-colored, self-luminous hand formed itself at Home's elbow. The medium Eusapia Paladino produced a third arm which emerged from her shoulders and then receded, and English medium and clergyman W. Stainton Moses was able to produce a second pair of fully formed arms, above his own, which retracted if an attempt was made to touch them.[27]

The literature documenting materializations of the kind described above is abundant. Newspapers of the period often published accounts of séance experiences, and public fascination with the subject became generalized and widespread. At his post in the Turners Lane Army Hospital in Philadelphia, Weir Mitchell did not fail to notice that there was some extraordinary affinity between the experiences of séance devotees and his own amputee patients, among whom the experience of phantom limbs was an everyday affair. There Mitchell began to make the connection between the experience of his soldier-patients, whose bodies refused to acknowledge the final loss of a departed member, with that of the tens of thousands of Spiritualists who refused to accept the loss of their departed loved ones.

Indeed, the experience of these phantom limbs shared striking similarities with their ghostly counterparts. Individual experience with them varied widely, and they seemed to come and go with a lack of predictability. Only occasionally was the entire limb present or continuous, so that, for example, the foot might be sensed to protrude directly from a knee or thigh stump with no perception of a calf connecting the two. Some Spiritualists and psychical researchers believed that the experience of the phantom limb offered a new, scientific demonstration of the reality of the ethereal body: the sudden and traumatic severing of the limb exposing to consciousness, for a period, a phantom self, the perception of which was ordinarily masked by the richer sensual experiences of physicality. In addition, the experience of some amputees who testified to a continued sensate connection with the severed limb itself seemed to demonstrate that telepathic communication, at least under certain circumstances, was possible.[28] American philosopher and psychologist William James, who founded the American counterpart of the London Society for Psychical Research in 1885, thought carefully about the implications of Mitchell's discoveries at the Stump Hospital. In an essay prepared in 1887, James reported the results of his own investigations, a survey undertaken by mail made with the assistance of a list of names supplied by the manufacturers of artificial limbs. Armed with a well-thumbed copy of Mitchell's *Injuries of Nerves*, James sought to interpret the responses in a way that would demonstrate some solid conclusions. He was disappointed, partly because the respondents were in many cases inarticulate, but also because their experience differed so widely. His closing paragraph is, nonetheless, remarkable:

> My final observations are on a matter which ought to be of interest to students of "psychical research." Surely, if there be any distant material object with which a man might be supposed to have clairvoyant or telepathic relations, that object ought to be his own cut-off arm or leg. . . . Of course, did such telepathic rapport exist, it need not be found in every case. . . . One man writes that he has dug up his buried leg eight times and changed its position. He asks me to advise him whether to dig it up again, saying he "dreads to."[29]

Like Mitchell, whom he read enthusiastically, Freud trained as a neurologist and took special interest in those nervous disorders which were thought to have environmental causes and in the mysterious symptoms of hysteria. Though he remarked in a footnote to an autobiographical sketch that his interest in the natural sciences, medicine, and psychotherapy had been merely a detour "to the cultural problems that had fascinated me long before, when I was a youth scarcely old enough for thinking,"[30] when Freud returned to the generalized philosophical problems that were his first love, he brought with him a baggage train of clinical observation and rationalization that forms the largest body of the standard edition of his work and for which he is most well known.

Freud's disdain for religion and any form of Spiritualism is well documented. He was convinced that religious belief of any sort was an illusion, that is, an outward projection of human mental life in general and of its wishes in particular. In this sense, Freud was firmly in the Enlightenment tradition, displaying in his epistemological assumptions the clearest distinction between subject and object, inside and outside, between self and other. In *The Future of an Illusion* (1927), he solemnly pronounced that

> Scientific work is the only road which can lead us to a knowledge of reality outside of ourselves. It is once again merely an illusion to expect anything from introspection and intuition; they can give us nothing but particulars about our own mental life.[31]

Thus, for Freud, the scientific method is characterized by the ability to rightly distinguish between phenomena which is interior, mental, and subjective and that which is external, extramental, and objective. Conversely, he perceived in prescientific thought "an intention to impose the laws governing mental life upon real things,"[32] and considered that "Spirits and demons . . . are only projections of man's own emotional impulses. [Man] turns his emotional cathexis into persons, he peoples the world with them and meets his internal mental processes again outside himself."[33]

Later, in *The Ego and the Id*, we meet this same construct applied to the history, not of culture, but of the individual. The infant has no ego or selfhood and experiences no boundaries between himself and the world. This condition Freud referred to as primitive narcissism. "An infant at the breast," he noted, "does not as yet distinguish his own ego from the external world as the source of the sensations flowing in upon him."[34] The process of ego development, by which the child comes to gradual realization of selfhood, is actually a process of progressive loss, as little by little the all-encompassing, world-embracing, undifferentiated ego of the infant suffers the trauma of a sort of amputation. This process of ego-crystalization is painful, but by the third year it has resulted in a discontinuity by which the original infantile bliss of cosmic oneness has been left behind. This process, according to Freud, is primarily tactile:

> One comes to learn a proceedure by which, through a deliberate direction of one's sensory activities and through suitable muscular action, one can differentiate between what is internal—what belongs to the ego—and what

is external—what emanates from the external world. In this way, one makes the first step towards the introduction of the reality principal which is to dominate future development.[35]

In this way, he continues,

The ego detaches itself from the external world. Or, to put it more correctly, originally the ego includes everything, later it separates off an external world from itself. Our present ego-feeling, then, is only a shrunken residue of a much more inclusive—indeed, an all-embracing—feeling which corresponded to a more intimate bond between the ego and the world around it.[36]

"All ego is bodily ego." Freud's famous dictum arose out of his conviction that the sense of self is ultimately derived from bodily sensations, chiefly from those which are experienced at the body's surfaces. [37] In a footnote to his essay *The Ego and the Id*, he noted that this bodily ego "may thus be regarded as a mental projection of the surface of the body."[38] Freud guessed that the determinative factor in the infant's sense of what was ego and what was not ego was rooted in the child's initial experience of what he could immediately enjoy (his own body) and what he desired but could not always enjoy (his mother's breast). The gradual move away from undifferentiated oneness toward clear and sharp boundaries represents, for Freud the rationalist, a progress toward both ego formation and acceptance of the reality principle.

Twentieth-century studies in the development of the bodily ego have confirmed many of Freud's basic insights.[39] Ego definition is now seen as a gradual process, advancing little by little from infancy as a result of three factors: tactile interaction with the world surrounding the body, interpersonal relationships, and visual data.[40] The work of Head and Schilder in particular have demonstrated that body image (an outwardly projected inward and mental structure) and body schema (the outward extension of the body reflected in an inward, mental map) are plastic.[41] As Freud had suggested in *The Ego and the Id*, pain and painful illnesses have indeed played a key role in our understanding of how we arrive at ideas about the extent of our body.[42] In particular, it has been the experience of the painful amputated limb which, from the moment when Weir Mitchell first described it in 1866, has not failed to provide researchers with a window on the development of the bodily ego; specifically, how the ego-construct responds to a sudden and traumatic alteration in the relationship between its own "idea" of itself (the outward projection of its extension and shape) and new data from the body's periphery which contradicts this idea and seeks to adjust it into correspondence with new external boundaries. The result, phantom limb phenomena shows, is a reluctance on the part of the ego to "believe" what it is being told and a tenacity with respect to the retention of its integrity in the face of deprivation. Despite the evidence of the senses, the amputee continues to meet, in the world of his experience, that image of his body which his ego has habitually projected outward, though, very likely, in a form that is disturbed and strangely changed—not quite itself, but still familiar as the self.

In an analysis of data collected by W. B. Haber in 1954, Seymour Fisher noted a link between the vividness and persistence of phantom limbs and the definiteness or firmness ascribed by each man to his body image boundaries.[43] He found that those amputees who displayed very well defined and firmly demarcated body image boundaries had significantly less vivid and persistent phantoms, while those who possessed vague and indefinite boundaries experienced a greater degree of hallucinatory distortion.

Thus, one way to explain phantom limb phenomena is as a result of the body's attempts to reestablish body image or ego equilibrium in the face of severe stress, and its vividness is somehow connected with the firmness or vagueness with which the amputee has previously experienced the boundaries of both his bodily and psychological ego.   Such an analysis could likewise be offered as an explanation for the experience of apparitions among persons whose diffuse body boundaries predispose them to such experiences. In his masterful and comprehensive 1941 essay on phantom limbs and body shape, George Riddoch articulated the terms of the problem:

> Knowledge of the persistence, as a phantom, of a limb which has been removed must be as old as survival from amputation. Nevertheless it is an interesting and, at first, surprising fact that medical literature up to comparatively recent times has been almost silent on the subject.[44]

Before undertaking his own survey of the attempts to understand and explain the phenomenon, Riddoch felt obliged to offer a solution to the problem of why the painful amputated limb attracted little attention until the mid to late nineteenth century. He divides his answer into two parts, first observing that the preternatural quality of the symptoms must have seemed to the surgeon "beyond reason" and that, in such a case, "it would not be surprising if the unfortunate patient was regarded as an obstinate, lying fellow or even possessed of the devil." From the point of view of the patient, Riddoch imagines that "dread of the unusual, of disbelief, or even of the accusation of insanity" may have provided sufficient motivation to keep his experiences to himself.

But these explanations are themselves problematic on several counts. First, Riddoch's assumption that the painful limb has always been experienced, or always been experienced in the same way, cannot be assumed. Second, that view of the human body which prevailed in the premodern world was one, as I have shown, which was amenable to notions of an animating soul existing side by side with the human body, and this view was not restricted to the uneducated.[45] Admiral Nelson, for example, believed that the phantom sensations he experienced in the fingers of his amputated arm provided "a direct proof of the existence of the soul."[46] In other words, the phantom limb experience was perfectly capable of explication within a soul-oriented thought structure. Third, the more generalized belief in the reality of apparitions and the supernatural during the prescientific period would not, it seems to me, have shrunk from an experience that tended to confirm its own assumptions.   Riddoch would likely have done better to reread "The Case of George Dedlow," in which Weir Mitchell made the original, critical, and correct judgement that phantom limb experience and the body apparitions of Spiritualism share some fundamental affinity.

In the experience of the painful lost limb, the amputee experiences vividly the tangible reality of his own bodily ego identity. While Freud believed that nothing was less real than the outward projection of a merely mental construct (the making of an object out of what was properly subject), the phantom limb argues with all the power of pain that this experience is real in the truest sense, despite the fact that strictly speaking the absent limb is merely hallucinated.

Studies performed on lepers who have lost limbs gradually due to attrition and on children with congenital limb loss have demonstrated that it is the sudden and traumatic loss of the limb that produces the phantom, that phantoms are not experienced when limb loss has been very gradual or has predated the firming of ego boundaries. With time, adjustments to new body boundaries may be made.[47] Weir Mitchell had observed in the Stump Hospital that eventually "even the most persistent phantoms must fade away" as adjustments are made to new perceptions of the limits of self.

In their essay on phantom limbs, Twombly and Price noted that, in their opinion, false pregnancy and imaginary playmates also belong in the category of the phantom experience. This is noteworthy because it demonstrates that the bodily ego is capable of embracing and making its own that which cannot be strictly said to belong to the body; that it can and often does reach out beyond the surface of the skin to lay claim to something "out there" as its own. I would suggest that further additions to the phantom category might include the experience many of us have had of stepping around the space once occupied by a table or chair which has been moved out of a long familiar spot in the home, or the experience of widow or widower who occasionally continues, even after years, to turn to speak to the departed spouse. Along this line, Lawrence Kolb notes that "in instances of dismemberment, one can expect mourning for the loss of a part, similar to that for separation of a significant person" and further remarks that "invariably, the loss of the body part leads to mourning, and to fantasies over the way in which the part is to be interred or destroyed."[48] How apt a description of the experience of the hallucinated limb! It is not mere poetry that calls it a mourning, a reluctance of the body to acknowledge the sudden and traumatic loss of that which long experience and habituation had convinced it to be self. Thus, a dramatic diminution of the body results in a tactile, visual, and, not least, psychological deprivation, which conflicts with a persistent sense of integral selfhood in the bodily ego and produces a confusion of subjective and objective realities resulting in the exteriorization or "dramatization" of the beloved lost member—the phantom limb.

This same confusion of inner and outer, subjective and objective, mental and substantive, Seymour Fisher describes as primary factors in the hallucinations of his schizophrenic patients, going so far as to say that "body image boundary disturbance is a factor basic to hallucinatory experience."[49] It is Fisher's conclusion that the hallucinatory experiences of a schizophrenic patient are grounded in a concern for bodily integrity:

> The body image organization which he has built up to deal with bodily experiences is often seriously disrupted. He becomes alarmed at the consequently altered quality of his bodily experiences and is aroused to the

possibility that his body is suffering radical transformation or damage of some kind. Within the setting of such alarm he may therefore find the projections of symbolic representations of his body via hallucinations to have reassurance value. That is, by populating the exterior world with rather autonomous symbolizations of his body he can defend against sensations of catastrophic dissolution.[50]

Combining the insights of Kolb and Fisher, then, we learn that hallucinations may occur either as mourning, that is, a reluctance to acknowledge the loss of a part of the body by dramatizing its continued existence, or as a defensive stratagem brought into play when the body senses an imminent threat to its own dissolution and populates the environment with symbolizations of its own durable being.

By the mid-nineteenth century, the body had been suffering enormous cultural stress as the focus of a raging controversy lasting nearly two hundred years. Long accustomed to an extension into the universe with which, according to the tenets of both science and religion, it had formed a substantial and psychological unity, it had endured at the hands of the field surgeons of the new science a most egregious series of amputations, by which it became isolated, disconnected, and objectified. Subsequently, it was faced with the trauma of mechanization and determinism and stripped of its image of deity. Alarmed at the altered quality of the bodily experience and aroused to the possibility that the body was suffering radical transformation (to use Seymour Fisher's words), a reaction, characterized by hallucination, in the form of romantic subjectivism, gothic ghost stories, and, most of all, Spiritualism, gripped large segments of American and European society. A pervasive sense of loss and bereavement experienced by romantics who longed to be reunited with the universe, by Spiritualists who could not abide the thought of extinction, and by ordinary people who mourned the loss of loved ones in wars waged on an unprecedented scale was the tragic result. [51]

Freud saw it and understood it, but he could not sympathize with it. He admitted to his friend Romain Rolland that he had never experienced that "oceanic feeling" that he took to be a remnant of primitive narcissism. It is likely that the reason for this is simply that his own ego was so firmly bounded, so unambiguous, so clearly cognizant of self and other that he was merely incapable of it. Fisher and Kolb have described how individuals with the most clearly defined boundaries are least likely to experience a merger of subjective and objective experience. In this regard Freud may be said to have been a classic case.

A neurosis, Freud reminded us, is not itself a problem—it is a solution to a problem. I am proposing that the personal and historical affinity between the hallucinated limb and the apparition is explicable when the two experiences are seen as bodily defenses unconsciously mobilized against essentially similar threats. On the one hand we have the amputee's personal dramatization of his lost limb as a response to the trauma of amputation and the schizophrenic patient's exteriorization of his unrecognized self in a hallucination. In each of of these cases the hallucination is experienced only by the individual. On the other hand we have the social body responding to extreme stress on its traditional, culturally defined boundaries by projecting its own anxiety of loss and disconnection into an epidemic of hallucinations, first in a spate of ghost stories and then in the materializations of the séance.

However, if we accept this explanation, it seems that we must be willing to accept a corollary principle which asserts that the continuity of the body and world is no mere cultural perception or historical habit, but is grounded in some persistent relation which is the source of our intuitions and which, when disturbed by incoming messages to the contrary, will assert itself in individual and cultural phenomena of denial, the forms of which have been the subject of this paper.

If this is true, and it seems as though scientific and philosophical trends of the twentieth century are in the process of bearing this out,[52] a radical reassessment of the subject/object relation must be undertaken by science, philosophy, and medicine. This reassessment would entail the reassertion of the subjective and the admission that no act of cognition can be undertaken without reference to the perceiver—indeed, that there is no object without a subject, that "the world of objects are full of our ideas" as the English realist Samuel Alexander admitted,[53] and that, as Bishop Berkeley said, we cannot contemplate the world without, at the same time and in some sense, contemplating our own ideas. Recognition of this fact will force us to reject the view that there is something primitive and subrational about the position that our bodies and minds—that is, our selves—remain the mediators of all experience with the world and, in fact, extend themselves as far into it as our senses reach.

Freud's idea that ancient men mistook the order of ideas for the order of nature must itself be seen as the product of a (partially) mistaken and outdated worldview; and the comment of Freud that the crystallized ego "separates off an external world for itself" creating in the adult an ego feeling that is "only a shrunken residue of a much more inclusive—indeed, an all embracing—feeling which corresponded to a more intimate bond between the ego and the world around it" will have to be seen, not only as the uncomfortable position of the modern individual, but as the epitaph on a generation that bore the brunt of the neuroses engendered by modern, scientific culture. This revised view will accept anew the long-intuited truth that the self is indeed intramundane—that the world sinks deeply into the ego, that the ego extends indefinitely into the world—and that between this extension of body into world and penetration of world into body, there emerges a dialectical definition of selfhood which is a real analogy of the act of cognition.

Notes

1   S. Weir Mitchell, *Atlantic Monthly,* July, 1866.
2   Mitchell, "The Case of George Dedlow," p. 128.

3   Mitchell, "The Case of George Dedlow," p. 131.
4   Mitchell, "The Case of George Dedlow," p. 137-39.
5   S. Weir Mitchell, "Phantom Limbs" *Lippincott's*, 8 (1871): 564.
6   Allen A. Bailey and Frederick P. Moersch, "Phantom Limb," *The Canadian Medical Association Journal* (July 1941): 41.
7   Douglas Price and Neal Twombly have recently uncovered evidence showing that the literature on the phantom limb phenomenon is somewhat more extensive than once thought, and have found over fifty references to it between the years 1610 and 1798. Douglas Price and Neil Twombly, *The Phantom Limb: An Eighteenth-Century Latin Dissertation Text and Translation with a Medical-historical and Linguistic Commentary*, Languages and Linguistics Working Papers no. 3 (Washington D.C.: Georgetown University Press, 1972).
8   Julia Briggs *Night Visitors: The Rise and Fall of the English Ghost Story.* (London: Faber, 1977), p. 16.
9   Briggs, *Night Visitors*, p.14. Likewise, in her work *The Gothic Imagination* (London and Toronto: Associated University Press, 1982), Linda Bayer-Berenbaum notes that "a basic orientation to reality is apparent in all Gothic works." See p. 10 f.
10   Briggs, *Night Visitors, p.* 17.
11   Briggs, *Night Visitors, p.* 16.
12   Sigmund Freud, *Totem and Taboo,* trans. James Strachey (1913; reprint, New York: W.W. Norton & Co., 1950), p. 75.
13   Freud, *Totem and Taboo,* p. 77.
14   Freud, *Totem and Taboo,* p. 87.
15   William Patrick Day, *In the Circles of Fear and Desire* (Chicago: University of Chicago Press, 1985)p. 10.
16   Mitchell, "Phantom Limbs," p. 8.
17   An excellent summary of the occult antecedents of Spiritualism including a discussion of demonism, witchcraft, alchemy, and Mesmerism is found in the article "Spiritualism" from *The Encyclopedia of Occultism and Parapsychology*. The most complete historical treatment of the origins of the movement in America can be found in Frank Podmore's *Studies in Psychical Research.*
18   Since I assert that Spiritualism proper appears to be native to America and came to France only later, the use of the French term here may seem anomalous, or at least anachronistic. In French its ordinary meaning is that of a convocation or conference of any sort—a "sitting." Its appropriation by the Spiritualists may derive from Mesmerism, itself an important precursor of both Spiritualism and dynamic psychiatry. On Mesmerism, see Henri Ellenberger, *Discovery of the Unconscious,* (New York: Basic Books Inc. Publishers, 1970), and Robert Darnton, *Mesmerism and the End of the Enlightenment in France* (Cambridge: Harvard University Press, 1968).
19   Ellenberger, *Discovery of the Unconscious*, p. 84.
20   Leonard Zusne and Warren H. Jones, *Anomalistic Psychology* (Hillsdale, N.J.: Lawrence Erlbaum Associates, 1982), pp. 270-71.
21   "Aura" is the term used to describe the slight extention of the ethereal body beyond the surface of the skin.
22   See articles "Psychic Body," "Ether," and "Etheric Double" in *The Encyclopedia of Occultism and Parapsychology.*
23   The list of prominent British philosophers, scientists, and literati who were either converted to Spiritualism or involved in its investigation is a long one. Those who were connected with the London founding, in 1882, or subsequent work of the Society for Psychical Research include such luminaries as F. W. H. Myers (who

coined the term *telepathy*), Henry Sidgewick, Edmund Gurney, Alfred Russell Wallace, Sir William Barrett, Walter Leaf, and Sir Oliver Lodge.

24 *Encyclopedia of Psychic Science*, s.v. "Materialization."
25 *Encyclopedia of Psychic Science*, s.v. "Materialization."
26 *Encyclopedia of Psychic Science*, s.v. "Materialization."
27 *Encyclopedia of Psychic Science*, s.v. "Materialization."
28 This, at least, was the opinion of British spiritualist and psychical researcher Sergeant Cox who came to this conclusion almost immediately after the publication of Mitchell's "Phantom Limbs" in 1871.
29 William James, "The Consciousness of Lost Limbs," *Essays in Psychology* (Cambridge: Harvard University Press, 1983), pp. 204-15.
30 From the postscript which Freud added in 1935 to his autobiographical study. See Sigmund Freud, *Standard Edition of the Complete Psychological Works of Sigmund Freud*, ed. James Strachey (New York: W. W. Norton & Company, 1971), 20:72.
31 Freud, *The Future of an Illusion* (New York: W. W. Norton & Company, 1928), pp. 31-32.
32 Freud, *Totem and Taboo*, p. 91.
33 Freud, *Totem and Taboo*, p. 92.
34 Freud, *Civilization and Its Discontents*, trans. James Strachey (New York: W. W. Norton & Company, 1961), pp. 13-14.
35 Freud, *Civilization and Its Discontents*, p. 14.
36 Freud, *Civilization and Its Discontents*, p. 15.
37 Freud, *The Ego and the Id*, p. 26.
38 The footnote appears on p. 26.
39 See the articles "Body Image" by Seymour Fisher and "Identity, psychosocial," in the *International Encyclopedia of the Social Sciences*. Note that in Fisher's brief but excellent bibliography he cites the full five volumes of Freud's collected papers.
40 See George Riddoch's "Phantom Limbs and Body Shape," *Brain* 64 (1941): 197-222, for a thorough survey of the development of body image theories and their debt to the phantom limb.
41 See Henry Head, et al. *Studies in Neurology* (London: Hodder & Stoughton, 1920); and Paul Schilder, *The Image and Appearance of the Human Body* (New York: International Universities Press, 1950).
42 Freud, *The Ego and the Id*, pp. 25-26.
43 W. B. Haber, *Effects of Loss of Limb on Sensory Organization and Phantom Limb Phenomena*. (PhD diss., New York University, 1954). Fisher's analysis of Haber's data appears in "Body Image Boundaries and Hallucinations," in *Hallucinations*, ed. Louis Jolyon West, M.D. (New York and London: Grune & Stratton, 1962), pp. 243-44.
44 Riddoch, "Phantom Limbs and Body Shape," p. 197.
45 For an early and fascinating treatment of the soul as ethereal body see Origen's "Dialogue with Heraclides," in *Alexandrian Christianity* (Oulton and Chadwick), pp. 437-455).
46 Riddoch, "Phantom Limbs and Body Shape," p. 197. It seems strange that Riddoch did not himself see the problem posed to his own analysis by this remark.
47 See Marianne L. Simmel, "Phantoms in Patients with Leprosy and in Elderly Digital Amputees." *American Journal of Psychology* 69, pp. 529-45.
48 Lawrence Kolb, "Phantom Sensations, Hallucinations, Body Image," in *Hallucinations*, ed. Louis Jolyon West, M.D. (New York and London: Grune &

Stratton, 1962), pp. 243-44.

49 Fisher, "Body Image Boundaries and Hallucinations," p. 252.

50 Fisher, "Body Image Boundaries and Hallucinations," p. 255.

51 In support of the view that the psychological perception of shrinking body boundaries results in symptomatic discomfort, see C. T. Tart, "Concerning the Scientific Study of the Human Aura," in *Altered States and Human Potentialities*.

In studies performed on the physical and psychological aspects of the human aura, the author demonstrated that persons convinced that their aura had shrunk to the surface of their skin experienced profound discomfort, anxiety, and even pain. Conversely, those who were convinced that their aura was indefinitely extended expressed a sense of happy well-being and contentment.

52 This is the position taken by Morris Berman in his book *The Reenchantment of the World* (New York: Bantam Books, 1988).

53 In his 1918 work *Space, Time, and Deity*.

4
Identity and the Subject in Performance
Body, Self and Social World

Loren Noveck

The place of the body in the signification and representation of identity is a contested site for contemporary theories of subjectivity. The body may be the site that produces a truth that escapes or exceeds the trap of realist representation, as in Elin Diamond's 1989 article "Mimesis, Mimicry, and the True-Real": "Can the body's true-real destabilize mimetic truth, or, put another way, can the body signify and also escape signification?" For Diamond, the female body, even under the representational regime of realism, can provide access to the true-real, Kristeva's *vreel*, by always signifying beyond that which it supposedly represents.

The body may be politically pliable, an emblem of a high consumerist postmodernism, a seductive realm of multiple identities enhanced by the unconstrained participation of the body, as it is for Lauren Berlant and Elizabeth Freeman in "Queer Nationalities": "[P]recisely because it *is* a body, [it] readily lends itself to any number of polymorphously perverse identities . . . unboundedness as a commodity identity exploits the way that the fantasy of being something else merges with the stereotype to confer an endlessly shifting series of identities upon the consumer's body." In both of these positions, the body becomes a site for restoring contingency or even volition to subjectivity.

By contrast, my other two examples present the body as the locus of a coercive perception of subjectivity; the subject is divorced from what might be a true context by virtue of its being read through a body. In one case, this happens by the postulation of identity only at the surface of the body, legible yet dispensable, ahistorical, meaningless: "This tendency to spectacle-ize Black bodies, to read race as a type of ephemeral surface narrative which need not be understood in the context of American history or culture is . . . constantly recurring" (Reid-Pharr, "The Spectacle of Blackness"). In the other the marked (particularly but not exclusively by gender) body is seen as trapped by spectacle into representation, a trap which some sort of radical subjectivity (also, importantly, figured through the body) can escape. I quote Jill Dolan, from *The Feminist Spectator as Critic*: "[R]epresentation . . . present[s] . . . the female body as spectacle. . . . In its refusal of heterosexuality the lesbian body cannot be narrativized as spectacle."

Each of these structures, obviously, makes certain assumptions about the extent to which subjectivity is necessarily constructed through the relationship between a body and identity categories, a body and representation, a body and the site of speech or the possibility of self-representation. Read together, they construct a particular way of using the idea of the body to intervene in a current theoretical debate between volitional (or even, in the words of one critic, inventional) and coercive models of subjectivity. This debate has been most clearly worked out in the debates ensuing from Judith Butler's *Gender Trouble.* Butler's own belated articulation that her much vaunted concept of gender performativity does not equate simply to a choice of how one inhabits one's gendered body has by no means shut down discussion on this subject.[1]

Although the writers cited above would most likely not place themselves squarely in either camp—rather, they seem to construct for themselves a tension between a coercive subjectivity from which one must escape into a volitional one—their positions suggest another problematic, which I would like to phrase in loaded language as the opposition between subjectivity as performative and subjectivity as spectacular. In the most reductive sense, performativity restores a public and visible agency to subjectivity; spectacularity denies it. Performativity alluringly promises one the power to enact (or at least to reenact) one's subjectivity. Spectacularity traps the subject in the gaze of the other, constructing a completely determined view of subjectivity, from which there is no escape. In both cases, the specific forces that produce different kinds of social subjects are elided; the performative model provides a way of reacting on an individual level to a monolithic set of social norms, while the spectacular model quashes even this level of intervention.

This very opposition, however, is itself built on a metaphorical relationship to the representational practices of performance; that is, the very terms of performativity and spectacle come out of the vocabulary of theatre and construct an unacknowledged but crucial paradigm of subjectivity as occurring at two sites at once: both for the subject itself (the performer or spectacle, to extend the metaphor) and for an external or social agency (the audience). The metaphoric nature of the relationship all too frequently disappears, however, as the idea of the performative is used to collapse the distinction between the representational and the real. I want to unpack the metaphor, to use concrete attention to performance practice, in its various twentieth-century manifestations, to construct a position that is not wedded to this opposition. I think the idea of performance theory allows one to hold a concept of the subject attentive to both its production and its reception, though the terms through which performance theory has historically done this themselves fall prey to the opposition.

The terms of this debate serve to link theoretically separate discursive realms as they engage with the problem of performativity, subjectivity, and the body: cultural theory dealing with the construction of subjectivity, twentieth-century performance, and performance theory. Theatre functions as a space to read the concrete structuring of the use of the body in constructing subjectivity by providing a location for the analysis of a clear distinction between the body of the actor and the speaking subject-position of the text, each logically prior to the moment of their conjunction.

Performance provides a critical site for the interrogation of the connection between subjectivity, as it has been theorized in discursive social frameworks, and the material body because it permits a separation between the two positions. In any text-based instance (although this term is awkward, it serves to link traditional theatre together with much contemporary performance art and to separate these forms from happenings, rituals, and other kinds of performed events where these boundaries are less clear), the spoken subject provided by the text is in relationship to, but not the same as, the material body provided by the outside agency of the performer.

The presumption of both the differential generation of the two fields and their determinate relationship allows a precision of analysis that avoids several different theoretical tendencies to universalize the legibility and specificity of a body in talking about the production of subjects. This analytic body is neither the Lacanian-generated psychoanalytic subject-in-language, which claims independence from bodily norms but takes its impetus from a determinate perception of the sexed body, a morphological imaginary; nor the over-determined Foucauldian body that is unable to be more specific than the level of the social episteme. But this object of study is also neither the intrinsically and essentially gendered, sexed, raced body, whether that is seen as a biological limitation or a political necessity; nor, certainly, the multiple, liminal, provisionally embodied subject who pervasively inhabits the metaphors of contemporary thought on subjectivity. In particular, this limited acknowledgment of the nonsingular site of production of the subject challenges the proposition that any kind of multiplicity is liminal, playful, performative, and therefore critically or politically progressive. A play provides a particular kind of object of study—one that is at the same time textual and (for lack of a better word) material, in the present tense and in a historical moment of its construction, one that provides all the elements we use to think about the meaning of subjectivity in a controlled and malleable space. And this peculiar place that is the stage provides a ground from which to interrogate the supposed radical tropes of the postmodern subject. Homi Bhabha's mimicry, Judith Butler's subversive repetition, Teresa de Lauretis's in-between and elsewhere feminist subject, Gloria Anzaldúa's mestiza, Donna Haraway's cyborg, Trinh Minh-ha's I/i. In their original incarnations these theories promise utopias; when applied to theatrical representations, they become simple descriptive categories for the representational-material constructs that dramatic characters become. The fictional subject, forced always into a relationship (a power struggle?) with the prefictional acting body, can serve as a corrective to the radical or utopian impulses of these theories.[2]

The logical extrapolation of this argument would be this: any dramatic text, especially in a moment where mimetic acting is both unquestioningly accepted by most theatre and stunningly displaced in the rest, creates theoretically bodiless, purely discursive subject positions, which then demand to be filled by bodies under a contract to suppress their "own" subjects. The question of what kinds of bodies are demanded and accepted by certain texts, what factors in the history or identity of the speaking dramatic character/subject are and are not seen to be enhanced, determined, located upon the surface of the body of the actor is not simply the question, as it is often posed, of whether to recuperate or reject mimesis. Without rejecting the convention of acting itself (which, make no mistake, is a powerful theme if a singularly disingenuous one in much performance art), mimesis is unavoidable. Nor are these questions simply or primarily about gender, though feminist work has come closest to asking them. I want to stress this point because it seems that a crucial intervention is restoring the ways in which a whole series of social regimes of the subject are produced as comprehensible through an invocation to the body in performance— not only the familiar addition to gender of race, not even (or perhaps especially not) the equally familiar cousins of class and sexuality, which have extremely different relationships of legibility to the body, but such disparate examples as illness and health, family, nationality, history, are produced through an equally wide series of relationships to the performing body. Rather, the question seems to be what, under the auspices of the postmodern, postcolonial, feminist subject, mimesis means, how it functions and fails, and how its significant interruptions can be understood.

The materiality of the body, then, can be read under the conditions and constraints of theatrical representation by producing a constant tension between the realist idea of phenomenological legibility of the character-body relationship and the necessary instability of any text's determination of subject positions; this provides a tool to rethink the meaning of performance and performativity in both performance theory and larger theories of subjectivity. At what level and with what degree of certainty does a text compel the bodies that fill its roles? What categories of identity rhetoric seem to read off of the body in unmediated ways in performance, and which need to be compulsively narrativized (for example, sexuality or ethnicity); which are denaturalized through an appeal to the performative (as in Judith Butler's erstwhile reading of gender); and which are naturalized through that same invocation in performance?

Different kinds of texts and performance practices demand and repress specific kinds of identity/subjectivity. The three genres showing these relationships most clearly are realism, performance art, and what I call late twentieth-century postrealism. The next section of the paper defines these three realms and sketches readings in each that show how these body problematics operate around, in this instance, the issue of race. Race is used because its operations are very clear in these texts and because it illustrates the problems in performance theory that are addressed in the final section of the paper by standing to the side of the gendered and sexual dynamics with which the theory is primarily concerned. Realism overdetermines the actor-character relationship by demanding that the two coincide in the fictional realm. Through its acting techniques and its conception of character psychology as embedded in character physique, it encourages the spectator to read the character upon the body of the actor. For this, it becomes the demon-figure of performance theory from Brecht to the present for refusing to provide the critical distance that allows social critique and for failing to provide the tools to effectively address the coercive social relationships maintaining its recognizable individual portraits. Langston Hughes's play *Mulatto* illustrates the tragic triumph of one such social relationship, that which maintains oppositional categories of race. This play shows a nuclear family of sorts: a white southern plantation owner in the 1920s, his black housekeeper/ mistress of long standing, and their four mixed-race children, whose differences in skin colors are clearly specified in the text. Their father, Colonel Norwood, both acknowledges his mulatto children—he pays for them to be educated in northern schools—and insists upon their blackness; in the summers, they return to the plantation and act as servants or field hands. The two daughters, minor characters, are both "light enough to pass," and in fact one (unbeknownst to her father) is in New York doing so, and the other is being educated for the same. They slip uneasily into the category of whiteness by leaving the text and the geography of the play. One son stays on the plantation, marries a black woman, and takes up his place, as a servant, in the bifurcated southern racial economy.

The second son, Robert, a light mulatto with "proud thin features like his father's"(2), refuses this opposition, insists on being visibly and physically recognized as the heir to his white half rather than his black half, insists on privileging the "wrong" portion of the contradictory message his body bears. This brings him into a violent conflict with his father; Robert insists on his resemblance to Norwood, his light skin and his gray eyes, while Norwood comments on both his physical and social position as a black man: "How come your skin is yellow and your elbows rusty? How come they threw you out of the post office today for talking to a white woman?" (23) The violent social conflict borne by Robert's refusal to submit to the appropriate regime of embodiment erupts, as it so constantly does in the dramatic economy of realism, in individual physical violence; he kills the Colonel and then shoots himself, one step ahead of a lynch mob.

Much performance art equally overdetermines the performer-performance relationship, albeit in the opposite direction. Especially in the currently chic realm of one-person monologues, performance art, despite its theoretically acclaimed deconstruction of traditional relationships between the artist and the audience and standard narrative conventions, relies on the authenticity provided by autobiography, by the projection of the subject behind the text as real and really present. An idea of the inherent subversiveness of a "pure performance," drawn from Artaud and later theorists like Peter Brook, underlies the work. The central location given to the performance artist, the projection of a relationship of continuity between the artist and the material, recreates belief in the necessity of certain subject-bodies to certain articulations. The reading suggested here is even more fragmentary than the one above, intended more to suggest a line of inquiry than to sufficiently address the text in question. Performance artist Robbie McCauley did sections from her piece "My Father and the Wars" at Brown University in the fall of 1994; this piece is a series of anecdotes, illustrated by slides, on the place of the black men in her family in various American wars and other individual conflicts at home. She uses the phrase "these are my stories" as something like a refrain, continually positioning herself, the artist, as in possession of these narrative fragments. During the question period after her performance, I asked what she meant by this phrase; I wanted to inquire by the question whether possession came in the telling, in performance, or whether these belonged to her, to Robbie McCauley, in one of several possible more concrete senses: as the inheritor of a genealogy, as an African-American person, as a person of a certain generation marked by some of the wars of which she told. She was unable to answer this question and, I think, perceived it as hostile in ways I never intended. They *were* her stories, and this was not to be questioned. The performance text functions as an extension of the performance artist; McCauley's legitimacy as a performer becomes crucially tied to her legitimate possession of these stories, these histories which define her.

The label "late twentieth-century postrealism" is admittedly a neologist's technique for avoiding the term "postmodernism" for the moment; the relationship between modernism and postmodernism is enormously complex in theatre and quite different from that of other literary genres. The term is meant to indicate that some recent texts do show a self-consciousness about the production of subject positions that could only follow both realism (with its "lamination" of actor to character) and performance theory's critiques of realism (Brecht's "alienation effect"). But they also show a willingness to reengage with the problematic of realism, the problem of narrative, and other levels of dramatic articulation that certain strains of performance theory would willingly dispense with. These texts operate in a tension with the assumptions of realism about the relationship between acting body and acted character; for example, the disjuncture between the male body and female character in Caryl Churchill's *Cloud Nine* is only significant against an expectation of conjuncture; this also operates at the level of social expectations in this text, so Edward's announcement that he is a lesbian (in act 2, where he is in fact played by a male actor) only means something if we the audience have an understanding of "lesbian" that demands a female body.

Suzan-Lori Parks's *Imperceptible Mutabilities in the Third Kingdom*, first produced in 1989, is divided into five sections. Sections 2 and 4 are choral fugues set on slave ships between worlds. Sections 1, 3, and 5 occur partially in darkness; rather than performers who simultaneously enact and speak lines, the lines are spoken as slides of these performers flash overhead in mechanical sequence. The geographical split between worlds that forms a key metaphor for sections 2 and 4, then, is transformed into a split between and among different social realms of subjectivity in the narrative segments. I want to focus briefly on section 1, which is further subdivided into six parts. In parts A and C, as I have described above, Mona/Molly, Chona/Charlene, and Verona/Veronica carry on a domestic conversation (about, among other things, Molly's unemployment as a result of her expulsion from a speech class), in a highly stylized version of urban black English, while slides flash overhead. Their language and their bodies, their representations and their selves, are not equatable. In parts B and D, lit normally on stage, a naturalist lectures to us about his scientific observation of "Molly" and "Charlene" (not, we know, their real names) in fluent officialese. But his expert testimony speaks of an observation we are being denied. Are the slides, then, the scientist's view of the women? What we would see, if we could? Something else entirely? Are they images of Molly, Charlene, and Veronica, the properly named, properly individuated subjects for analysis, or of Mona, Chona, and Verona, the echoing fragments of a historical narrative that makes black women into disciplinary objects? In part E these two worlds collide on stage, as the naturalist enters Mona and Chona's house to retrieve his camera. Two worlds, two different realms of language, interact; the naturalist's purpose seems to be the motor of the scene, but he is thwarted by the women and by a robber, who steals his cockroach-on-the-wall camera. And in the final segment, Verona speaks at the naturalist's podium, sliding between the two kinds of language, the two kinds of performance, the two kinds of space. Neither is produced as natural to her; we know where she learned to enact each subject position. But this duality, multiplicity, we might say, is also not valorized; the uneasy inhabitance of two worlds, in and across the text, is a struggle for Verona to maintain and difficult for us, as spectators, to take in.

The kinds of readings outlined above serve as the impetus for a rethinking of the terms of performance theory, especially feminist performance theory, in an attempt to produce a way of thinking about performance that neither uncritically valorizes a kind of pure, untextual performativity nor assumes mimesis to be a trap, in short, a way of theorizing performance that is able to think with a high degree of specificity about the ways in which individual instances of performance produce particular kinds of operative social relationships of subjectivity. This, in turn, provides a wedge for investigation into the claims made by larger theories of postmodern subjectivity.

The founding writers of performance theory, Brecht and Artaud, begin with the assumption that bourgeois realist representation is corrupt and unable to present the necessary truths for an audience. They focus on the theatrical apparatus as a whole, as a technology of reproducing a social world which they would see changed utterly. Brecht's concern is primarily with the production of contingency, of restoring a sense of the theatre as story and as product rather than as a partial and flawed reflection of the social world which takes itself for whole. His project is not antimimetic, but rather the search for a better mimesis, one which more accurately illustrates the produced and therefore changeable nature of both the stage image and the social world it describes. He wants to restore critical perspective, intellectual distance, to the relationship between the audience and the performance. Artaud, on the contrary, wants to shatter the boundaries between actor and spectator; his critique sees language, referentiality itself, as the basis for the despised social order, and therefore his ideal theatrical practice would operate by direct and nonlinguistic sensory communion. Artaudian representation neither describes nor reflects reality, but rather denies representation. Where Brecht would use theatre as a tool to change reality,

Artaud would destroy theatre in an attempt to destroy the social order.

Despite the enormous usefulness of their work, Brecht's in particular, in thinking about theatre as a whole and about the relationships of spectatorship, their models have certain conceptual flaws that have been retained in performance theory to the present. Both idealize specific non-Western performance practices as the cornerstones of their new theories of performance. Brecht turns to Chinese theatre and Artaud to Balinese, but in both cases these models serve as the radical and superior other by virtue of postulating a different relationship between actor and performance, one which leaves unnatural the relationship between the performance and the real. Although it is impossible to know whether this foundational denaturalization comes from their inability to understand the languages and conventions of the theatres in question, these models provide something they see as unlocatable within Western theatre.[3] This insistence legitimates a blind spot around a careful consideration of Western acting itself.

Feminist performance theory combines a Brechtian critique of the apparatus of theatre with a theory of spectatorship and identity constructed out of a tangled and problematic relationship with film theory, the result of which is the production of the theatre apparatus as a coercive technology of gender. Its main concern is investigating the way in which Western theatre is incapable of dealing with the question of difference at the level of subjectivity (rather than, as in Brecht, difference at the level of social change). One enormous problem for this field is its reliance on a disenabling concept of gender as spectacle, gender as trap, which I believe to come largely from a dehistoricized reading of feminist film theory. The idea of gender as spectacle for the production of narrative on behalf of a male spectator, an argument made first by Laura Mulvey, makes its claims only for a particular kind of cinematic practice and theory and in a context of prior writers on film who were painstakingly aware that the models of spectatorship and of representation being constructed for film did not apply in theatre and, in fact, did not apply precisely because the material presence of the actor intervened in the spectatorial relationship. Yet the move in performance theory seems to be to overlay Brecht's apparatus critique with Mulvey's, to say that if a particular kind of theatre practice can be critiqued as an apparatus for the kind of relationship it produces with spectators and if a kind of film practice can also be so critiqued, then a transitivity applies. This loses both the intense specificity of psychoanalytically inflected feminist film theory and, perhaps more disenabling, the always crucial emphasis in Brecht on the mutability of theatre form as form. This fear of being trapped in the psychoanalytically defined machine of gendered spectatorship, a fear of spectacle, leads to two different tendencies in feminist performance theory, each of which seeks to restore the freedom of the performative through some theoretical operation.

The first is seen most prominently in the work of Jill Dolan and Sue-Ellen Case: the use of the lesbian body as an inherently disruptive and deconstructive force in theatrical representation. Positing the lesbian as a subject outside of the gender traps of realism enables a strange theoretical alliance between anti-mimesis and essentialism; that is, lesbian desire, or lesbian identity, existing both inside and outside the theatre, becomes a necessarily antimimetic and therefore radical force. Theatre and the street together become the subversive spaces for the radical performativity of "lesbianity," that is, a state of being a lesbian that is both on the street and on the stage, that comes from neither the set of sexual practices referred to by lesbianism nor a particular political alliance such as the "woman-identified-woman" of certain strains of feminism. When lesbian desire or identity is "real" (whatever that means) and materialized in a community or audience of mutual desire, the referentiality of the female body disappears. It's especially striking in Dolan's *The Feminist Spectator as Critic* because she's gone to such lengths to assert that there is no transcendental feminist signification possible around the always historically conditioned female body, and yet, in her discussion of Split Britches and other lesbian work, lesbian identity, legible to the lesbian spectator, performed by and only by a body that materializes itself as a lesbian outside the theatre, becomes disengendered, loses the troubled qualities of the female body, and takes on the subversive resonances of the lesbian body. Dolan does admit the troubling implications of this reification of both the lesbian performer and the lesbian spectator in her later work, but her response to this is to explore the potential for training the heterosexual woman in the strategies of the lesbian, rather than questioning the usefulness of the lesbian body itself.

Case's work depends more on the postulation of the butch-femme couple as this transcendent lesbian subject, but the effect is quite similar: the lesbian body is not subject to the significations of the female body, is able in some unmediated way to speak and perform not only lesbian identity but also class difference, relationships to maternity, etcetera. It is the offstage identities, for example, of the members of Split Britches that speak to an audience through the production of collective identity. For Case, any attempt to alienate (in the Brechtian sense; that is, to distance so as to analyze) gender must be motivated by lesbian desire or else fail on the grounds of essentialism.

The other strand of feminist work seeks to reclaim the tool of psychoanalysis from film theory, instead of positing a particular predefined kind of subject position as subversively performative. Some of Elin Diamond's work, for example, posits an unspecifiable or invisible psychic excess, located either in the hysteric body speaking through the text or on the instability of the relationship between the performer/role complex and the spectator. The performative apparatus becomes a process of repression of the original dangerous insight psychoanalysis provides about subjectivity. Performance, then, opens a space through which the body can slip into a "better" signification.

Peggy Phelan's book *Unmarked* comes close to asking the right questions, but is still concerned with undoing the trap of the visible. She seeks to challenge the legibility of identity on the body, and I am in complete sympathy with her desire to complicate the assumption that the relationship between identity, visibility, and representation is simple and carries political effectivity. But for Phelan the question of identity is inextricably connected with the question of identification, of the processes by which like recognizes like in language and the visible together. The spectator is always searching for herself, and the way to question or problematize this process is to chart that which cannot be seen or said, that which is powerful in its absence. I am more interested in the contradictions between the seen and the said.

I believe that the theatre texts themselves present a site for the analysis of these contradictions. The changing relationship between text and enactment seems to point the way to theorizing the "limits and pressures" of the identity-body-subject field—the limits of performativity and the pressures of spectacle; a subjectivity that is neither endowed with complete agency to manipulate the signifiers of identity upon the body nor condemned to live out a relationship of oppression and domination in the body. I believe performance theory can produce a kind of critical reading of enacted and embodied subjectivity that is sensitive to more determinants of identity than gender, more, indeed, than the litany of gender-race-class-sexuality. And I believe this kind of thought about subjectivity is crucial in ongoing theoretical debates about the political and social relationships in which identity engages.

Notes

1 See particularly *Bodies that Matter*: "performativity . . . consists in a reiteration of norms which precede, constrain, and exceed the performer and in that sense cannot be taken as the fabrication of the performer's 'will' or 'choice'."(p. 234).
2 I would very much like to pay more attention to the countertendency noted above; that is, I think this deconstructive or critical effect is also possible in relationship to spectacle. However, I'm not sure how to approach that here, except through the problems in performance theory as a discipline.
3 This quest for answers outside of the space of Western theatre has been institutionalized in the discipline of Performance Studies, an anthropological-theatrical hybrid whose main methodology is reading social actions and rituals of other cultures.

Bibliography

Anzaldúa, Gloria. *Borderlands/ La Frontera: The New Mestiza*. San Francisco: Aunt Lute Books, 1987.

Artaud, Antonin. *The Theatre and Its Double*. Translated by Mary Caroline Richards.New York: Grove Weidenfeld, 1958.

Berlant, Lauren, and Elizabeth Freeman. "Queer Nationality." In *Fear of a Queer Planet: Queer Politics and Social Theory,* edited by Michael Warner, 193-214. Minneapolis: University of Minnesota Press, 1993.

Bhabha, Homi. "Of Mimicry and Man: The Ambivalence of Colonial Discourse." *October* 28 spring, 1984: 125-33.

Brecht, Bertolt. *Brecht on Theatre.* Translated by John Willett. New York: Hill and Wang, 1964.

Butler, Judith. *Gender Trouble: Feminism and the Subversion of Identity.* (New York and London: Routledge, 1990.

——. *Bodies that Matter: On the Discursive Limits of "Sex."* New York and London:Routledge, 1993.

Case, Sue-Ellen. "Toward a Butch-Femme Aesthetic." In *Making a Spectacle: Feminist Essays on Contemporary Women's Theatre,* edited by Lynda Hart. Ann Arbor: University of Michigan Press, 1989.

Churchill, Caryl. *Cloud Nine.* In *Plays: One.* New York: Routledge, 1985.

de Lauretis, Teresa. "The Technology of Gender." In *Technologies of Gender: Essays on Theory, Film, and Fiction,* 1-27. Bloomington: Indiana University Press, 1987.

Diamond, Elin. "Mimesis, Mimicry, and the 'True-Real.'" *Modern Drama* 32, no. 1 (1989): 58-72.

Dolan, Jill. *The Feminist Spectator as Critic.* Ann Arbor: UMI Research Press, 1988.

Haraway, Donna. "A Manifesto for Cyborgs: Science, Technology, and Socialist Feminism in the 1980s." In *Feminism/Postmodernism,* edited by Linda J. Nicholson, 218-30. New York: Routledge, 1990.

Hughes, Langston. *Mulatto.* In *Five Plays,* edited by Webster Smalley, 1-35. Bloomington: Indiana University Press, 1968.

McCauley, Robbie. "My Father and the Wars." Performance, Brown University, 1994.

Mulvey, Laura. "Visual Pleasure and Narrative Cinema." In *Visual and Other Pleasures.* 1973. Reprint, Bloomington: Indiana University Press, 1989.

Parks, Suzan-Lori. *Imperceptible Mutabilities in the Third Kingdom.* In *The Best of Off-Broadway: Eight Contemporary Obie-Winning Plays,* edited by Ross Wetzsteon, 239-304. New York: Mentor, 1994.

Phelan, Peggy. *Unmarked: The Politics of Performance.* New York and London: Routledge, 1993.

Reid-Pharr, Robert F. "The Spectacle of Blackness." *Radical America* 24, no.4 (1993): 57-65.

Trinh, T. Minh-ha. *Woman, Native, Other: Writing Postcoloniality and Feminism.* Bloomington: Indiana University Press, 1989.

5
What Meaning in Her Breast?

Ambivalence of the Body as Sign and Site of Identity in *Beloved* and *The Woman Warrior*

Michele Janette

In both *The Woman Warrior* and *Beloved,* a woman's body bears an inscribed story of oppression on the back, which the woman cannot read without an interpreter, and which is in tension with the signifiers on the front, the breasts, that determine identity in terms of gender. In this paper, I pair these figures as explorations of the ways raced and gendered bodies negotiate an identity among often conflicting cultural narratives. Does a body generate its own story or is it determined by externally imposed narratives? How does a body participate in the narrative of history which it inherits and passes on? These questions, once posed in a nature/nurture binary, now framed by the discourse of essentialism and constructionism, have long been of interest to thinkers and scholars from various professional and theoretical perspectives.[1] I read *The Woman Warrior* and *Beloved* as sophisticated fictional explorations of these questions. Maxine Hong Kingston and Toni Morrison literally flesh out the metaphor of "cultural inscription" in the scarred, written-on backs of Sethe and the woman warrior. The bloody, painful signing of these bodies shocks us into fresh vision of the ways bodies gain and are given meaning. With our eyes thus trained, the novels then ask us to look further, to see cultural inscription, not only in the scarred backs of these two women, but also in their signifying breasts. When placed in dialogue with one another, these writers offer alternative valuations of the body, and reveal the dangers in each other's models.

Sethe's back, which has been whipped and scarred to mark her permanently as slave (to sentence her as told text, not author), and the woman warrior's back, which has been carved with characters telling the story of the crimes against her family, render legible the bodies of these two women and provide them with their own explanatory texts. Yet these texts are thoroughly ambiguous, their meaning unstable and fluid. The scars are indeed marks inflicted by an external hand, but they are also produced by the body itself, as it heals the wounds that the knives or whip inflicted. Intended by slave master or family to brand ownership or announce vengeance, the marks, the body's own response to the cuts, commemorate not only victimization but also the strength of these women who have survived. Sethe's scarred back is a palpable memorial to the physical violence done to her as a slave, the reminder of brutal whippings performed by plantation overseers. But when Amy redescribes the wounds as a blossoming chokecherry tree or Paul D sees the scars as wrought iron sculpture "too passionate for display,"[2] Sethe's back comes to signify not her status as slave but as passionate, strong, life-giving survivor. Similarly, the woman warrior's back is literally legible as historical record: the family carves into her skin characters which tell of the crimes against her family. But while the tale *on* her back tells of atrocity and victimization, the tale *of* her carved back is a story of filial responsibility, of resistance, and of the connection between bodies and history (story).

To this multiplicity of meanings, Kingston and Morrison add still another layer of signification. In both *The Woman Warrior* and *Beloved*, at the moment when these backs are exposed and these texts find a reader, the inscriptions get trumped by another bodily sign, the breasts. The ambiguity of the written-on backs, whether they be imposed definitions or emanations from within, is superseded by the breasts, familiar signifiers of femininity.

The two scenes are remarkably alike: the woman warrior exposes her back to the perpetrator of the crimes carved into her skin, only to find that he does not even read the words, but sees instead only her revealed breasts; Sethe stands over the stove while Paul D explores the scars of her back with his lips, yet she feels nothing of this, knowing only that her breasts are cradled in his hands. For both authors, embodiment involves another, a reader, since neither Sethe nor the woman warrior can see the texts at their backs. But these scenes also differ powerfully from each other in the contrasting reactions of the characters to the attention given their breasts. For Sethe, this is a moment of relief and amelioration. Paul D's touch redresses the violation done to Sethe's breasts earlier in the novel. For the woman warrior, the exclusive focus on her breasts is itself the violation she cannot forgive. Seeing the baron's "startled eyes at [her] breasts,"[3] she decapitates him for attending to the sign of her gender rather than the history of her activism. These reactions indicate the way gender and its relation to the body are imagined in these novels. Morrison (at least with Sethe) posits the body as prior to the social constructions placed on it, while Kingston battles the idea that identity is determined by biological sex. Morrison endorses an idea of gender identity as essentially determined by the body. Kingston supports a more constructionist view.

Body and Gender Identity

A tension between body and costume as determinants of gender identity runs throughout the mythology from which Kingston develops her woman warrior. The tale of the girl soldier has been embellished in its several centuries of modification, but even in its earliest known version, the fifth-century "Ballad of Fa MuLan," the poem is centrally concerned with the disruption of gender roles occasioned by MuLan's passing as a boy soldier. In the ballad, MuLan enters the army to spare her aging father, who has no sons to send. As Joseph Allen has shown, the energy of the poem derives not from celebration of MuLan's military exploits, but from the need to return this errant girl from the battlefield to her domestic sphere.[4] Her passing as male is the conflict which drives the plot towards its resolution, and is also a potentially titillating secret which gives the poem an erotic dimension. Allen locates this erotic energy primarily in the (historically male) reader of the MuLan tradition,[5] whom he imagines as a knowing voyeur, in on the secret hidden beneath the armor. He notes the frequency of battle illustrations which draw attention to MuLan's wide spread legs, astride her charging battlehorse or garbed in provocative male leggings. This imagining of the knowledgeable gaze as the desiring gaze is then transferred from the voyeuristic reader to MuLan's soldier comrades within the poem. When the war is over, MuLan dresses herself "in robes of old" and comes "out the door to see my camp mates, / My camp mates so shocked at first? / They'd traveled together for many a year / Without knowing MuLan was a girl!"[6] Allen imagines this scene as a sudden coming to awareness by MuLan's fellow soldiers of sexual potential in their relationship: "One can almost hear the sighs of missed opportunity in the lines."[7] Although I tend not to believe that biological sex determines one's critical stance, I am intrigued by the gender politics of reader identification here. Allen's reading requires that we see the exposure of MuLan's "pass" from the perspective of the male camp mates who discover that she is female. In reading this passage, I myself identified not with the male spectators but with the newly feminized MuLan. I read the scene as tense not with sexual excitement, but with the risk of punishment for her duplicity. Rather than sexually provocative, the revelation that MuLan had been passing as male seemed to me potentially dangerous. My reaction was thus not arousal, but relief that the consequence of disrupting gender systems is no more than short-lived surprise: the "so shocked at first" fading benignly into acceptance in the poem's final metaphor: "two rabbits running side by side. / Who can tell which is the he and which the she?"[8] Frank Chin, too, finds gender equality in this image, but also sees between the lines a "romantic drama" about a Confucian ideal marriage between soldier-individuals.[9] The happy resolution at the end seemed to me not a metaphor of flirtation, but of possible androgyny in which bodies in action are indistinguishable by sex. Kingston's interpretive revision of the MuLan tale, however, validates neither utopian visions of gender neutrality nor the sexual frisson seen by Allen and Chin. Her version reminds us that what is at stake here is not titillation or participatory anonymity, but power.

On first reading, Kingston's revision of "The Ballad of Fa MuLan" appears to develop the ballad's model of androgynous equality into a Superwoman ideal.

The warrior's success in the public, military, explicitly male realm achieves not only innocuous participation across gender norms, but ostentatious triumph. Not a soldier under another's command, Kingston's heroine is chief general: leading the army, deposing the emperor, determining the strategies, wielding the magic tools given her by her mentors. This fantastic warrior gets to have her career and a family, too. In a delightful moment of wish fulfillment, the warrior is joined, at the height of her career, by her adoring husband. She spends a year with him, bears their child, and brings the entire family to work, none of which impedes her from getting her job done: she charges into battle with her nursing infant swaddled under her armor, the dried umbilical cord fluttering among the battle flags. The novel thus seems to endorse a version of female empowerment that had much currency during the period in which *The Woman Warrior* was published. The image of the Superwoman pervades that cultural moment. Captured succinctly in the Enjoli perfume ad which chorused, "I can bring home the bacon, fry it up in a pan, and never, never let you forget you're a man 'cuz I'm a WOMAN," the early 1970s images of strong women were celebrations of power defined as being able to do everything at once, and superbly. Three years before *The Woman Warrior* was published, Helen Reddy won the Grammy award for her hit record "I Am Woman," and Billie Jean King defeated Bobby Riggs in a tennis match billed as "The Battle of the Sexes." Feminist literature titled itself with strength and power: *Revolt of the Second Sex* (Julie Ellis), *The Bold New Women* (Barbara Allen Wasserman), *Woman Power* (Celestine Ware), *Sisterhood Is Powerful* (Robin Morgan). Lawsuits proclaimed female strength by challenging heavy-lifting requirements which had been used to bar women from promotion in industry and communications.[10]

But even as it participates in this cultural mythology, Kingston's text presciently qualifies and critiques the possibility of "having/doing/being it all." The warrior can charge into battle carrying her child, only because child care can be imagined as making no demands. The wish-fulfillment compatibility of marriage and career is predicated on seeing the family as only supplemental: her double life goes undetected because maternity can be imagined as invisible.

To be a powerful woman in the public sphere is to conform to established masculinity. The warrior succeeds in precisely the same measure that she disguises her femaleness. She has her family only so long as it doesn't interfere. Even in fantasy, there is no space for a femininity that might resurrect stereotypes of weakness and irresponsibility. Kingston's "White Tigers" chapter thus participates in a long tradition of narratives which have little patience for amazons who slip into feminine distraction. As far back as Virgil's Camilla, such weakness leads only to catastrophe. Like Camilla, whose "girl's love of finery"[11] fatally diverts her attention from overall victory to the capture of an eye-catching helmet, Fa MuLan, sick with longing and love for her husband, wanders off distractedly to pick wildflowers. Camilla never sees the arrow which brings her down. Kingston's warrior snaps out of her daze just in time. Although she has foolishly allowed herself to be ambushed (not coincidentally by a man so antimaternal that he has killed his own sons to melt them into magical swords), she regains her proper focus and defends herself successfully, putting aside her familial longings and returning to her filial duty. Camilla's femininity is fatal. The warrior manages to suppress hers, rearmoring herself in her masculine persona. In this action, the warrior does not redefine but rather postpones femininity. The Superwoman model redivides into familiar masculine and feminine possibilities, whose boundaries remain firm. The warrior sends her child to his grandparents to await the end of the war, when she will resume the role traditionally assigned to women: "'Now my public duties are finished,' I said. 'I will stay with you, doing farmwork and housework and giving you more sons'" (*WW*, 45). Feminine is feminine, masculine is masculine, and ne'er the twain shall meet.

The woman warrior triumphs not by being a successful woman in a male world (the exception which proves the rule or the token which solidifies convention), nor by transcending gender difference in androgynous equality, but by passing as a man, denying her biological sex altogether. She manipulates her appearance to hide the gender which society interprets as powerless, exposing instead a persona of greater social power. This act of passing is presented as a positive act of self-creation, giving agency to the self, allowing an individual to write her own story and to choose her own terms of self-definition. Further, by explicitly performing an identity of her own making, the warrior exposes the constructedness of all identities. In its self-conscious creation of identity, passing can be seen as subverting all assumptions of "the natural." Identity, this incident implies, is not inherent but grafted.[12]

Passing as male, the woman warrior would refuse her body the power to determine her identity. But the problem here is that to be successful, in order not to give itself away, the self-constructed masculine identity must conform to already familiar conventions of masculinity.[13] Survival depends on being undetected, as Kingston acknowledges: "Chinese executed women who disguised themselves as soldiers or students, no matter how bravely they fought or how high they scored on the examinations" (*WW*, 39). Whereas the traditional "Ballad of Fa MuLan" offered gender difference as possibly insignificant, in Kingston's world (as in ours), there are often very material risks to insisting that sex is not determinative.

In her version, Kingston omits the scene from the traditional ballad in which MuLan returns to her feminine robes before the audience of her fellow soldiers. She replaces that benign exposure with one much less comforting. After winning her national battles and overturning the central government, the woman warrior returns to her village where she has a final showdown with the local, evil baron, perpetrator of the crimes carved into her back. The warrior offers her body as testimony: she exposes her back to refute the baron's claim that "I've done nothing to you" (*WW*, 43),[14] her scarred skin embodying her connection to the story etched into her flesh. But when she tears open her shirt in accusation, he doesn't even see the list of atrocities to which her body bears witness. That text is overridden by the unexpected sign of her gender:

"You've done this," I said, and ripped off my shirt to show him my back. "You are responsible for this." When I saw his startled eyes at my breasts, I slashed him across the face and on the second stroke cut off his head. (*WW*, 44)

At the moment of her familial and cultural triumph, when she has successfully escaped the gender restrictions which so threaten her, when she has redefined herself as warrior, mother, wife, magician, general, daughter, avenger, scourge, and savior, the baron's startled gaze reconfines her into the single category "female." Where she offers a contextualized, self-scripted body, he sees only an essential sex characteristic. In frustration at this privileging of gender, at the fact that 'female' trumps all other forms of identification, the warrior narrator lashes out with violence. The baron's inability to see beyond gender signs is his last crime—the one which ends their dialogue and proves him irredeemable (unlike those members of the baron's troupe who were spared if they "proved they could be reformed" [*WW*, 44]). Kingston presents the warrior's reaction as impulsive and instinctive: the warrior lashing out in her fury before thinking; so upset, in fact, that despite ten years of training in control, her first stroke is wild, and she has to strike again to kill. But a precise logic undergirds this appearance of frenzy so that the punishment fits the baron's crime with Dante-like aptness. The decapitation metaphorically castrates the baron, punishing his exclusive focus on the anatomy of gender. Yet in the very fact that this castration is figurative, and allows the head to substitute for the penis, this punishment also enacts the layering of signification and figurative representation that the baron is unable to achieve.

Kingston's heroine experiences this privileging of the natural over the disguise as a denial of her own identity, shunting her back into society's constructions. The sight of the breast under the armor does not merge the story of this heroine with her body; it contradicts it. The scene is one in which a body appears to have an essential truth which will overcome disguise. But to see the episode from that perspective is to occupy the position of the baron. The observer who believes the body holds essential truth is the reader as villain. The particular villainy of such misreading is that it takes as essential and natural what is in fact already socially constructed.

But the validation of self-creation which such a reading supposes itself contains the danger that the body will ultimately be dropped out altogether. Passing not only allows but in fact insists that the body be ignored in favor of construction. The woman warrior's fury is that her body has to matter. Her training is largely about overcoming the body—learning to ignore hunger and pain, materially expelling fear by turning it into a sword with which to do battle, regarding the body as separate from the self. The warrior learns from a rabbit, who sacrifices itself in her fire so she can eat, that the self is not circumscribed within one's own body, but is a force that transcends the body. It is located in each of us but also exceeds our individuality—like the paradoxical dragon which "lives in the sky, ocean, marshes, and mountains;" and yet "the mountains are also its cranium" (*WW*, 29).

Morrison, too, creates a scene in which the heroine's exposure of her marked back becomes instead attention to her breasts. While the trajectory of the scenes is the same, the meanings invested in this shift are nearly opposite for Kingston and Morrison. In *Beloved*, it is the woman who is focused on her breasts while the man attempts to read the text of her back. The scene is not one of revenge and violence but of recompense and healing. Sethe stands weeping into the stove while Paul D touches "every ridge and leaf of [her scarred back] with his mouth" (*B*, 18), undoing the oral violence done to her breasts earlier in the novel, when Schoolteacher's nephews take her milk. While Paul D's attention is directed to the story on Sethe's back, she has a different experience of his caresses, "none of which [she] could feel because her back skin had been dead for years. What she knew was that the responsibility for her breasts, at last, was in somebody else's hands" (*B*,18).

As Anne Goldman and Jean Wyatt have shown, Sethe's identity is grounded in her sense of herself as a mother, and her breasts become the symbol and location for this essential maternal identity.[15] She sees her body as vehicle, home, and sustenance for her unborn baby. Her need not to abandon her maternal role keeps her going:

> "I believe this baby's ma'am is gonna die in wild onions on the bloody side of the Ohio River.". . . And it didn't seem such a bad idea, all in all, in view of the step she would not have to take, but the thought of herself stretched out dead while the little antelope lived on—an hour? a day? a day and a night?— in her lifeless body grieved her so she made the groan that made the person walking on a path not ten yards away halt. (*B*, 31)

The self-alienation of this passage is really quite remarkable. Already defining herself solely by her maternal relationship ("this baby's ma'am"), Sethe would happily forego the continuation of her own life. Her anguish comes from the sense that her own release would be a betrayal of her child. Unendurable is the image of her body as suffocating sepulchre rather than source of nurture.[16] Sethe's body is essentially maternal—by which I mean both that maternity is the necessary condition for Sethe's continued desire to live and that it is the innermost core of Sethe's bodily self-definition.

The climactic trauma of Sweet Home, that which Sethe will not withstand in silence, that which sends Halle into madness, is the rape of Sethe's breasts: a violation of her maternal body, a stealing of that motherly nurture which defines her as human. Schoolteacher's nephews pin her down on the barn floor, and with Schoolteacher watching, forcibly nurse her breast milk. These "boys with mossy teeth" (*B*, 31, 70) milk her like a cow.

Morrison emphasizes this insult through its contrast with the respect for Sethe's sexuality, individuality, and humanity earlier shown by the Sweet Home men. When Sethe arrives on the plantation, all the men desire her sexually, but all wait a "long, tough year of thrashing on pallets, eaten up with dreams of her" (*B*, 10) until she makes her choice among them. Leaving her be, they take out their sexual frustration on the plantation calves.

The nephews' actions reclassify her as one of the abusable livestock. Sethe has already, at this point in the novel, been infuriated by learning that one of schoolteacher's assignments for his nephews is for them to list in opposing columns all of Sethe's human and animal characteristics. In response to being seen as half-animal, Sethe determines to run away—to prevent such classification of characteristics from being performed upon her children (again, her actions are motivated by maternal concern). The nephews' milking treats her as entirely animal. Her response to this is both to continue in her action of escaping and also literally to *respond*—to speak to Mrs. Garner about their action—to reclaim her humanity through speech. Sethe's body becomes the site of a discursive battle: whose definition, whose label, will determine Sethe's physical relation to the world? Is she a woman, or is she a cow?

Antislavery literature frequently invoked this comparison to garner abolitionist sympathy. The *Liberator* generated outrage at the sexual abuse of female slaves by publicizing that they were "exposed to all the violence of lust and passion—and treated with more indelicacy and cruelty than cattle."[17] Morrison's dramatization of such treatment shows that it wasn't just a matter of comparison—whether women were treated *worse than* cattle—but a matter of constitution—whether women were *defined as* cattle. As Karen Sánchez-Eppler points out, etymologically the very word "cattle" refers not only to bovine animals but to all "movable property or wealth."[18] Cattle = chattel = livestock = slaves. The nephews' behavior logically and horribly brings to life the semantics of slavery.[19]

The scene also invokes the tradition of wet nursing which deprived the birth child of its mother's milk in favor of white children. Morrison exposes the gratuitous selfishness of that tradition, since the milk—so needed by Sethe's beloved baby—is utterly unnecessary to the grown boys nursing from her.[20] This inability to determine the recipient of her milk echoes Sethe's own infancy, her own experience of being deprived of her mother's milk: "My mother," she tells Denver, "must of nursed me two or three weeks—that's the way the others did. Then she went back in rice and I sucked from another woman whose job it was" (*B*, 60).

The route to recovery from the trauma at the hands and mouths of the white boys involves returning, retracing those actions, but with a difference. Mouths and hands again touch Sethe's breasts and back, but in reverse: hands to breasts, mouth to back. Paul D's hands hold her breasts, countering with a recompensing caress of support the violence done to her back by the nephews' cowhide-brandishing hands. His lips kiss the scars of her back, tasting her unique strength and sorrow. This gesture of generous respect counters the selfish guzzling of the slave-owning boys. The nephews touch Sethe's body in order to render it only a body—a thing, an animal, not human like themselves, but of a separate, and lesser, order. Paul D touches her in order to connect with her humanity.

This is, after all, a love scene. It is a moment in which emotional, even spiritual connection is figured through physical contact—exemplified in Paul D's touching her back, "learn[ing] that way her sorrow" (*B*, 18). Throughout the novel, touch parallels, or indeed enacts, the psychic experience of the characters. Sethe begins each day kneading bread; the rhythmic pounding of the dough is her best way to "start the day's serious work of beating back the past" (*B*, 73). When she massages Paul D's knee, the kneading motions have the same effect: that act of touch beats back his past, seals off his history. It reminds him that he is in the presence of an other, and he doesn't finish his story, doesn't tell the worst of what happened to him. The metaphor is made literal through touch.

Morrison uses this technique again in this love scene. Paul D's caress of Sethe's breast is a bodily enactment of their intimacy. If, as I have argued, Sethe's essential self-definition is as mother, and that identity is synecdochically figured by her breast, then Paul D has literally touched the core of her self.

Paul D, sympathetic and welcome reader, interprets Sethe's body as she herself does, his touch furthering their intimacy. Kingston's baron, reading against the grain of the warrior's self-definition, emphasizes their animosity and alienation. Paul D attends to Sethe's breasts, and this attention ameliorates the violation done her. The baron attends to the warrior's breasts, and this attention is the violation which costs him his life. The difference reveals, not only the differences in the crimes done to these women, but also the differences in the ways these authors view gender. Where Sethe's essence is violated, the warrior's violation occurs in the very act of essentializing. The rape of Sethe's breasts violates her essence as a woman. The baron's exclusive attention to the warrior's breasts violates by essentializing her as "Woman."

In their treatment of race, too, Morrison tends towards celebration; Kingston, toward skepticism. Morrison celebrates a black American tradition, urging critics to read her work in the African-American context: "I would much prefer that they [her books] were dismissed or embraced based on the success of their accomplishment within the culture out of which I write."[21] She endorses connections between her early work and that of Zora Neale Hurston, despite her not having then read Hurston, because such connections prove that "the tradition [of black women's writing] really exists."[22] Kingston's relationship to her ethnicity is more wary. Less something to be claimed, racial identity is, like gender, something to tease out from confusing data and conflicting constructions. "I could not figure out what was my village," her autobiographical narrator claims in an oft-quoted passage (*WW*, 45). "I continue to sort out what's just my childhood, just my imagination, just my family, just the village, just the movies, just living" (*WW*, 205). There is as much anger as love toward the ethnic culture which informs and constrains her. "Even now, China wraps double binds around me" (*WW*, 48).

Some previous criticism of Kingston, most notoriously that of Frank Chin, has accused her of not getting her culture right—of misquoting the ancient legends or furthering a racist view of Asian Americans.[23] I think Chin misreads Kingston, but that misreading is useful in revealing what is at issue in Kingston's creation of a projected self poised amid conflicting cultural scripts. Chin's desire for Kingston to be "accurate" (which is really a desire for her to agree with *his* vision), seeks to make Kingston's characters exemplary, representative. He would have her posit didactic and generalizing truths. Her novels instead explore the contradictions already existing in the particular. To wholeheartedly embrace a Chinese ethnic identity would be simultaneously to accept a devalued female identity. As Kingston's narrator experiences it, her racial identity is radically sexist. Kingston captures this clash in her deconstruction of the Chinese language: "There is a Chinese word for the female *I* —which is 'slave.' Break the women with their own tongues!" (*WW*, 47).

And philosophy endorses what the language implies: "'Chinese smeared bad daughters-in-law with honey and tied them naked on top of ant nests,' my father said. 'A husband may kill a wife who disobeys him. Confucius said that.' Confucius, the rational man" (*WW*, 193). Confucius and the father: cultural and familial patriarchs both tell the daughter who would love and revere them that their culture does not value her. The female body is a source for the father's obscene curses. To be a daughter is to be an embarrassment. To be one of six granddaughters is to be less than human. As the narrator recounts:

> When my sisters and I ate at [the great-grandfather's house], there we would be—six girls eating. The old man opened his eyes wide at us and turned in a circle, surrounded. His neck tendons stretched out. "Maggots!" he shouted. "Maggots!   Where are my grandsons?   I want grandsons! Give me grandsons! Maggots!" He pointed at each one of us, "Maggot!   Maggot! Maggot! Maggot! Maggot! Maggot!" (*WW*, 191)

Surrounded by such tensions, Kingston's female characters are defined by conflict and paradox. The woman warrior herself is introduced as a model of cultural opposition, an alternative to the more prevalent misogynist lore: "[My mother] said I would grow up a wife and a slave, but she taught me the song of the warrior woman, Fa MuLan. I would have to grow up a warrior woman" (*WW*, 20). Yet, as we have seen, even within this feminist fable, gender remains a locus of trouble rather than triumph. The woman warrior embodies not wholeness but tension, not coherence but contradiction.

Such tension doesn't exist for Sethe. She embodies a coherent identity, whose experiences in the world as a raced body and a sexed body are complementary rather than contradictory. She embodies her self: black, woman, mother, ex-slave—these identities become whole in her embodiment of them all.

For Kingston's warrior, race and gender are externally constructed entities which one struggles to fit with, without being fixed by. For Sethe, they are internal determinators which one must fully claim. Danger to identity in *Beloved* comes in denying the experiences of the body. In *The Woman Warrior* it comes from cultural privileging of the body. Story and body come powerfully together in the breasts of these two characters. For both Sethe and the warrior, the moment of bodily exposure is a moment of contest, over the meaning of her body and over who will construct that meaning. For Sethe, the body is the source of truth and the grounding in material context. For the woman warrior, the body grounds a person's story not by keeping it material but by fixing it— and fixing it in someone else's narrative. Sánchez-Eppler describes this tension as follows: "the recognition of ownership of one's own body as essential to claiming personhood is matched by the fear of being imprisoned, silenced, deprived of personhood by that same body."[24] Interestingly, this formulation, which parallels Kingston's treatment of the body, actually refers to the historical bodies about whom *Morrison* writes. Sánchez-Eppler is talking about the dangers faced by black bodies under slavery, when the body's coloring was legal justification for enslaving a free body.

This skeptical, paradoxical attitude toward the body does not characterize Morrison's imaginative strategy. Her characters tend neither to fear nor deny their bodies, but rather to revel in them. Her novels abound with rich descriptions of black bodies, from Pilate's "trembling unhampered breasts" and "smooth balloon of a stomach" with no navel,[25] to Eva's one "magnificent" leg: "stockinged and shod in all weather" and "always in view."[26] Characters celebrate each other's bodies: Sula focuses her thoughts during lovemaking on a fantasy of bodily layers: gold leaf shining through the black ledge of her lover's cheekbone; under the gold, alabaster giving his face "its planes, its curves"; and through the cracked alabaster, "loam, fertile, free of pebbles and twigs."[27] Joe Trace loves the "flesh, heavily despised by the brothers" of his girlfriend Dorcas: "She had long hair and bad skin. . . . I liked it like that. Little half moons clustered underneath her cheekbones, like faint hoofmarks. There and on her forehead."[28] In *Beloved*, Sethe's body is the source and foundation for her identity, her family, and her connection with others. She figures her nurturing strength as having "milk enough for all" (*B*, 100). This joy in the body is most thoroughly articulated by Baby Suggs, holy. In her clearing, she sermonizes about "flesh that dances on bare feet in grass." In response to centuries of brutalization and degradation of black bodies by white ones, she urges her followers to celebrate their bodies themselves: "Love it. Love it hard. Love your hands! Love them. Raise them up and kiss them. Touch others with them, pat them together, stroke them on your face. . . . *You* got to love it, *you!*. . . This is flesh I'm talking about here. Flesh that needs to be loved" (*B*, 88).[29]

Kingston's project is less reclamation than circumvention. It has been argued, again most cogently by Joseph Allen, that Kingston's reimagination of the MuLan tale increases the material reality of the woman warrior's body. He argues that over time, the story of MuLan has developed from its early emphasis on costume to increasing contemporary acknowledgment of and interest in corporeality, a shift most noticeable in the fact that Kingston's warrior menstruates, becomes pregnant, and gives birth. I would argue, however, that these are the very moments in which the warrior's body is *least* real. The warrior at first mistakenly assumes that her menstrual bleeding is the result of "cut[ting her]self when jumping over [her] swords" (*WW*, 31). That the warrior could imagine herself as noticing only retrospectively that she has received knife wounds to the genitalia which she didn't feel at the time does *not* persuade me that this is a real body.[30] Where Allen sees attention to the body in the warrior's armor adjustments during pregnancy, I see the instantaneous (and unremarked) transformation from stout commander to slim young man as further evidence of this body's cinematic shape shifts. Kingston herself refers to this chapter of her novel as like a "kung fu movie"—not real life.[31] It is worth remembering, in this regard, that even within the fictional world of the novel, the woman warrior has no body—she exists only as a fantasy of the narrator.

This de-emphasis of the body appears frequently in Kingston's work. To make only two brief comparisons to scenes already mentioned in Morrison: whereas Sethe reconnected with her bodily self through her sense of maternal reproduction, one of *The Woman Warrior's* most graphically embodied moments is in fact insistently a scene of bodily self-alienation. A crazy grandfather is prone to interrupting meals in order to interrogate his body's refusal to engender girls: "He used to put his naked penis on the dinner table, laughing" (*WW*, 10-11). The text here dismembers the body even as it invokes it. And in contrast to the elaborate evocation of Sula and Ajax's lovemaking—Sula imagining delving into the fertile depths of Ajax's being as she attempts to delay her sexual climax—Kingston's most tenderly imagined love scenes operate through tactful omission. As if the privacy of physical contact precludes even narrative description, the scene of the warrior's reunion with her husband is only hinted at adverbially: "I turned around and touched his face, loving the familiar first" (*WW*, 39). The paragraph ends there. The text resumes almost blushingly, "And so for a time I had a partner"—leaving to the white space between paragraphs, to the blank, unworded parts of the page, the consummation which results in pregnancy. Kingston coyly invokes with that "first" a sequence she declines to continue. As the narrator says in another chapter, "I have believed that sex was unspeakable" (*WW*, 15).

Morrison's texts celebrate the body as where it all begins and why it matters. Kingston's texts do not endorse such location of truth value in bodies. The moment of embodiment is a moment of limitation, of encounter with the interpretations always already applied to bodies.

In her latest book, Judith Butler has argued for an understanding of identities as "constituted" by societal and cultural influences interacting with material bodies.[32] I am persuaded by her argument that increasing attention to the processes and mechanisms of this constitution will allow us greater possibilities of contestation, of subversion, and of individual control. The concern, of course, lies in the question of who will have that control. If reality becomes a discursive spin, if bodies signify with infinite mutability, where do we locate responsibility? The warrior's battle with the baron is over who will construct the meaning of her body. He wants the body to be meaningful; she wants it to be irrelevant. It is a struggle to the death, and I want her to win. I want her self-determination to triumph. But there is also anxiety in that triumph. Bodies should not be irrelevant. Morrison plans her next book to be about a place where race exists but doesn't matter.[33] I see the world in which we live as one in which the constructions we call race and gender only exist *because* they matter. Bodies exist in a social web of connections with other people—the threads of that web having everything to do with our mutual or opposed perceptions, assumptions, and behaviors toward each other.

We need to keep real bodies in mind because they keep us in touch with consequences. With pleasure. With pain. The literal presence of bodies reminds us that the world we have constructed is nonetheless real, that our awareness of constructions hasn't yet rendered them obsolete. Abstraction away from the body is dangerous, in taking us away from the ways material bodies hurt, in forgetting actual lived experiences.

The body is necessary to ground identity, to keep us aware of the real material world and the consequences for real people of the cultural scripts among which we play out our lives. It is by claiming the body as under our own control that we establish that there is a self—and yet, that self is always in danger of being overwritten by an external significance imposed on that same body. Morrison's emphasis on Sethe's body as essentially connected to her identity is a reclaiming of that body from the slavery which would claim ownership and the power to define. Kingston's emphasis on construction is an attempt to keep her body from imprisoning or determining her identity for her. Kingston appears to resolve the tension between her inscribed back and signifying breasts by exorcising the reader who would privilege the wrong text. Morrison appears to achieve harmony by connecting back to front, by telling on the back the story of the breast. And yet when compared to one another, these scenes reveal flaws in each other's logic. Sethe's body, always so tangible in the novel—not only the focus of so much narrative description, but also actively and physically interacting with the world of the novel: giving birth, bleeding, dripping milk, shaping food, expressing milk intermingled with blood—Sethe's body which won't go away, reminds us that it is in our physical bodies that identity is felt; it questions by its inescapable presence the ephemerality of Kingston's fantasy warrior. And the warrior's body, site of definitions in contest rather than ground of identity, reminds us that the body has no "natural" significance. It questions in its anger the assumption that there is ever original or essential meaning.[34]

Notes

1 See, for example, the work of Judith Butler and Maurice Merleau-Ponty. And nearer to hand, see the papers in this volume—particularly those by Loren Noveck and Ed Casey, which address questions of bodily subjectivity through the discursive lenses of performance theory, cultural analysis, and psychology.

2 Toni Morrison, *Beloved* New York: Plume, 1987), p. 17. Hereafter cited in text as *B*.

3 Maxine Hong Kingston, *The Woman Warrior* (New York: Vintage, 1975), p. 35. Hereafter cited in text as *WW*.

4 Joseph R. Allen, "The Sartorial Story of the Chinese Woman Warrior," *Positions* (forthcoming).

5 Literally translated as the "MuLan Works" (MuLan Shi), this tradition extends from the early anonymous ballad to contemporary comic books and cartoons appearing on Taiwan television—see Allen for a full delineation of historical alterations to the tale.

6 William N. Nienhauser, trans., in *Sunflower Splendor,* Wu-Chi Liu and Irving Lo, ed.c, (Bloomington: Indiana University Press, 1975).

7 Allen, "The Sartorial Story," p. 10.

8 Frank Chin, trans., in "Come All Ye Asian Writers of the Real and Fake," in *The Big Aiiieeeee!* ed. J. P. Chan, F. Chin, L. F. Inada, S. Wong (New York: Penguin, 1991), p. 6.

9 Chin, "Come All Ye Asian Writers," p. 6.

10 For example, *Weeks v. Southern Bell* (1968-69), *Thelma Bowe et al v. Colgate Palmolive Co.* (1967, 1969), *Megelkoch v. Industrial Welfare Commission of California* (1971).

11 Virgil, *The Aeneid,* trans. Robert Fitzgerald (New York: Vintage, 1980), XI, 1066.

12 My thinking here is strongly indebted to Judith Butler's work on the constitution and performance of gender identity. See especially *Gender Trouble: Feminism and the Subversion of Identity* (London: Routledge, 1990); "Contingent Foundations: Feminism and the Question of 'Postmodernism,'" in *Feminists Theorize the Political,* ed. J. Butler and J. Scott (New York: Routledge, 1992); and *Bodies That Matter: On the Discursive Limits of "Sex"* (New York: Routledge, 1993).

13 Such a strategy and the stakes involved in its pursuit are exemplified in Jennie Livingston's 1991 film *Paris Is Burning* by Venus Extravaganza, whose hopes for success (in the form of a rich husband) depend upon the absoluteness with which "she" embodies conventional femininity. Another contemporary play (and film), *M. Butterfly* (David Hwang, 1986), explores these conventions as always only a projected male fantasy, which, when exposed, leads to madness for the man who wants to believe in his fantasy. *Butterfly* gets away with his act of passing by readopting a macho male identity, from which he mocks his dupe. *Paris Is Burning* offers no such sanguine escape for the transvestite. Exposure of Venus's "secret" does nothing to its discoverer, who vanishes anonymously. It is Venus who pays for linking the "wrong" gender to body: Venus left strangled on the hotel floor.

14 My thanks to David Hillman for drawing my attention to this exposure of bodily inscription as also validating the body as source of knowledge.

15 See Anne E. Goldman, "'I Made the Ink': (Literary) Production and Reproduction in *Dessa Rose* and *Beloved,*" *Feminist Studies* 16 (1990): 2; Jean Wyatt, "Giving Body to the Word: The Maternal Symbolic in Toni Morrison's *Beloved,*" *PMLA* 108, (May 1993): 3.

16 Cf. David Hillman's discussion (in this volume) of King Hamlet's death by a poison which, as it kills, imprisons his soul within an impermeable bodily cage.

17 Quoted in Karen Sánchez-Eppler, *Touching Liberty: Abolition, Feminism, and the Politics of the Body* (Berkeley: University of California Press, 1993), p. 20.

18 See Sánchez-Eppler, *Touching Liberty.* n. 24.

19 Mae Henderson notes that Schoolteacher's account of Sethe's child murder furthers this sense of her as animal. For an account of the way Sethe refashions that narrative "by privileging specifically female tropes" to "reconstitute her self and her-story," see Henderson, "Toni Morrison's *Beloved*: Re-Membering the Body as Historical Text," in *Comparative American Identities,* ed. Hortense Spillers (London: Routledge, 1991).

20 On the importance of Sethe's milk and of the way Sethe sees herself as maternal vessel, see Goldman, "'I Made the Ink'"; Wyatt "Giving Body to The Word", and Lorraine Liscio, "*Beloved*'s Narrative: Writing Mother's Milk," *Tulsa Studies in Women's Literature* 11 (spring 1992):1.

21 Toni Morrison, "Rootedness: The Ancestor as Foundation," in *Black Women Writers (1950-1980)* p. 342.

22 Toni Morrison and Gloria Naylor, "A Conversation," *Southern Review* 21 (summer 1985).

23 See Chin, "Come All Ye Asian Writers."

24 Sánchez-Eppler, *Touching Liberty* p. 33.

25 Toni Morrison, *Song of Solomon* (1977, rpt, New York: Plume, 1987) pp. 143, 147.

26 Toni Morrison, *Sula* (1973; rpt, New York: Plume, 1982), p. 31.

27 Morrison, *Sula,* p. 130.

28 Toni Morrison, *Jazz* (New York: Knopf, 1992) p. 130.

29 Morrison claims such a motive herself to explain her expansion beyond familiar fictional possibilities: "I didn't like the imposition that had been placed on black women's sexuality in literature. They were either mothers, mammies, or whores. And they were not vulnerable people. They were not people who were supposed to enjoy sex, either. That was forbidden in literature—to enjoy your body, be in your body, defend your body." ("Chloe Wofford Discusses Toni Morrison," *New York Times*, 11 September 1994.)

30 My attention to the unreality of this menstruating body owes greatly to Elaine Scarry's speedy deconstruction of the absurd treatment of menstruation in adverstising: "a tampax, which (according to its advertisers) enables one to hurl and spin through the air as though one had just been transformed into Kathy Rigby and the inserted product had just been transformed into a supercharged battery" (*Resisting Representation* [Oxford: Oxford University Press, 1994], p. 17). Scarry's point here is the contrast between such hyperbole and the understatement of advertisements for painkillers. But her description drew my attention to the way in which menstruation's (often surprising) reminder of our bodiness becomes a location for exaggerated denial of the body. The tampon ad transforms menstruation from a potentially messy bodily function which one wants to sop up as efficiently and undramatically as possible into the occasion for gymnastic metamorphosis, implying that we will not only be able to continue our normal routines, but will suddenly have newly improved, superpowerful bodies with which to leap and handspring along the seashore.

31 Maxine Hong Kingston, "Cultural Misreadings by American Reviewers, " in *Asian and Western Writers in Dialogue,* ed. Guy Amirthanayagam (London: Macmillan Press, 1982), p. 57.

32 See Butler, *Bodies That Matter.*

33 The working title of this next novel is *Paradise.* See *New York Times*, 11 September 1994, p. 73.

34 I am grateful to the many colleagues and mentors who have helped me to think, talk, and write through these questions. I thank Margaret Homans, Suzanne Keen, Melinda Gough, David Southward, Chris Cobb, Michelle Stephens, Margery Sokoloff, Deborah Karush, Cristina Ruotolo, Sharon Palmer, and Franny Nudelman for their generously critical responses to this paper in its many stages. And I also thank Michael O'Donovan-Anderson, enthusiastic and sage catalyst for the interdisciplinary dialogue which the Theories and/of Embodiment conference, at which this paper was originally delivered, so helpfully embodied.

6
Hamlet, Nietzsche, and Visceral Knowledge

David Asaf Hillman

Misanthropy and love:—One speaks of being sick of man only when one can no longer digest him and yet has one's stomach full of him. Misanthropy comes of an all too greedy love of man and "cannibalism"; but who asked you to swallow men like oysters, Prince Hamlet?

—Friedrich Nietzsche,
The Gay Science

From the opening moments of *Hamlet*, with Francisco's command to a muffled figure in the night, "Stand and unfold yourself" (I.i.2), a persistent concern throughout the play is with what cannot be seen, or known—what is beyond a threshold or "bourn" (III.i.79).[1] The question of what lies within—within, for example, the armor of the Ghost, beneath the smiling exterior of a person, or, as this paper argues, within the very bodies of the different protagonists—occupies a number of the play's characters, not least among them Hamlet himself. For him, it seems to me, the problem of other minds, of the truth of other minds, is inseparably a problem of other bodies; these bodies have their own truth, and access to this truth is to a remarkable extent equated with access to the interior of the human body. What is anatomically and physiologically inside people—inside himself no less than inside others—is something Hamlet harps on repeatedly.

This preoccupation with corporeal innards ties together a number of the play's—and its protagonist's—obsessions. We can include among these the problem of death and mourning and of what happens to the body after death, as well as the problem of birth and bodily origins; the difficulties of sexuality and of Hamlet's distaste at the idea of the sexual act; a concept of gender which is based on the contents of the body; and a deep concern with truth and truthfulness, with the sorting out of appearance and reality. All these are associated, in this "incorps'd" (IV.vii.86) play, with what we might call visceral knowledge: a sense of one's own as well as others' entrails, understood as ineluctably connected to the core of one's being, one's innermost truth.

In taking the idea of viscerality in the play to be central and complex, I am taking issue with an idea which has become practically a commonplace of *Hamlet* criticism: the idea that Hamlet feels "a disgust at the physical body of man,"[2] a "despairing contempt for the body"[3] as such. Hamlet's ubiquitous and somewhat grotesque oral fantasies, coupled with his apparent "sexual disgust,"[4] have led many critics of the play to think of him as having, as Francis Barker puts it, a "desire to refine away the insistent materiality of the body."[5] But distinctions need to be made between Hamlet's attitudes to bodies which are healthy or sick, open or closed, full or empty, paternal or maternal. Hamlet's aversion to the state of corporeality is far less absolute and more specific than such descriptions of his "hatred of the flesh"[6] might suggest; it is rather, we could say, the pervasive lies that people tell about their bodies, with their bodies, that he hates: the possibility of giving someone "the lie i'th' throat / As deep as to the lungs" (II.ii.569-70).

Hamlet's Entrails

I take as my point of entry a comment made by Stanley Cavell in his piece on the play, in which he speaks of "the everyday, skeletal manner in which human beings present themselves to [Hamlet]." He adds: "I think of this in connection with Nietzsche's statement in his autobiography (I mean *Ecce Homo*) that one trait of his nature that causes difficulty in his contacts with others is the uncanny sensitivity of his instinct for cleanliness, or, say, truthfulness, so that the innermost parts, the entrails (we might perhaps say drives) of every soul are *smelled* by him."[7] I would like to stick with the idea, specifically, of entrails, avoiding (at least partially) the movement manifested in Cavell's brackets ["("we might perhaps say drives)"]. Nietzsche, after all, speaks specifically of "entrails"—and of his sensitivity to them as "physiological."[8] "The inmost parts," those least accessible to epistemological inquiry, are used again and again by Nietzsche as his central metaphor for the undecipherability or opacity of human thoughts and actions:

> "However far a man may go in self-knowledge, nothing however can be more incomplete than his image of the totality of *drives* which constitute his being. He can scarcely name even the cruder ones: their number and strength, their ebb and flood, their play and counterplay among one another, and above all the laws of their *nutriment* remain wholly unknown to him . . . our moral judgements and evaluations too are only images and fantasies

based on a physiological process unknown to us, a kind of acquired language for designating nervous stimuli."[9]

Elsewhere, for instance in the fragment "On Truth and Lie in the Extra-Moral Sense," he points out the irony involved in the fact that "the urge for truth" is so often a product of "our proud, deceptive consciousness, far from the coils of the intestines, the quick current of the blood stream, and the involved tremors of the fibers."[10]

Nonetheless, any hermeneutic undertaking must, for Nietzsche, begin from the body—and, moreover, from its interior, which is why he speaks of the "hard, unwanted, inescapable task" of philosophy as a kind of vivisection; Socrates, for example, is "the old physician and plebeian who cut ruthlessly into his own flesh, as he did into the flesh and heart of the 'noble.'"[11] The body, though, for Nietzsche, is useful less as a physiological foundation than as a principle of interpretation: since "soul is only a word for something about the body," it is "essential: to start from the *body* and employ it as a guide. It is the much richer phenomenon, which allows of clearer observation. Belief in the body is better established than belief in the spirit."[12]

The words of a dead man
Are modified in the guts of the living[13]

Hamlet, we could say, starts from the body; as Coleridge was, I believe, the first to note, the opening scene is filled with "the language of *sensation* . . . the broken expressions of a man's compelled attention to bodily feelings." The entire play, Coleridge adds, is "a tragedy the interest of which is eminently *ad et apud intra* [towards and about the inside]."[14] Coleridge doesn't go on to explain this somewhat enigmatic comment any further, and the question of how to understand his remark echoes that of what we make of Hamlet's own rather opaque, "I have that within which passes show" (I.ii.85).[15] Both point to an internality the contents of which are unspecified; "*Hamlet*," as T. S. Eliot famously complained, "is full of some stuff that the writer could not drag to light, contemplate, or manipulate into art."[16] Certainly, Hamlet's statement involves an insistence upon the insufficiency of the merely external, though it has never to my knowledge been taken to imply a corporeal "inmost part" (III.iv.19). My argument here is that Hamlet's celebrated introspection includes an intensely visceral self-consciousness; within the context of his preoccupation with bodily innards, his "that within which passes show" can be understood as referring to, among other things, a strong sense of "the pith and marrow" (I.iv.22) of "the inward man" (II.ii.6).

The play opens under the pall of the felt absence of Hamlet's father. In the Ghost's return to the prehistory of the play, in his relation of his own murder, we can find a number of indications of Hamlet's bodily state. His account is vivid in its details:

> Sleeping within my orchard,
> My custom always of the afternoon,
> Upon my secure hour thy uncle stole
> With juice of cursed hebenon in a vial,

And in the porches of my ears did pour
The leperous distilment, whose effect
Holds such an enmity with blood of man
That swift as quicksilver it courses through
The natural gates and alleys of the body,
And with a sudden vigour it doth posset
And curd, like eager droppings into milk,
The thin and wholesome blood. So did it mine,
And a most instant tetter bark'd about,
Most lazar-like, with vile and loathsome crust
All my smooth body.
Thus was I, sleeping, by a brother's hand
Of life, of crown, of queen at once dispatch'd,
Cut off even in the blossoms of my sin,
Unhousel'd, disappointed, unanel'd,
No reck'ning made, but sent to my account
With all my imperfections on my head.
O horrible! O horrible! most horrible!
                  (I.v.59-80)

The account strikingly depicts the effects of the poison upon the body of Old
Hamlet: first, an internal thickening ("it doth posset / And curd . . . The thin
and wholesome blood"), followed immediately by a hardening of the boundaries
of the body. The formerly markedly open body of the King, the "porches" of
whose ears and "gates and alleys" of whose body have easily received the poison,
is now "bark'd about," "All" enclosed in a "tetter," a "vile and loathsome crust."
The speediness of the whole rigor-mortis-like process is repeatedly underlined.
The "sudden[ness]" of the action and the absoluteness of the closure combine to
give the effect of a trapping within—as if something which should have been
allowed to issue forth has been stopped up inside the instantly mummified body.
And the Ghost himself, through his piling up of negative prefixes, stresses not
so much the loss "Of life, of crown, of queen" as his own unpreparedness, the
"Cut off" or obstructed nature of his death; this is what seems so "horrible!"

What has not taken place here is the preparation which is thought of as
crucial to the passage into death. Hamlet later returns to this aborted process
when he refuses to kill Claudius during just such an attempt at purgation: "[He]
took my father grossly, full of bread, / With all his crimes broad blown, as flush
as May. . . . And am I then reveng'd, / To take him in the purging of his soul, /
When he is fit and season'd for his passage?" (III.iii.80-86). The fullness ("full
of bread"—perhaps recalling the Ghost's use of the phrase "loathsome crust") is
what is galling to Hamlet, as it is contrasted to a "purging" which would
prepare Claudius for the "passage" to the other world. Perhaps there is a clue here
as to why Hamlet eventually forces the already dying Claudius to drink the
poisoned cup of wine. The apparently excessive act may be understood as a final
act of vengeance, filling the very body of Claudius with his own sin-tainted
liquid and thus not allowing the emptying-out prior to death which Claudius has
denied Old Hamlet. (As Hamlet says to Horatio early on in the play: "We'll
teach you to drink deep ere you depart" [I.ii.175]. Does the "deep" here refer to

the emptying of the cup or to the filling of the body?) When told later that Claudius is "marvellous distempered . . . with choler," Hamlet puns on the word "choler," using it in its physiological sense of a bodily humor: "for me to put him to his purgation would perhaps plunge him into more choler" (III.ii.293-98), he replies. Old Hamlet, asleep during the moments preceding his death, is unable to "season" himself prior to it; he is thus consigned to purgatory, where he is "confin'd to fast in fires, / Till [his] foul crimes . . ./ Are burnt and purg'd away" (I.v.11-13).

Fasting, purging, and burning away are purification rituals which have been connected with death in almost all cultures. Such last rites are at least partially an emptying-out, originally of the body, later (in confession, e.g.) of the soul, a discharge seemingly entailed by the process of dying.[17] This fantasied emptying-out seems to be Janus-faced in its uses: it is meant to allow both the passage of the deceased into the next world and a form of continued existence of the dead person in this world. Death is symbolically overcome by a continuity in the very bodies of the survivors, and the latter are able to retain a contact with the one they have lost, to almost literally fill the gap created by the loss, by taking what is emptied-out symbolically into their own bodies; hence, the widespread existence of funerary feasts.[18] It is the emptying-out of the deceased which— imaginatively—makes possible the taking-in by the survivors, a process described by Freud, in "Mourning and Melancholia,"[19] as an "incorporation" which is followed by a bit-by-bit disengagement of the libido from the lost object. Perhaps, too, what is being imagined in this purging is an opening, at least at the last moment before death, of one's innermost being, an acknowledgement, as Nietzsche might put it, of the truth of one's innards—an enabling of the "cleanliness" of one's death.

Death, then, involves a ritual emptying-out of the body of the deceased; mourning, a symbolic reincorporation of the corpse into the bodies of the survivors. In his reading of *Hamlet*, Lacan points out both the predominance of the theme of mourning in the play and the fact that this theme is characterized by an "insufficiency": "in all the instances of mourning in *Hamlet*, one element is always present: the rites have been cut short and performed in secret."[20] These "maimed rites" (V.i.219) are epitomized in Hamlet's description of the proximity of his father's funeral and his mother's wedding: "Thrift, thrift, Horatio. The funeral bak'd meats / Did coldly furnish forth the marriage tables" (I.ii.180-81). We may wonder at the exact nature of the relation between the "bak'd meats" and the body of Old Hamlet, remembering that a "coffin" meant, at that time, both a burial chest and the crust of a pie or meat casserole.[21] The implication of Hamlet's comment is not only that there has been an overhasty transition from "dole" to "delight" (I.ii.13); the fact that the same meats furnished both the funeral and the wedding implies that they were *not* consumed at the earlier occasion. Neither end of the "bargain" of dying has been allowed: both the opening and purging of Old Hamlet's body, and the symbolic "incorporation" demanded by mourning, have been aborted. There is thus no sense of there having been any real grieving—it is not only the meat but also the mourners who are cold.

Old Hamlet's flesh, however, is eventually symbolically eaten—at his widow's wedding.[22] And Gertrude's coldness towards her former husband is repeatedly and specifically portrayed as a transferring of her feeding from the body of Old Hamlet to that of Claudius: "Could you on this fair mountain leave to feed / And batten [grow fat] on this moor?" (III.iv.66-67; cf. 163-64). It is primarily, of course, Hamlet who upbraids his mother in this way—in terms of who she is ingesting: "Why, she would hang on him / As if increase of appetite had grown / By what it fed on; and yet within a month— / Let me not think on't" (I.ii.143-46; cf. I.v.55-57).

Yet "think on't" he does, and, in trying not to dwell on it, his fantasies take on a compulsive quality. The comment about the "funeral bak'd meats" not only perfectly encapsulates the problematic status of mourning in the play but also marks the beginning of Hamlet's angry preoccupation with the idea of male innards as food, from his avowal to feed "all the region kites" with Claudius's "offal" (II.ii.575-56) to his disquisitions upon the "worm that hath eat of a king" and the progress of an emperor "through the guts of a beggar" (IV.iii.27-31).[23]

The association of human innards with food in *Hamlet* is almost exclusively limited to male bodies. It may not be enough, therefore, to simply call attention, as Janet Adelman does, to "the play's fusion of eating and death and sex."[24] Such a formulation collapses important differentiations, such as those between who is being consumed and who is doing the eating. For while the maternal body may indeed, as Adelman argues, be "always already sexual" and the *source* of death in the world, it is the paternal body which is consistently fantasized as being at the other terminus of death—as being posthumously eaten.[25] Maternal and paternal bodies are associated, respectively, with the bodily origins and ends of death—the two poles, as it were, of the process of dying: "To be" and "not to be."[26] Hamlet is habitually interested in this way-of-all-flesh. His pleasure-in-putrefaction—his delight in reminding everyone around him of the existence of the abject ("How long will a man lie i'th'earth ere he rot?" [V.1.15]; "if the sun breed maggots in a dead dog" [II.ii.181-82]; "we fat ourselves for maggots" [IV.iii.22], and so forth) may be connected to the fact that through decomposition, and the idea of the generativity of decomposing matter, the two ends of the process are brought together:[27] as Georges Bataille writes, in archaic societies "decay summed up the world we spring from and return to, and horror and shame were attached both to our birth and to our death."[28]

The play as a whole and Hamlet in particular repeatedly stress the beginnings of this process of decay in the body's afflictions; and, with some consistency, the metaphor is one of *internal* sickness:[29] "Something is rotten *in* the state of Denmark" (I.iv.90). This "something" remains slightly vague, hidden within the body, thus Hamlet's explanation of Fortinbras's Polish expedition:

> This is th'impostume [abscess] of much wealth and peace,
> That inward breaks, and shows no cause without
> Why the man dies.
>
> (IV.iv.27-28)

Like Hamlet's "that within which passes show," this too "shows no cause without." Again, Hamlet warns his mother that her avoidance of the truth

> will but skin and film the ulcerous place,
> Whiles rank corruption, mining all within,
> Infects unseen.
>
> (III.iv.149-51)

There is presumably in these perceptions a recollection of the manner of Old Hamlet's death—the poison working first within, then shutting off the body's boundaries.

But "to the quick of th'ulcer" (IV.vii.123): Hamlet's cannibalistic fantasies are in part an attempt on his behalf to grieve for his father; in the absence of any community of mourners, they are also his insistent, angry rejoinder to the symbolic nonincorporation of his father's body by its survivors; to these he defiantly opposes the image of a grotesquely open and edible paternal corpus. The closure of his father's body and the foreclosure of the grieving leave Hamlet alone in a world of surfaces, surrounded by figures whom he sees as rejecting not only emotional but also corporeal openness to himself. It is not that he imagines these figures to be closed in any absolute way—he depicts his mother, for example, as feeding on Claudius's body, the two of them as "one flesh" (IV.iii.55)—but that he thinks of them as closed or inaccessible *to him*. This lack of any open bodies to turn to or identify with, a lack of what I will call "visceral matching," leaves Hamlet with a sense of bodily as well as spiritual isolation; his "doubts about the mother and the holding environment," as the psychoanalyst Adam Phillips has written in a different context, "are transferred onto the body, turned against it, as it begins to represent a new kind of internal environment, a more solitary one"; he is left "in the solitary confinement of his body."[30] Nor is his solitude in any sense "benign": his environment is described by Hamlet as a kind of "prison"; the whole world, indeed, is for him nothing but a prison "in which there are many confines, wards, and dungeons" (II.ii.243-46). In this perception he seemingly matches the pent-up condition of his father, his blood thickened and body "bark'd about" by the poison, "confin'd," as we've seen, in his posthumous "prison-house" (I.v.11-14).

Immediately before and immediately after his encounter with the Ghost in act 1, Hamlet signals a kind of internal stiffening: "My fate cries out / And makes each petty artire [artery] in this body /As hardy as the Nemean lion's nerve" (I.iv.81-83); "Hold, hold, my heart, / And you, my sinews, grow not instant old, / But bear me stiffly up" (I.v.93-5).[31] There is here, as elsewhere in the play, a forced rigidifying of his own body, a countermovement to the urge to "burst in ignorance" (I.iv.45). This corporeal hardening literally embodies a state of skepticism, a doubting of the environment, of its capacity to acknowledge him, or him it. So, as Elaine Scarry has shown in relation to the Hebraic Scriptures, "disbelief or doubt . . . is habitually described as a witholding of the body, which in its resistance to an external referent is perceived as covered, or hard, or stiff."[32] This stiffening is inevitably accompanied by an impulse on Hamlet's behalf to "burst in ignorance," "to shatter all his bulk [trunk] / And end his being" (II.i.95-96). This is one way of understanding Hamlet's use of the phrase "this mortal coil" (III.i.67): the constriction implied by it is, among other things, specifically corporeal. His "too too solid flesh"[33] (I.ii.129) may be taken in a similar fashion: the wish to "have shuffled off" the coil, like the one to "melt, / Thaw, and resolve" the flesh, expresses his anguish over his solitary imprisonment within what he calls "this machine" (II.ii.123), his body: he is indeed too much *in* the son.

There is a striking congruence between the kind of corporeal confinement and hardening described here and standard early-modern views of melancholy. Timothy Bright, for instance, whose *A Treatise of Melancholy* (1586) was the most widely available Elizabethan text on the subject, speaks of the "hardness whereof the flesh of melancholy persons is": such people "shut up the hart as it were in a dungeon of obscurity . . . and locketh up the gates of the hart, whereout the spirits should breake forth upon just occasion, to the comfort of all the family of their fellow members."[34] Hamlet's heartfelt declaration, "O God, I could be bounded in a nutshell and count myself a king of infinite space—were it not that I have bad dreams" (II.ii.254-56), immediately follows his decription of the world as a "confine." The image of a nutshell perfectly encapsulates the ambivalence Hamlet feels about the hardening of the body: alongside the defensive need for a protective shell around "my heart's core, ay . . . my heart of heart" (III.ii.73), there is a concomitant wish to be cracked open (and, perhaps, devoured); portraying himself as "bounded in a nutshell," while allowing a matching of his closed-off father ("and count myself a king"), is surely also a plea of this kind.[35]

Through much of the play, Hamlet displays a profound doubt about what is within not only himself, his own body, but also within the various figures around him, paternal and maternal. His early plea—"Let me not burst in ignorance" (I.iv.45)—expresses a relation between *not* knowing and a need to be open—a need for "the hatch and the discharge" (III.i.168) of whatever lies within, for the closure of the figures surrounding him exacerbates his own uncertainty as to the accuracy of his sensitivity to others' entrails—their corporeal refusal frustrates what Nietzsche might call his "sense of smell." Hence (in part) Hamlet's famous idleness. Hence also an urge to penetration, which he exhibits repeatedly throughout the play—an urge which finds its sources both in the frustrating environment and in his own uncertainty. Hamlet's epistemophilic impulse, as we shall see in a moment, is persistently imagined in both violent and bodily terms.

Hamlet's Nero Complex

Ever since Freud's footnote on *Hamlet* in *The Interpretation of Dreams*, there have been numerous interpretations of Hamlet's sexuality—of his incestuous impulses, of his disgust at the corporeal aspects of sex, of his possible homosexuality: these have practically become commonplaces of *Hamlet* criticism. Such interpretations often place a wide range of "bodily" material under the category of the sexual. Here, I take the sexual in *Hamlet* as one aspect of what I have called visceral knowledge, understanding the urge to penetration as an urge to open up the other, to know or connect with the insides of the body of another—*carnal* knowledge in the fullest sense of the term.

Freud, followed by Ernest Jones and many later critics, portrayed Hamlet's desires as Oedipal—indeed, as prototypically Oedipal.[36] If we try to imagine what the Oedipus complex would look like from the perspective of what I've called visceral knowledge—or, more accurately, frustrated visceral knowledge—we might come up with something like this: the desire to know one's mother and one's father can manifest itself as a desire to inhabit, or to find a way into, their bodies; this may have a tendency to be sexual in the former case and to be violent in the latter. Biblically at least, the taboos against incest and violence antecede a more primary taboo against knowing.

In any event, in turning to the play for evidence of Hamlet's Oedipus complex, we find not so much an incestuous impulse as what we might call a Nero complex: a desire to open the parental body—to know one's parents' entrails—a desire inseparable from a wish to have one's own entrails known (less, perhaps, a sexual complex than a "Nerosis"). Here is Hamlet, on his way to his mother's chambers, at "the very witching time of night":

> Now could I drink hot blood,
> And do such bitter business as the day
> Would quake to look on. Soft, now to my mother.
> O heart, lose not thy nature. Let not ever
> The soul of Nero enter this firm bosom;
> Let me be cruel, not unnatural.
> I will speak daggers to her, but use none.
> (III.ii.381-87)

There is here no hint of a sexual desire. What Hamlet expresses in this prayer is a violent impulse, suppressed only with difficulty, to use daggers on his mother: on her body. We can call the daggers phallic, the Neronian impulse an incestuous attempt to reach the mother's womb, but neither the immediate nor the wider context requires such a reading. Elsewhere in Shakespeare, Nero appears simply as the type of cruelty, without reference to incest. During the following scenes, first with his stepfather and then with his mother, Hamlet reveals, above all, a barely stifled penetrative urge—a desire for aperture.

When we turn to the closet scene (*not* "the bedroom scene," as many critics have referred to it since John Dover Wilson's *What Happens in Hamlet*[37], we see, for the first time, a Hamlet unable to suppress his violent impulses. Here again we can find no evidence of direct sexual intent; on the contrary, as Adelman points out, Hamlet attempts in this scene to separate his mother from her sexuality. His penetrative wish is here coupled with an attempt at closing his mother's body, primarily (though not only) sexually, to Claudius: "Not this, by no means, that I bid you do: / Let the bloat King tempt you again to bed" (ll.183-84). This may be simply a matter of shutting out Claudius in order to open his mother to himself, but it involves two different kinds of aperture—the 'merely' sexual, which for Hamlet is "rank" (l.150), "enseamed, . . . / Stew'd in corruption" (ll.92-93), and the kind of carnal knowledge described above. Thus, his desexualization of Gertrude is by no means incompatible with an imagined penetration of her body:

> Peace, sit you down,
> And let me wring your heart; for so I shall
> If it be made of penetrable stuff,
> If damned custom have not braz'd it so,
> That it be proof and bulwark against sense.
>   (III.iv.34-38)

This expresses a desire, more than anything, for ingression, without any sense of the transgression which would accompany an incestuous sexual desire. And Hamlet is insistent about this wish to fashion a mother whose heart consists of "penetrable stuff": "You go not till I set you up a glass / Where you may see the inmost part of you" (ll.18-19). (Hamlet's rather convoluted syntax here—"I set you up a glass"—leaves open the possibility that he is positioning *himself* as the mirror for his mother's "inmost part.") What this "inmost part" is precisely we never learn; Hamlet's language, though, throughout this scene, is relentlessly body-bound. He speaks of his mother's appetites in specifically inner-bodily terms ("the heyday in the blood," "a matron's bones" [ll. 69, 83])—"his version," as Adelman writes, "of her soiled inner body"[38].

The closet scene, of course, contains not only this metaphorical penetration of Gertrude, but also the killing—the physical penetration—of Polonius. As Gertrude describes it, Hamlet

> In his lawless fit,
> Behind the arras hearing something stir,
> Whips out his rapier, cries "A rat, a rat,"
> And in this brainish apprehension kills
> The unseen good old man.
>   (IV.i.8-12)

Hamlet turns from an agonizing confrontation with his mother, at the moment when he comes closest to doing violence to her physical person ("What wilt thou do? Thou wilt not murder me? / Help, ho!" [III.iv.20-21]), and thrusts his rapier through the arras. The surge of penetrative anger is turned away from his mother and towards a symbolically obstructive object. Rather than attacking "the mobbled [muffled or veiled] queen" (II.ii.498), he attacks another "mobbled" body. The action strikingly brings together two associated strands of the play's imagery: a separating integument (the arras), and a penetrative instrument (the rapier). Several critics have commented upon the play's stress on skin and its relation to the multiple images of seals and sealing.[39] These images, along with a number of others evoking obstructive membranes,[40] can be understood to symbolize for Hamlet the sense of other people's veiled or closed-off bodies. Their concomitant is a plethora of piercing weapons and tools—"the pass and fell incensed points / Of mighty opposites" (V.ii.61-62)—a plethora which bespeaks the violence born of the frustration of inaccessibility.[41] Many of these objects appear as actual props on stage, making not only metaphorically but physically present the sharpness, the "keen . . . edge" (III.ii.243-44), of Hamlet's desire. Walter Benjamin speaks of "the precision with which the passions themselves take on the nature of stage-properties" in baroque drama—if this is so, the play's passions are nothing if not penetrative.[42]

This is most obviously the case when the idea of revenge is foremost. When Hamlet thinks of catching the conscience of the king, he thinks in terms of penetrating to the very center of his body: "I'll tent him to the quick" (II.ii.593),[43] he says, as he plans the staging of "The Mousetrap." But, as the earlier part of this soliloquy reveals, access to Claudius's "offal" seems inseparably linked to access to Hamlet's own entrails, "As deep as to the lungs":

> Am I a coward?
> Who calls me villain, breaks my pate across,
> Plucks off my beard and blows it in my face,
> Tweaks me by the nose, gives me the lie i'th' throat
> As deep as to the lungs—who does me this?
> Ha!
> Swounds, I should take it: for it cannot be
> But I am pigeon-liver'd and lack gall
> To make oppression bitter, or ere this
> I should ha' fatted all the region kites
> With this slave's offal.
> (II.ii.566-76)

Here again there is a kind of visceral matching. Coming as it does at the end of this self-castigating tirade (which began with Hamlet calling himself a "slave" [l.544]) and after the repeated mention of his own viscera (lungs, liver, gall), "this slave's offal" may sound for a moment like a reference to himself—almost as if there is some confusion between killing the king and killing himself. Indeed, Hamlet's suicidal impulses may be thought of as partially a desire to reveal his own innards. His imagined method of suicide—"a bare bodkin" (III.i.76)—entails the opening up of the body (we might say: the baring of the body, noting that a "bodkin" meant not only a dagger but also a "body")[44]. Shuffling off the constrictive "mortal coil" through suicide would thus be not only, as Freudian psychoanalysis would say, an aggressive act misdirected inward instead of outward,[45] but also a vengeful injunction to look (analogous to his verbal foregrounding of putrefaction)—the embodiment of a wish to be known.

In his "O what a rogue and peasant slave" soliloquy, however, Hamlet's self-accusation takes the form of seeing himself as *lacking*, quite literally, guts: "for it cannot be / But I am pigeon-liver'd and lack gall / To make oppression bitter." He is "A dull and muddy-mettled rascal . . . unpregnant of [his] cause" (II.ii.562-63). Hamlet's sense of visceral poverty alternates, in his fantasy, with a contrary sense of visceral plenitude. Freud, in his interpretation of the "complex of melancholia" (in "Mourning and Melancholia"), describes an "alternation of melancholic and manic phases" (p. 174). Hamlet, of course, displays just such a vacillation, between suicidal despair and an "antic disposition" (I.v.180). (Heinz Kohut, in his brief discussion of the play, depicts Hamlet's "traumatic state" as "characterized (a) by discharge phenomena, ranging from sarcastic punning to reckless, aggressive, outbursts [the killing of

Polonius]; and (b) by retreat phenomena, ranging from philosophical brooding to deeply melancholiac preoccupations.)"[46] What we are now in a position to see is the bodily correlatives of these two phases.

We can call the depressive pole of this dialectic Hamlet's "Stoic" disposition, noting Nietzsche's definition of the Stoic as one who "wants his stomach to become ultimately indifferent to whatever the accidents of existence might pour into it."[47] Associated with this attitude are what we have described as the closure and hardening of the body and the concomitant sense of internal corruption or emptiness. It is when in this state that Hamlet feels the world to be a prison, his own body a constriction; and it is this mood that his self-castigations spring from. Benjamin, describing the paradigmatic baroque attitude of *acedia*, speaks of "the desolation with which the practice of stoicism confronts man. The deadening of the emotions, and the ebbing away of the waves of life which are the source of these emotions in the body, can increase the distance between the self and the surrounding world to the point of alienation from the body."[48]

The manic pole of the dialectic, Hamlet's "antic disposition," is accompanied by a sense of visceral plenitude. This is manifested from his early "I have that within which passes show" to his "though I am not splenative and rash, / Yet have I in me something dangerous / Which let thy wiseness fear" (V.i.254-56). The "discharge phenomena" associated with this attitude may stem from Hamlet's need to "discharge" some of this fullness. In this humor the penetrative urge is inescapable, and the violence barely under control.

But this mood at last meets its maker in the graveyard scene. Here the ultimate "truth of entrails" finally seems to have a calming effect on Hamlet's penetrative temperament, as his very viscera react with revulsion to the fragments of bodies in the graveyard. Wherever he has broken through a surface, he has encountered death—beneath the earth in which his father was buried, behind Polonius's arras, beneath the seal of his own death warrant; now he finds death inside the body itself, and he realizes that the body hidden beneath its skin is not altogether desirable. His own bodily interior reacts less than favorably to Yorick's skull and the other human remains: his "bones . . . ache to think on't" (V.i.90-91)—on, that is, corpsehood, the living body's terminus; his "gorge rises at it" (l.181); and, he finds, mortality stinks:

> Hamlet: Dost thou think Alexander looked o' this fashion i'th'earth?
> Horatio: E'en so.
> Hamlet: And smelt so? Pah!
> (ll.191-94)

"But who asked you to swallow men like oysters, Prince Hamlet?"—Nietzsche's own sense of smell seems to be informing his gnomic comment on the play. Perhaps what he means when he speaks of Hamlet's "misanthropy and love" is something akin to the alternation between the two dispositions depicted above— the Stoic and the antic, the Senecan (at least, the Senecan of the moral essays) and the Neronian (the Senecan of the revenge tragedies). Nor are the two as different, or as separable, as they may seem at first glance: like misanthropy and "an all too greedy love of man," there is here too an all-too-human oscillation between isolation and fusion.[49] Hamlet's "cannibalism" is an expression of his overwhelming desire to inhabit, and to be inhabited by, the other—to escape his condition of bodily solitude. We can describe him, as Nietzsche described Socrates, as one "who cut ruthlessly into his own flesh, as he did into the flesh and heart of the 'noble,' with a look that said clearly enough: 'Don't dissemble in front of me! Here—we are equal.'"[50] "Don't dissemble": the stakes of acknowledgment are, for Hamlet, screwed to their highest pitch, reaching into his "inmost part," his "heart's core." "The death of our capacity to acknowledge as such," as Cavell has written, is "the turning of our hearts to stone or their bursting."[51] This is Hamlet's heartbreaking choice: to shut himself off within his "too too solid flesh"—or to "burst in ignorance." Neither alternative holds the promise of satisfying his desire to know, and to be known by, the other—hence the impasse at which Hamlet finds himself for most of the play. "We are all," in Emerson's words, "discontented pendulums"; Hamlet's pendulum swings not so much between killing the king and not killing him as between the two Hamlets these would entail being. Caught between hard-hearted "misanthropy" and heart-shattering "greedy love," he can only adopt, while simultaneously rejecting, alternating strategies of self-protection—Stoic isolation and antic aggression—until, we could say, he breaks apart—internally, where else?—"Now cracks a noble heart" (V.ii.364).[52]

Notes

1   All quotations from *Hamlet* are from the Arden edition of the play, ed. Harold Jenkins (London: Routledge, 1982).
2   G. Wilson Knight, "The Embassy of Death: An Essay on *Hamlet*," in *The Wheel of Fire: Interpretations of Shakespearean Tragedy* (London: Methuen, 1949), p. 23.
3   John Hunt, "A Thing of Nothing: The Catastrophic Body in *Hamlet*," *Shakespeare Quarterly* 39 (1988): 27-44; p. 27. Though Hunt does see an eventual redemption for bodily experience in the play, in his view Hamlet's overwhelming attitude is one of "disdainful, alienated contempt" for the "corrupt and corrupting" flesh (p. 37).
4   Janet Adelman, "'Man and Wife Is One Flesh': *Hamlet* and the Confrontation with the Maternal Body," in *Suffocating Mothers: Fantasies of Maternal Origin in Shakespeare's Plays, Hamlet to The Tempest* (New York: Routledge, 1992), p. 250, n. 14.
5   Francis Barker, *The Tremulous Private Body: Essays on Subjection* (London: Methuen, 1984), p. 40. Cf. Hunt's characterization of Hamlet as wishing "to remove himself from the compromising infection of corporeality" (p. 38).
6   Adelman, "'Man and Wife Is One Flesh,'" p. 250 n. 14.
7   Stanley Cavell, "Hamlet's Burden of Proof," in *Disowning Knowledge: In Six Plays of Shakespeare* (Cambridge: Cambridge University Press, 1987), pp. 179-91;

p. 186 (emphasis in the original). My reading of Hamlet is indebted to Cavell's *The Claim of Reason: Wittgenstein, Skepticism, Morality, and Tragedy* (Oxford: Oxford University Press, 1979), where tragedy is understood as "a kind of epistemological problem" and where "the problem of knowledge" is inextricable from the embodied condition of humanity (p. 482).

8   Friedrich Nietzsche, *On the Genealogy of Morals and Ecce Homo*, the latter trans. Walter Kaufmann (New York: Vintage Books, 1989), p. 233: "My instinct for cleanliness is characterized by a perfectly uncanny sensitivity so that the proximity or—what am I saying?—the inmost parts, the 'entrails' of every soul are physiologically perceived by me—*smelled*." On Nietzsche's repeated use of a "gastroenterological metaphor," see Eric Blondel, *Nietzsche: The Body and Culture. Philosophy as a Philological Genealogy*, trans. Seán Hand (Stanford: Stanford University Press, 1991), pp. 201-38; esp. pp. 219-20.

9   Friedrich Nietzsche, *Daybreak: Thoughts on the Prejudices of Morality*, trans. R. J. Hollingdale (Cambridge: Cambridge University Press, 1982), pp. 74-76 (§ 119).

10   Friedrich Nietzsche, "On Truth and Lie in the Extra-Moral Sense," in *The Portable Nietzsche*, ed. and trans. Walter Kaufmann (New York: Penguin Books, 1954), p. 44. The idea of an inherent connection between truth and entrails is at least as old as the practice of haruspices (or, in the case of human entrails, anthropomancy). See, e.g., Walter Burkert, *Homo Necans: The Anthropology of Ancient Greek Sacrificial Ritual and Myth*, trans. Peter Bing (Berkeley: University of California Press, 1983), pp. 5-6; Jean-Louis Durand, "Greek Animals: Towards a Topology of Edible Bodies," in *The Cuisine of Sacrifice among the Greeks*, ed. Marcel Detienne and Jean-Pierre Vernant, trans. Paula Wissing (Chicago: University of Chicago Press, 1989), pp. 87-118. In both Old and New Testaments, as Elaine Scarry has shown, "the interior of the body carries the force of confirmation [of belief]." *The Body in Pain: The Making and Unmaking of the World* (New York: Oxford University Press, 1985), p. 215. Elsewhere she speaks of "the mining of the ultimate substance, the ultimate source of substantiation, the extraction of the physical basis of reality from its dark hiding place in the body out into the light of day, the making available of the precious ore of confirmation, the interior content of human bodies, lungs, arteries, blood, brains" (p. 137).

11   Friedrich Nietzsche, *Beyond Good and Evil: Prelude to a Philosophy of the Future*, trans. Walter Kaufmann (New York: Vintage Books, 1989), pp. 137-39 (§ 212): "By applying the knife vivisectionally to the chest of the very *virtues of their time*, they [philosophers] betrayed what was their own secret: to know of a *new* greatness of man."

12   Friedrich Nietzsche, *Thus Spoke Zarathustra*, in *The Portable Nietzsche*, p. 146; *The Will to Power*, trans. Walter Kaufmann and R. J. Hollingdale, ed. Walter Kaufmann (New York: Vintage Books, 1968), p. 289; emphasis in the original.

13   W. H. Auden, "In Memory of W. B. Yeats."

14   Samuel T. Coleridge, *Coleridge's Writings on Shakespeare*, ed. Terence Hawkes (New York: Capricorn Books, 1959), p. 140; emphasis in the original.

15   "Within," rather oddly, is capitalized in the Folio; the opacity here extends to the grammar—the context allows the word to be taken as either an adverb or a preposition.

16   T. S. Eliot, "*Hamlet*," in *The Selected Prose of T. S. Eliot*, ed. Frank Kermode (New York: Harcourt Brace Jovanovich, 1975), p .48.

17   See R. B. Onians, *The Origins of European Thought: About the Body, the Mind, the Soul, the World, Time, and Fate* (Cambridge: Cambridge University Press, 1951),

pp. 254-91, esp pp.   279, and 283-85.

1 8   See Burkert, *Homo Necans*, pp. 48-58; esp. p. 50: "The most widespread element in funerals—so obvious it may seem hardly worth mentioning—is the role played by eating, i.e., the funerary meal. . . . The ritualization of hunting made possible a twofold transferral: the dead could take the place of the quarry. . . but in the subsequent feast, his place could in turn be taken by the sacrificial animal." Georges Bataille discusses the cannibalistic impulse underlying the taboo regarding the touching of corpses: "The taboo protected the corpse from other people's desire to eat it. This is a desire no longer active in us, one we never feel now. Archaic societies, however, do show the taboo as alternately in force and suspended. Man is never looked upon as butcher's meat, but he is frequently eaten ritually." *Erotism: Death and Sensuality*, trans. Mary Dalwood (San Francisco: City Lights Books, 1986), p. 71.

1 9   Sigmund Freud, "Mourning and Melancholia" [1917], trans. Joan Riviere, in *General Psychological Theory: Papers on Metapsychology*, ed. Philip Rieff (New York: Macmillan, 1963), pp. 164-79. References to this paper are bracketed in the text. Freud's essay has been juxtaposed with *Hamlet* numerous times; see especially Stephen A. Reid, "Hamlet's Melancholia," *American Imago* 31, no. 4 (winter 1974):, 378-400; Arthur Kirsch, "Hamlet's Grief," *ELH*. 48, no. 1 (1981): 17-36, esp. 22-24); and Steven Mullaney, "Mourning and Misogyny: *Hamlet, The Revenger's Tragedy*, and the Final Progress of Elizabeth I, 1600-1607," *Shakespeare Quarterly*, 45, no. 2 (summer 1994): 139-62.

2 0   Jacques Lacan, "Desire and the Interpretation of Desire in *Hamlet*," trans. James Hulbert, in *Literature and Psychoanalysis: The Question of Reading: Otherwise,* ed. Shoshana Felman (Baltimore: Johns Hopkins University Press, 1982), pp. 11-52, pp. 39-40.

2 1   The word has both meanings in *Titus Andronicus* (I.i.35; V.ii.188); see Alexander Schmidt, *Shakespeare Lexicon and Quotation Dictionary*, 3d. ed. (New York: Dover Publications, 1971), I:212.

2 2   The poet Erich Fried, who translated *Hamlet* into German, claims that in his "funeral bak'd meats" comment, "Hamlet is suggesting that his father's flesh was eaten at his mother's wedding." *Is Shakespeare Still Our Contemporary?* ed. John Elsom (London and New York: Routledge, 1989), p. 31.

2 3   We have seen Hamlet speaking about Claudius's being "fit and season'd for his passage" (III.iii.86). "Season'd" in Shakespeare usually means "to spice, to give relish to" when used as a transitive verb: see Schmidt, *Shakespeare Lexicon and Quotation Dictionary*, II:1017. Hamlet may thus punningly refer to Claudius as being readied to be eaten. Indeed, there seems to be a fairly specific culinary fantasy in Hamlet's mind—of a dead body being prepared for eating by first being "season'd" as well as, perhaps, stuffed ("full of bread"), then "bak'd" till a crust has formed around it. Cf. the "blood of fathers, mothers, daughters, sons, / Bak'd and impasted [made into a crust] . . . Roasted with wrath"—in Hamlet's part of the Pyrrhus speech (II.ii.455-57): and his later "Now could I drink hot blood" (III.ii.381) soliloquy.

2 4   Adelman, "'Man and Wife Is One Flesh'" p. 28.

2 5   Adelman, "'Man and Wife Is One Flesh'" p. 27. The play's imagery of the insides of the body (as opposed to its surfaces) not surprisingly focuses on the torso; here too we can sense a tenuous distinction between male and female insides: images of the maternal inner-body tend to point to the upper half of the torso ("those thorns that in her bosom lodge" [I.v.87]; "in her excellent white bosom" [II.ii.112]; "such love must needs be treason in my breast" [III.ii.173]; "let me wring your heart . . . if it be made of penetrable stuff" [III.iv.35-36]) or to the womb (I.i.140 and, implicitly,

III.ii.385); images of the paternal inner-body are most often gastro-enteric ("guts" [III.iv.214; IV.iii.31], "offal" [II.ii.576], "garbage [entrails]" [I.v.57], "stomach" [I.i.103], etc.). (I exclude from this list most of the play's many references [36] to "heart" and its derivatives.)

26 Cavell sees "Hamlet's question whether to be or not, as asking first of all not why he stays alive, but first of all how he or anyone lets himself be born as the one he is" ("Hamlet's Burden of Proof," p. 187). Both he and Adelman (in her concern with the "devouring maternal womb" and the "fantasy of spoiling at the site of origin" ["'Man and Woman Is One Flesh,'" p. 23]) are primarily interested in the question of the origin of the individual. The distinction between the problem of death and the problem of being born is, I think, important in the play, though it is hardly a simple binary: as Adelman says, in *Hamlet* "birth itself . . . immerses the body in death" (p. 27).

27 Note the cyclical structure of many of Hamlet's comments about decomposition: "Not where he eats, but where he is eaten . . . we fat all creatures else to fat us, and we fat ourselves for maggots. . . . A man may fish with the worm that hath eat of a king, and eat of the fish that hath fed of that worm" (IV.iii.19-28).

28 Bataille, *Erotism*, p. 56. The body's decomposition is intimately connected to the idea of the contagiousness of death, an idea which recurs in Hamlet's imagery. (See ibid., pp. 46-47; and cf. the uses of "pestilence" and "contagion" in the play: "a foul and pestilent congregation of vapours" [II.ii.302]; "pestilent speeches of his father's death" [IV.v.91; cf. V.i.173]; "hell itself breathes out / Contagion to this world" [III.ii.380-81]; "I'll touch my point / With this contagion, that if I gall him slightly, / It may be death" [IV.vii.145-47; cf. I.iii.42].)

29 Among the most prominent critics who have noted this strand of imagery are Caroline Spurgeon (*Shakespeare's Imagery and What It Tells Us* [Cambridge: Cambridge University Press, 1935], pp. 133-34, 316-19) and Wolfgang Clemen (*The Development of Shakespeare's Imagery* [London: Methuen, 1977], pp. 112-18).

30 Adam Phillips, "On Risk and Solitude," in *On Kissing, Tickling, and Being Bored: Psychoanalytic Essays on the Unexamined Life* (Cambridge, Mass.: Harvard University Press, 1993), pp. 31, 28.

31 The Ghost has already signaled a kind of internal matching with his son, when characterizing his tale as one that should "freeze thy young blood" (I.v.16; cf. the similar effects of the poison on Old Hamlet's own blood: I.v.65-70). His "Remember me" (l. 91) may thus be taken literally as an injunction to his son to "re-member"— i.e., bodily reproduce—himself.

32 Scarry, *The Body in Pain,* p. 202. Scarry's examples are plentiful, but see especially Exod. 32:9; Zech. 7:11-12; Neh. 9:29; Isa. 48:4.

33 I here adopt the Folio reading (rather than the Second Quarto's "sullied").

34 Timothy Bright, *A Treatise on Melancholy*, reprinted Facsimile Text Society (New York: Columbia University Press, 1940; orig. London: Thomas Vautrollier, 1586), pp. 128, 100.

35 Cf. the German playwright Heiner Müller's *Hamletmachine*, where Hamlet declares: "I want to force open my sealed flesh. I want to dwell in my veins, in the marrow of my bones, in the maze of my skull. I retreat into my entrails." *Hamletmachine and Other Texts for the Stage*, trans. Carl Weber (New York: Performing Arts Journal Publications, 1984), p. 57.

36 Sigmund Freud, *The Interpretation of Dreams*, trans. James Strachey (New York: Basic Books, 1959), pp. 263-66; Ernest Jones, *Hamlet and Oedipus* (New York: Doubleday, 1954).

37 The Queen's "closet" was her private apartment, not her bedroom. John Dover Wilson's influential *What Happens in Hamlet* (Cambridge: Cambridge University Press, 1935) was, I think, the first to call this "The Bedroom Scene" (p. 246, chapter heading). Twentieth-century interpretations have more often than not gone along with this and used a bed as central prop, following (perhaps) Freud's reading of the scene as portraying Hamlet's incestuous impulses.

38 Adelman, "'Man and Wife is One Flesh,'" p. 34.

39 E.g., Maurice Charney, "The Imagery of Skin Disease and Sealing," in *Hamlet's Fictions* (New York: Routledge, 1988), pp. 120-30.

40 To take some salient examples, apart from the many images of skin and sealing: the arras behind which Claudius and Polonius hide together (II.ii.263), the one behind which Polonius hides, the "inky cloak" (I.ii.77) of seeming, the multiple layers enclosing the body of Old Hamlet (armor, "crust," "cerements," coffin, "sepulchre"), and the "mobbled queen" of the Pyrrhus speech (a phrase over which Hamlet muses, interrupting the performance).

41 Penetrative instruments are ubiquitous in *Hamlet*, from Marcellus's "partisan [a long-handled spear]" (I.i.143), through Pyrrhus's "antique sword" (II.ii.465), Hamlet's "slings and arrows" and "bare bodkin" (III.i.58, 76; cf. IV.vii.21; V.ii.239), Laertes's poisoned "knife" (IV.vii.141) and "sword unbated" (IV.vii.137; the play's other references to swords are: I.v.154, 156, 162, 166, 167, 169; II.ii.469, 473, 487, 510; III.i.153; III.iii.88; IV.iii.64; IV.v.211; IV.vii.139), Gertrude's "words like daggers" (III.iv.95; cf. III.ii.387), and Claudius's "great axe" (IV.v.215; cf. V.ii.24), to the final trial by "rapier and dagger" (V.ii.142) or "foils" (IV.vii.135; V.ii.250) the play is full of sharp weapons; there are, too, images of pins (I.iv.65), thorns (I.iii.48; I.v.88), a "tent [a surgical probe]" (II.ii.593), a "worthy pioner [a foot soldier who preceded the main army with spade or pickaxe]" (I.v.171), and "a sexton's spade" (V.i.88).

42 Walter Benjamin, *The Origin of German Tragic Drama*, trans. John Osborne (London: Verso, 1977), p. 133. (Benjamin later [pp. 157-58] speaks of *Hamlet* as perhaps the supreme example of the baroque *Trauerspiel*.) The ubiquitous presence of weapons works to ensure the audience's re-membering of the hidden parts, the interior of the human body; as Scarry writes: "As an actual physical fact, a weapon is an object that goes into the body and produces pain; as a perceptual fact, it can lift pain and its attributes out of the body and make them visible" (*The Body in Pain* p. 16).

43 "Tent" "probe": "A *tent* was an instrument for examining or cleansing a wound" (Arden). "The quick" is "the tender or sensitive flesh in any part of the body. . . the tender part of a sore or wound" (*OED*). Claudius has spoken of himself as "the owner of a foul disease, [who,] / To keep it from divulging, let it feed / Even on the pith of life" (IV.i.21-23) and of the raging of "the hectic [fever] in my blood" (IV.iii.69); Hamlet calls his uncle "this canker of our nature" (V.ii.69). In Claudius's case at least, Hamlet's assumption of internal corruption seems to be an accurate assessment of the truth.

44 As it does 150 lines earlier, at II.ii.524.

45 Cf. Freud, "Mourning and Melancholia," p. 173: "No neurotic harbours thoughts of suicide which are not murderous impulses against others re-directed upon himself."

46 Heinz Kohut, *The Analysis of the Self* (New York: International Universities Press, 1971), pp. 236-37.

47 Friedrich Nietzsche, letter to Franz Overbeck, 31 March 1885; cited in Blondel, *Nietzsche*, p. 221.

48 Benjamin, *Origin of German Tragic Drama*, p. 140.

49   Cf. Gordon Braden, *Renaissance Tragedy and the Senecan Tradition: Anger's Privilege* (New Haven: Yale Univerity Press, 1985), p. 219: "Hamlet's case in effect shows that the unsuccessful avenger is also going to be . . . the unsuccessful Stoic. Stoicism is the natural alternative to revenge because it is a twin endeavor, a complementary strategy for establishing the self's belief in its own dignity and power." Cf. also Marjorie Garber's comment that Hamlet is "caught between cannibalism and anorexia, spewing forth in language what he cannot swallow." *Shakespeare's Ghost Writers: Literature as Uncanny Causality* (New York and London: Methuen, 1987), p. 150.

50   See note 12 above.

51   Cavell, *The Claim of Reason*, p. 493.

52   I would like to thank Stanley Cavell, Marjorie Garber, Nick Halpern, Jeff Masten, Carla Mazzio, Curtis Perry, and Scott Stevens for their valuable comments at various stages of this essay. Above all, I am deeply grateful to Ruth Nevo for her (as always) wonderful counsel and support.

Part III

Knowledge Incorporated

7
Living Words
Physiognomy and Aesthetic Language

Colin Sample

Since Western philosophy first conceptually sundered soul and body—canonically, with Plato's arguments for the soul's immateriality—there has been a sense that something about aesthetic comportment tended toward their reintegration.[1] The urge to attain an understanding of the interpenetration of sensuality and reason was a motivating force in the development of modern aesthetics. For Kant, the faculty of imagination (*Einbildungskraft*) mediates between sensibility and understanding in such a way as to provide pleasure and to introduce novelty into our concepts. Imagination possesses "the ability to exhibit *aesthetic idea*s; and by an aesthetic idea I mean a presentation of the imagination which prompts much thought, but to which no determinate thought whatsover, i.e. no determinate *concept*, can be adequate, so that no language can express it completely and allow us to grasp it."[2] The term "aesthetic idea" implies the intertwinement of the sensual and conceptual domains, since "aesthetic" stems from *aisthesis*: sensory perception.

But how does this chiasmus work? What does the presentation of an aesthetic idea *do* such that "it is a presentation that makes us add to a concept the thoughts of much that is ineffable, but the feeling of which quickens our cognitive powers and connects language, which otherwise would be mere letters, with spirit"?[3] Kant's answer is that the aesthetic idea awakens our sensitivity to a range of affinities or correspondences. It presents what he calls an "aesthetic attribute" of a concept of reason. Unlike a logical attribute—a quality predicated of something, for example, "The lectern is wooden"—the aesthetic attribute is a phenomenon that *stands in* for an idea; it has an *allegorical* or *metaphorical* function. The metaphorical relation, Kant argues, opens the understanding to a broad field of phenomena that, through some family resemblance (Wittgenstein), can also stand in the metaphorical or allegorical relation of presentation to the concept in question: "Through these attributes, we do not present the content of our concepts . . . but present something different, something that prompts the imagination to spread over a multitude of kindred presentations that arouse more thought than can be expressed in a concept determined by words. These aesthetic attributes yield an aesthetic idea, which serves the mentioned rational idea as a substitute for logical exhibition, but its proper function is to quicken the mind by opening up for it a view into an immense realm of kindred presentations."[4]

The claim that I shall argue for is the following: This ability to open a vista onto "an immense realm of kindred presentations" is something that language possesses by virtue of what I shall call its physiognomic dimension. It is at least partially because language is spoken by embodied, sensual human beings, because the human body is itself expressive, because human communication resonates with affective and dynamic nuances, that words can become windows onto sensual significance that far exceeds their conventional or determinate sense. The aesthetic use of language is closely related to the sensual and affective significance that we experience as living bodies in the world, to the indeterminate sense of which we are aware through our abilities for physiognomic and affective perception and that we can express mimetically by making our own bodies—the qualities of the sounds that we produce or the posture and gestures we adopt—into symbolic vehicles. It is the sensual, essentially embodied dimension of language which brings into unmistakable focus the intertwining of sensuality and reason.

My argument presupposes the classification of linguistic behavior into two (theoretically) distinct signifying functions. The first we could call the *semiotic*: a sign conveys a meaning by virtue of arbitrary,[5] conventional consensus as to its correct use. The second is what I shall call the *mimetic* function of language. Here, the symbolic vehicle is itself somehow expressive of its meaning; it conveys its meaning by virtue of some resemblance to it, by somehow presenting an image of it. In mimetic language, then, there is an intimate, internal relation between signifier and signified.

Both ontogenetic and phylogenetic reconstructions of the origins of language can trace a development from the mimetic to the semiotic function.[6] But it is clear that the mimetic function persists in the physiognomic dimension of language: in the expressive nuances contained in linguistic interaction. Those expressive nuances originate in the interrelated capacities for perceiving physiognomic qualities in the environment and for utilizing the body as a symbolic vehicle to produce expressive correspondences to those qualities by generating iconic representations of physiognomic aspects. Fully developed semiotic communication still contains this mimetic function in its material substratum: in the sensuous stuff and the affective background of verbal communication. Thus conventional verbal language can be used in a non-conventional manner as aesthetic, poetic, or imaginative language in order to articulate physiognomic perception. Aesthetic language dips into the resources of the mimetic function and becomes thereby expressive of physiognomic correspondences. By seeking to present its meaning iconically instead of referring to it arbitrarily, aesthetic language presents "aesthetic ideas" that lend sensuous life to verbal language.

In what follows, I will discuss the primary capacity for phsyiognomic perception and its genesis in preverbal communicative interaction. I'll then utilize this understanding of the physiognomic dimension of language to explore the capacity of aesthetic language to present what Kant called "an immense realm of kindred presentations" in the "aesthetic idea."

Physiognomic Perception

What is physiognomic perception? Essentially, it lies in discerning in the environment expressive qualities such as those that we attribute to the faces, gestures, and vocalizations of other persons: mood, intensity, affect, texture, coloration, rhythm, etc.—qualities expressive of subjective character. We note, for instance, that a circle drawing is sad, a landscape threatening, a line of music dancing, a motion heavy or flowing, inner- or outer-directed, that a scent is silky or thick, a color brassy, et cetera. Physiognomic perception is often synesthetic, or cross-modal, as in the last examples. It has been shown to be prevalent in the early stages of ontogenesis. Daniel Stern has discovered that infants discern in their environments what he calls "vitality affects": dynamic-vectorial properties of motion and tone that convey affective associations.[7] Infants' perception of physiognomic properties is indicated by the employment of their own capacities for affective and dynamic expression as a primitive mode of symbolizing activity. Preverbal children seem to grasp those aspects of the environment that bear some similarity to the affective and gestural-postural expressive possibilities of their own bodies. They employ these expressive possibilities in order to craft iconic symbolic vehicles, at first merely instinctively, but then increasingly intentionally. Thus, for instance, one infant initially rejected proffered objects with an involuntary gesture of pushing away; at thirteen months, this had become an intentional, nonpragmatic gesture of negation; and with the acquisition of verbal language it became incorporated into speech as a gestural accompaniment to verbal negation.[8]

Similarly, opening/closing seems to be a dynamic relationship grasped early on in conjunction with the the infant's own motor capacities. Heinz Werner and Bernard Kaplan report that opening and closing of the eyes was noted by an infant and responded to by opening and closing of the eyes, hands, and mouth; a flickering light was reproduced by rapidly opening and closing the eyelids. Involuntary mimesis of this sort is quickly replaced by intentional representation, as when a slightly older infant models the shape of an orange by inflating his cheeks.[9] Neonates appear to be highly sensitive to the idiosyncratic qualities of the mother's voice and to patterns of vocalization which they can't, of course, recognize as discrete symbolic units.[10] Their ability to recognize verbal patterns corresponds to a capacity for bodily listening. In videotape studies to which we'll return in discussing mimetic communication, W. S. Condon has shown that neonates respond to the discrete phonemes of a speaker with precise micromovements of the body and changes in facial expression.[11] Infants have been shown to correlate bright light with loud sound, and an interrupted tone with an interrupted line, a continuous tone with a continuous line.[12] By the age of four months, infants can distinguish between representations of normal faces and those in which mouth, eyes, and nose are incorrectly ordered. This suggests that they are able to recognize the parts of the face as parts of a single pattern.[13] About the same time, they demonstrate the ability to distinguish basic facial expressions of surprise, joy, and sadness and to correlate facial expression with verbal expression of basic affects.[14] Synaesthetic correspondences between the haptic and visual modalities have been demonstrated as early as twenty days: neonates were given a pacifier with little knobs and shown pictures of a pacifier with and one without knobs. They gazed significantly longer at the former.[15]

Such evidence strongly suggests that infants are acutely aware of synesthetic, physiognomic, and affective elements of their environment and that the infant's tactile-kinaesthetic body responds to those elements with a kind of protosymbolic activity. Thus affective and dynamic qualities, often cross-modally related to their "referents," are the building blocks of what we might call "paleo-symbolization." I have already mentioned the example of a pragmatic gesture of refusal that becomes a gestural part of the linguistic expression of negation. Similarly, Werner and Kaplan have noted that very young children asked to depict the quality of "sharpness" will often represent it *dynamically* by the action of penetrating paper with pencil.[16] These dynamic, physiognomic, affective and synesthetic associations allow for the establishment of correspondences among a broadening range of things, such that the mimetic symbol can depict an indefinite range of similar things. Werner and Kaplan cite the case of a child who initially used the phoneme "fff," "(in imitation of the blowing noise of putting out a match), as a name for smoke, steam, later on, for funnel, chimney, and finally for anything standing upright against the sky, as for instance, a flagstaff."[17] Physiognomic associations of this sort also emerge when adults are asked to symbolize affective states, objects, actions, or qualities by means of simple line drawings. Some sensual quality of the symbolic vehicle—the line drawing—is seen as bearing a physiognomic affinity to its meaning. For example, two line drawings quite different from a geometric viewpoint were used by two of Werner's subjects to symbolize the idea of "longing." They were able to perform this mimetic function because both drawings manifested for the subjects "the physiognomic characteristic of 'reaching for something far away and out of reach.'"[18]

These physiognomic aspects of things correspond closely, as I've already suggested, to the expressive possibilities of our own bodies. A particular line drawing is expressive of "longing" because its vector is that of an arm reaching out to grasp something and trailing away in dejected failure. The early forms of symbolic activity are, in this sense, quite close to such line drawings. Symbolization originates in inborn gestures, expressions, and vocalizations and in onomatopoetic representations of things constrained by the phonetic resources of a mother tongue. (Thus the dog is "bow-wow" in English, "wau-wau" in German.)[19] There is a developmental trend toward distancing of signifier and signified, moving from onomatopoetic representation through the depiction of physiognomic properties to conventional reference.[20] It is at the stage of physiognomic depiction that the creativity of mimetic symbolization is at its greatest. Whereas onomatopoeia more or less straightforwardly imitates its referent, physiognomic symbolization discerns cross-modal affinities between the body's expressive vocabulary and an aspect of the referent. A vowel in a primitive noun, for instance, may be lengthened in order to indicate the size of the object; intonation and the posture of the mouth can also depict size and shape.[21] With the gradual transition from idiomorphic to conventional speech, some of these mimetic patterns are preserved, so that conventional speech retains a dimension of physiognomic depiction that can be creatively exploited. That possibility is exemplified ontogenetically in the transitional stage from idiomorphic baby talk to conventional speech. It is a developmental stage of linguistic playfulness, in which idiomorphic forms are grafted onto conventional syntactic and lexical forms, resulting in such hybrids as "pochmacher" for "workman," from the infant's onomatopoetic "poch" for "hammering."[22] Eventually, the mimetic idioms become largely submerged under the lexical and syntactic rules of conventional language. They reappear in some fashion when we seek to use language creatively and expressively. We are able to return to the transitional stage and utilize the potential of linguistic behavior for phsyiognomic coloration in order to individualize and concretize conventional language. In fact, there is some evidence that elements of conventional verbal language may be perceived physiognomically. In experiments in which words were flashed repeatedly on a screen for micro-seconds, Werner was able to show that the subjects perceived such qualities as warmth, direction, weight, brightness, et cetera, *before* they were able to recognize the discrete words.[23] In more conclusive tests, it was found that normal perception of nonsense words turned up physiognomic association; there was a remarkable degree of consensus on such properties as size, shape, brightness, texture, motion, and affect-mood with regard to many of the invented sound patterns.[24] This research suggests that, at least within the the framework of a single language, particular phonetic patterns can function to convey "naturally" certain physiognomic senses.

What is the relevance of infantile experience for our subject? What the studies I have mentioned show in common is that there exists an ontogenetically primary mode of experience centered around the discernment of what we can broadly call physiognomic properties. These properties correspond to the expressive and gestural possibilities of the human body. That correspondence provides for a primitive mode of symbolization that is initially rooted in inborn expressive behavior, but quickly becomes intentionally and culturally modified. The bodily mode of physiognomic or mimetic symbolization soon gives way to the conventional symbolic order, but it also helps to shape the acquisition of that order and remains present within it as an expressive background.

The physiognomic dimension of language connects it to the felt context of a sensual human being in the world. The permeation of language by domains of felt associations affords it resources for imaginative creativity and sensuous and affective concretion. Because there are so many associations bound up with a particular symbolic vehicle, it can be connected up along lines of similarity with a plurality of distinct referents, all of which can be seen as coalescing in it by virtue of physiognomic correspondences. At the same time, a plurality of distinct physiognomic aspects can be perceived in most of the things of our environment. Hence different symbolic vehicles can be expressive of the *same* thing, since they share physiognomic correspondences with various of its aspects. The individual symbolic vehicle resonates on the one hand with a perhaps inexhaustible wealth of associations, while, on the other hand, the particular, variegated thing calls for perhaps indefinite further symbolic characterization. In this way, the physiognomic dimension of language and perception opens language in two directions to that "immense realm of kindred presentations" of which Kant spoke.

Mimetic Communication

Much of the felt context of verbal language is constituted by the bodily dimension of mimetic communication.[25] This includes facial expression, gesture, posture, qualities of vocal intonation and inflection, rhythm, dynamic properties, vector, shape, texture, et cetera. Such properties, as we've seen, are meaningful elements of the infant's experience prior to the acquisition of conventional verbal language. And subsequent to the acquisition of conventional language, they remain as a constant accompaniment to verbal communication. These properties envelop verbal utterances in a felt context of emotion and physiognomic qualities. And it is this context which makes verbal communication resonate with physiognomic associations, makes the spoken word a vista onto a domain of felt significance far exceeding conventional meaning.

Verbal communication is not merely the exchange of propositional contents. It is also a meticulous dance, so to speak, in which physiognomic significance is expressed by the bodies of the interaction partners; a dance that has come under scrutiny in the discipline of kinesics.[26] In the above-mentioned studies performed by W. S. Condon, it was discovered that subjects accompany their own speech and that of their communication partners with minute, discrete movements that can be segmented into video stills at intervals of 1/23 second to reveal a rich lexicon of movement. Condon was thus able to display what he called "a precise isomorphism" between vocalization segments and movement segments, both in speech and listening.[27] In extending his studies to infants, he found that even two-day-old neonates move in correspondence to the elemental phonemes of perceived speech over a whole 125-word sequence.[28] The kinesic accompaniment of one's own speech and that of communication partners was found to be a cross-culturally universal phenomenon.[29] It seems, then, that, prior to the acquisition of verbal language, humans are educated in networks of phylogenetically rooted, culturally refined mimetic communication. Long before words are comprehensible as signs communicating propositional contents, the sensuous qualities of vocal patterns are recognized and associated with mimetic significance.[30] These associations persist even after their communicative function has been largely superseded by propositional language, forming a sensual, expressive background dimension of verbal communication.

The primary bearer of prepropositional content, then—the paleo-symbolic vehicle—is the body. The body conveys expressive meaning in communicative interaction through the above-considered physiognomic aspects of rhythm, intensity, shape, flow, dynamics, et cetera.[31] Martha Davis and others have found that Rudolf Laban's well-known system of notating movement in dance—the basic categories of which capture physiognomic aspects of shape, direction, and quality—can be used to analyze the expressive content of mimetic communication.[32] Laban analysis can provide a diagram, for instance, of the physiognomic characteristics of communication when a person enters a room and greets another: the overbearing exuberance of the newcomer and the restrained, slightly hostile politeness of the addressee are discernible in the representation of the qualities of their motions.[33]

Of course, it is not only in kinesis that the body forms a sensual subtext to spoken language. Vocal inflection and rhythm as well as facial expression also contribute enormously to the felt context of linguistic interaction and are important bearers of meaning early in ontogenesis. It has been shown, for instance, that three-and-a-half-year-old children identify correctly vocal expressions of sadness, joy, anger and fear conveyed through differently inflected repetitions of the same sentence.[34] Furthermore, the rhythmic and dynamic qualities of vocalization can provide communicative correspondences to the kinesthetic and affective states of preverbal children, as when a mother accompanies the delighted, rhythmic movements of a child slamming a toy against the floor with a "Kaa-bam!" expression that cross-modally mirrors the rhythm and quality of the movement.[35] Such cross-modal attunement of physiognomic qualities establishes a communicative bond and functions as "social referencing,"[36] investing an action, state, or object with intersubjectively shared physiognomic meaning. And as everyone knows intuitively, facial expression lends a felt context of associations to linguistic interchanges. Significant evidence has been presented in defense of the claim that there exist cross-culturally consensual facial expressions of so-called primary affects: happiness, sadness, anger, fear, disgust/contempt, surprise, interest, and shame.[37] These have been anatomically codified as distinct positions of the mimic musculature, and the codification has been used to investigate videotaped segments of communicative interaction, thereby revealing a mimetic dimension of communication that contributes greatly to speakers' understanding of their own and their partners' affective states.[38]

The body, then, through kinesis, vocalization, and facial expression, presents physiognomic aspects the perception of which, however subconscious, helps to constitute the felt context of a communicative situation. It is by existing in such a felt context that words come to life in a particular situation, so that we understand how propositional contents fit into the situation at hand. The body's innate and culturally articulated expressivity enables us to grasp whether we're being playfully flirted with or earnestly courted, genuinely threatened or engaged in a mock fight; whether a statement such as "I have an appointment to go to now" is meant straightforwardly or is a delicate way of extracting oneself from an uncomfortable encounter. It is by grasping physiognomic aspects of kinesis, vocalization, and facial expression, by associating meaning with these sensuous qualities, that we understand the meaning of a felt context. In all communication, there is an indefinite horizon of such associations of physiognomic meaning. Because it exists in that horizon, the use of a shared language is always individuated by a felt context arising out of the language of sensual, interacting bodies in the world. In this physiognomic horizon, meanings are not denoted according to conventional rules of fixed use; they are shown, presented, portrayed through sensual qualities.

Aesthetic Language

To return to the initial and ultimate question, then: What do physiognomic perception and mimetic communication have to do with aesthetic language? What, for that matter, do I mean by aesthetic language? There are no particularly sharp boundaries here. The very broad concept I have in mind refers to the imaginative or creative use of language such that we are able to perceive or understand something in a new manner and such that the words and their meaning appear to be intimately bound in an internal relation. The aesthetic use of language, whether in literature, criticism, or other contexts, is guided by the attempt to give voice to the mutely speaking things, to use language in order to transcend the limitations of language and respond to the way in which the things "wish" to be expressed. Paul Valéry has succinctly described this seeming unity of sign and sense: "The value of a poem lies in the fact that its sound and its sense together make up an indissoluble whole—a condition which seemingly demands the impossible. There is no connection between the sound and sense of a word . . . . Yet it is the business of the poet to give us the feeling that there does exist the closest possible unity between word and sense."[39]

Aesthetic language achieves that unity and gives voice to the things in two manners. First of all, it articulates our usually subconscious, fleeting physiognomic perceptions, giving shape to our vague apprehensions of the sensual, felt quality of situations. The physiognomic characteristics of things strike us as their own voices, their faces, their intrinsic characters. They startle language out of the fixity of determinate, arbitrary meanings and open it to the indefinite horizon of sensual associations, the webs of correspondences and interlaced felt contexts in which language occurs. Second, aesthetic-language use tends to portray or depict its sense, either by seeking words that correspond to the physiognomic perceptions or by presenting those physiognomic meanings in its own sensuous qualities. Onomatopoeia is the most obvious and least refined instance of such presentative language. But linguistic creativity consists more in the construction of word patterns that depict their meaning cross-modally or synesthetically.[40] This can remain on the strictly sensuous plane, as when the accented repetition of the "w" and "im" phonemes portray something like dancing light on water in *Ulysses*: "Wavewhite wedded words shimmering on the dim tide."[41] The intimate unity of word and sense can also be achieved through what Benjamin called "nonsensuous correspondences," that is, through the webs of associations that allow language to be used metaphorically and metonomically. Aesthetic language delineates new associations, allowing us to discern things in a new light.

A passage from T. W. Adorno's book on Mahler illustrates nicely, I think, the way in which language articulates physiognomic perceptions—a crucial function for writing on art as well as for poetic language.

The First Symphony opens with a long pedal point in the strings, all playing harmonics except for the lowest of the three groups of double basses. Reaching to the highest A of the violins, it is an unpleasant whistling sound like that emitted by old-fashioned steam engines. A thin curtain, threadbare but densely woven, it hangs from the sky like a pale gray cloud layer, similarly painful to sensitive eyes . . . . The tempo suddenly quickens with a pianissimo fanfare for two clarinets in their pale, lower register, with the weak bass clarinet as the third voice, sounding faintly as if from behind the curtain that it vainly seeks to penetrate, its strength failing. Even when the fanfare is taken up by the trumpets it still remains, as the score directs, *in sehr weiter Entfernung*. Then, at the height of the movement, six measures before the return of the tonic D, the fanfare explodes in the trumpets, horns, and high woodwinds, quite out of scale with the orchestra's previous sound or even the preceding crescendo. It is not so much that this crescendo has reached a climax as that the music has expanded with a physical jolt. The rupture originates from beyond the music's intrinsic movement, intervening from outside. For a few moments the symphony imagines that something has become reality that for a lifetime the gaze from earth has fearfully yearned for in the sky. With it Mahler's music has kept faith; the transformation of that experience is its history. If all music, with its first note, promises that which is different, the rending of the veil, his symphonies attempt to withhold it no longer, to place it literally before our eyes.[42]

Surely this is language that heeds the voice of its object, bringing it to speech. The symphony comes to life in Adorno's words, which trace its physiognomic qualities: thin screeching, vain attempts to break free, yearning expectation, et cetera. The words seem to emerge naturally from the sounds and to open them up to our understanding.

The same sort of unity of word and sense is often found in the poetic use of physiognomic qualities in a writer like Joyce. Consider, for instance, the way in which the sensuous qualities of his language coalesce into a living image in the famous description of Stephen Dedalus urinating on the beach:

In long lassoes from the Cock lake the water flowed full, covering greengoldenly lagoons of sand, rising, flowing. My ashplant will float away. I shall wait. No, they will pass on, passing, chafing against the low rocks, swirling, passing. Better get this job over quick. Listen: a fourworded wavespeech: seesoo, hrss, rsseeiss, ooos. Vehement breath of waters amid seasnakes, rearing horses, rocks. In cups of rocks it slops: flop, slop, slap: bounded in barrels. And, spent, its speech ceases. It flows purling, widely flowing, floating foampool, flower unfurling.[43]

In such passages we can see how the aesthetic use of language draws upon the prepropositional capacity for physiognomic perception and enriches that capacity with the articulatory resources of conventional language creatively exploited. I have argued that this primary capacity for physiognomic perception is closely tied to the body's role in mimetic communication consisting of kinesis, facial expression, and vocalization. The physiognomic qualities we perceive in the environment correspond to those from which we read the felt context of our communicative exchanges with one another. The physiognomic perception that contributes greatly to the aesthetic use of language, then, is dependent upon the expressive possibilities of our own bodies. Genuine aesthetic language, of course, is more than just the utilization of a primordial capacity for physiognomic perception, more than just the exploitation of a primordial dimension of linguistic interaction. We are not, by virtue of being expressive bodies, all artists. But the articulation of novel associations and apparent unity of sense and significance that characterize aesthetic language do draw upon those capacities for bodily expressivity and physiognomic perception. Aesthetic language carries the web of felt associations expressed in mimetic communication over into the domain of verbal language, in such a way that words come to evoke the presentation of a range of physiognomic and affective correspondences. It draws us into a context of sensuous associations that is never completed, never fully determinate.

To return, then, to our starting point: It is this fundamental indeterminacy of the range of associations evoked by aesthetic language that makes it what Kant called "the animating principle in the mind."[44] This dimension of language holds our thought open to new sense, preventing it from becoming frozen in fixed, determinate usage. And it holds language in an intimate connection with the living body.

The embodiment of language brings us back to a dimension of play. We abandon everyday conceptual determinations, comporting ourselves neither instrumentally nor theoretically-objectifyingly toward the things. Instead, we cathect the things themselves, comporting ourselves erotically towards them: that is, we seek to use the expressive resources of our embodied language to bring them to speech. The indeterminate, always-open character of this mode of comportment enlivens language by keeping conceptual determinations in a constant state of unrest, giving us simultaneously a sense of the incompleteness of all processes of understanding and constant access to the discernment of new sense in sensual qualities. Though there is no room to make this argument here, I believe that the aesthetic comportment here outlined is an elemental dimension of rationality.

Notes

1   Thus Plato valorizes the aesthetic dimension in certain contexts even while denigrating it for the sake of a politics of disembodied rationality. In *Phaedrus*, he praises poetry and love as species of prophetic mania, allowing insight from which the rational intellect is barred. Cf. *Phaedrus* 244 ff. And in the *Symposium*, Plato traces an unbroken progression from the love of a single beautiful body to the love of beautiful knowledge. On this, cf. Herbert Marcuse, *Eros and Civilization* (Boston: Beacon Press, 1955), p. 211. Plato's trepidations concerning the loss of reason through love are echoed by Iago's sentiments, which might give us pause to consider the possible connection between radical evil and the rejection of that loss of self-sufficiency that accompanies love. "If the balance of our lives had not one scale of

reason to poise another of sensuality, the blood and baseness of our natures would conduct us to most preposterous conclusions. But we have reason to cool our raging motions, our carnal stings, our unbitted lusts; whereof I take this, that you call love, to be a sect or scion." Shakespeare, *Othello*, I.iii.316.

2   Immanuel Kant, *Critique of Judgment*, trans. W. Pluhar (Indianapolis: Hackett, 1987), p. 182 (314).

3   Ibid., p. 185 (316).

4   Ibid., pp. 183-84 (315).

5   Arbitrary, i.e., in the sense that no particular symbolic vehicle stands in an internal relation to its referent.

6   For reasons of brevity I won't go into the phylogenetic dimension here. But cf., e.g., M. Sheets-Johnstone, *The Roots of Thinking* (Philadelphia: Temple University. Press, 1990); Heinz Werner and Bernard Kaplan, *Symbol Formation: An Organismic-Developmental Approach to the Psychology of Language* (Hillsdale, N.J.: Lawrence Earlbaum, 1984); M. L Foster, "The Symbolic Structure of Primordial Language," in *Human Evolution: Biosocial Perspectives* , ed. S. L. Washburn and E. R. McCown, (Menlo Park, Calif.: Benjamin/Cummings, 1978), pp. 76-121; Wilhelm Wundt, *The Language of Gestures* (The Hague/Paris: Mouton, 1973); Karl Bühler, *Ausdruckstheorie* (Stuttgart: Gustav Fischer, 1968); and A. Marshack, "Some Implications of the Paleolithic Symbolic Evidence for the Origin of Language," in *Origins and Evolution of Speech and Language*, ed. S. R. Harned, H. D. Steklis, and J. Lancaster (New York: The New York Academy of the Sciences, 1976), p. 309.

7   Cf. Daniel Stern, *The Interpersonal World of the Infant* (New York: Basic Books), pp. 53 ff.

8   Heinz Werner and Bernard Kaplan, *Symbol Formation: An Organismic-Developmental Approach to the Psychology of Language* (Hillsdale, N.J.: Lawrence Earlbaum, 1984), p. 90.

9   Ibid., pp. 87 ff. Werner/Kaplan refer to the formation of these sets of associations as an "inner-dynamic schematizing activity which shapes and intertwines the sensory, postural, affective, and imaginal components of the organismic state." Ibid., p. 18.

10   Martin Dornes, *Der kompetente Säugling* (Frankfurt: Fischer, 1993), p. 41. Intrauterine recognition of mother's voice was demonstrated. A group of mothers repeatedly read a particular story out loud while in the latter stages of pregnancy. After birth, the infants were able to turn on a tape recorder by sucking on a specially constructed pacifier; according to the rhythm of sucking, they could listen to the mother's or a stranger's voice reading the story. They preferred significantly the mother's voice. In similar experements, a story that was heard in uterus was preferred over a new story read by the same voice, indicating that there is intrauterine capacity for distinguishing patterns of vocalization.

11   Cf. W. S. Condon, "Speech Makes Babies Move," in *Child Alive*, ed. R. Lewin, (Anchor Books), pp. 75-85; and   W. S. Condon and L. W. Sander, "Synchrony Demonstrated between Movements of the Neonate and Adult Speech," *Child Development* 45, no. 2 (June 1974): 456-62.

12   Cf. Dornes, *Der Kompetente Säugling,*: pp. 41 ff.

13   Ibid., p. 39. This trivial-seeming discovery is of importance for psychology as evidence contrary to the psychoanalytic theory of "partial objects," according to which the infant is unable to correlate different body parts as those of one whole person.

14   Ibid., pp. 40, 46.

15   Ibid., p. 43.
16   Werner and Kaplan, *Symbol Formation*, p. 91.
17   Ibid., p. 107.
18   Ibid., p. 341. In the same way, one might note a physiognomic resemblance in two musical figures as distinct as the repeated three-note figure in the Adagio of Shostakovich's Fifth Symphony and the slow piano chord progressions in the second movement of Beethoven's Fourth Piano Concerto. In both cases, the music breathes in and reaches out, though in the first case more with a pleading and in the latter a soothing gesture.
19   Ibid., p. 102.
20   Ibid., pp. 99 ff.
21   Ibid., pp. 104-5. Julian Jaynes speculates that the first real words were modifiers formed by such physiognomic depiction. A warning cry "wah" might have been modified, he surmises, into "wahee" to depict the increasing intensity of an approaching tiger or bear, and "wahoo" to depict the waning intensity of a departing animal. Cf. "The Evolution of Language in the Late Pleistocene," in *Origins and Evolution of Language and Speech*, ed. S. R. Harned, H. D. Steklis and J. Lancaster (New York: The New York Academy of the Sciences,), p. 317.
22   Werner and Kaplan, *Symbol Formation*, p. 108.
23   Ibid., pp. 215ff. I would not want to claim that *all* words can be physiognomically perceived. It is likely that the experiment was biased by the choice of test-words with a relatively high degree of sensuous concretion, e.g., "blanke Waffe," in place of more abstract terms such as "atomic particle."
24   Ibid., pp. 219 ff.
25   The use of the term "mimetic" here oscillates between two meanings. On the one hand, it derives from the notion of imitative representation of things, occurrences and feelings; on the other hand, it borrows from the anatomical notion of the mimic musculature responsible for facial expression. (Cf. C.-H. Hjortsjö, *Man's Face and Mimic Language*, trans. W. F. Salisbury [Studentlitteratur: Lund, 1969], pp. 40ff.) A further point of reference is the conception of mimesis suggestively sketched by Benjamin and Adorno. On this, cf. Josef Früchtl, *Mimesis: Konstellation eines Grundbegriffes bei Adorno* (Würzburg: Königshaus und Neumann, 1986).
26   Cf. Raymond L. Birdwhistell, *Introduction to Kinesics* (Louisville: University of Kentucky Press, 1952).
27   Condon and Sander, "Synchrony Demonstrated," p. 457.
28   Ibid., pp. 460-61.
29   "Interactional synchrony appears with frame-by-frame analysis as the precise 'dance-like' sharing of micro-body-motion patterns of change between speaker and listener. Like self-synchrony, it has been observed in all normal human interaction thus far studied, including films of Mayan Indians, Kung Bushmen, Eskimos, etc. It has also been observed in group behavior, for example, seven listeners moved in synchrony with an eighth who was talking." Ibid., p. 459.
30   "If the infant, from the beginning, moves in precise, shared rhythm with the organization of the speech structure of his culture, then he participates developmentally through complex, sociobiological entrainment processes in millions of repetitions of linguistic forms long before he will later use them in speaking and communicating. By the time he begins to speak he may have already laid down within himself the forms and structures of the language system of his culture." Buck, *op. cit.*, p. 462.

31 Cf. Maurice Merleau-Ponty: ":he body does not constantly express the modalities of existence in the way that stripes indicate rank, or a house-number a house: the sign here does not only convey its significance, it is filled with it; it is, in a way, what it signifies" *Phenomenology of Perception*, trans. Colin Smith (London: Routledge, 1989), p. 161. Also ibid., p. 166: "If we therefore say that the body expresses existence at every moment, this is in the sense in which a word expresses thought. Anterior to conventional means of expression . . . we must . . . recognize a primary process of signification in which the thing expressed does not exist apart from the expression, and in which the signs themselves induce their significance externally. In this way the body expresses total existence, not because it is an external accompaniment to that existence, but because existence realizes itself in the body. This incarnate significance is the central phenomenon of which body and mind, sign and significance are abstract moments."

32 Cf. Martha Davis, "Laban Analysis of Nonverbal Communication," in *Nonverbal Communication*, ed. S. Weitz, 2d ed. (New York: Oxford, 1979), pp. 183-206.

33 Ibid., p. 185.

34 Cf. R. v.Bezooyen, *Characteristics and Recognizability of Vocal Expression of Emotion* (Dordrecht: Foro, 1984), p. 118.

35 Cf. Dornes, *Der Kompetente Säugling*, p. 154.

36 Cf. ibid., pp. 153 ff. The term refers to the apparent tendency of infants to garner an affective interpretation of objects from primary caregiver figures. When presented with an unknown object or person or a possibly frightening situation (e.g., an apparent deep drop in their path), infants will observe the affective expression on the caregiver's face. If it is fearful, they refrain from further investigation; if joyful, they give themselves over to curiosity.

37 Cf. Buck, p. 38.

38 Cf., e.g., Carrol E. Izard, *Measuring Emotions in Infants and Children* (Cambridge: Cambridge University Press, 1986). As Iago well knew, the mimetic subtext of communication can be manipulated so as to disguise and fabricate physiognomic meaning: "For when my outward action doth demonstrate / The native act and figure of my heart / In complement extern, 'tis not long after / But I will wear my heart upon my sleeve / For daws to peck at. I am not what I am." Shakespeare, *Othello*, I.i.51. The nervus facialis, which innervates the mimic musculature of the face, is influenced both by regions of the cortex associated with voluntary, conscious impulses and by the involuntary limbic system associated with the neurophysical dimension of emotion. Thus facial expression of emotion can be controlled to some degree. In fact, studies of adults have found that pure expressions of any one of the primary affects are quite rare. Emotions of which subjects are consciously quite aware are often masked by expressions of contrary emotions, and the most common expressions are "blends" in which two distinct codifiable expressions appear simultaneously or in the same second. Cf. C. Z. Malatesta and C. Izard, *Emotion in Adult Development* (Beverly Hills: Sage Publications, 1984), pp. 261ff.

39 Paul Valéry, *Poésie et Pensée abstraite* (Oxford: Clarendon Press, 1939), p. 20; English tr. *Poetry and Abstract Thought* (London: Wingate, 1947), p. 101. Valéry has also formulated nicely the function of aesthetic language as an attempt to give expression to the physiognomic aspects of the things, the ways in which they strike us as expressive visages. He describes poetry as "the attempt to represent, or to restore, by means of articulated language those things, or that thing, which cries, tears, caresses, kisses, sighs, etc., try obscurely to express, and which objects seem

to want to express in all that is lifelike in them or appears to have design." P. Valéry, *Selected Writings* (New York: New Directions, 1950), p. 147. And in his conception of the apparent unity of sound and sense, Valéry captures the incessant movement between sensuality and understanding that gives us simultaneously a feeling of wholeness and makes aesthetic language a constitutively incomplete process, never coming to rest in determinate sense: "Entre la Voix et la Pensée, entre la Pensée et la Voix, entre la Présence et l'Absence, oscille le pendule poétique." *Poésie et Pensée abstraite*, p. 20.

40 In this sense, language can function similarly to dance, music, or nonfigurative visual arts, in which sense is borne by the physiognomic qualities of the sensory material; as when the tonally and dynamically rising and falling vector of a musical line expresses yearning.

41 James Joyce, *Ulysses* (New York: Random House, 1986), p. 8.

42 T. W. Adorno, *Mahler: A Musical Physiognomy*, trans. E. Jephcott (Chicago: University of Chicago, 1992), pp. 4-5.

43 Joyce, *Ulysses*, p. 41.

44 Kant, *Critique of Judgment*, p. 182 (313).

8
The Mindful Body
Embodiment and Cognitive Science

Evan Thompson

Several years ago, in the introduction to our book *The Embodied Mind,* Francisco Varela, Eleanor Rosch, and I wrote: "If we examine the current situation today, with the exception of a few largely academic discussions cognitive science has had virtually nothing to say about what it means to be human in everyday, lived situations."[1] I think it is fair to say that this statement is no longer true. Since 1991, when these words were published, cognitive scientists have increasingly turned their attention to consciousness, and so have begun to discuss issues of embodiment and lived experience. What I would like to do here is to look at a few of these discussions in light of the project that we undertook in *The Embodied Mind.*

Embodiment and Enactive Cognitive Science

Let me begin by citing a remark from a recent article by the philosopher Mark Johnson about metaphor and our knowledge of mind. Johnson writes: "our very cognition of the mental is metaphorically defined. . . . The knowledge we think we have of how the mind works is always knowledge entailed by the projected structure of the source domains of the metaphors that jointly make up our conception of the mind."[2]

Johnson's point about the role that metaphor plays in our conceptualizations of the mind can be illustrated by looking at cognitive science. From its very beginning cognitive science has been deeply committed to a certain system of metaphors. I will call this metaphoric system *representationism.* Representationism rests on an invocation of the spatial metaphor of outside and inside.[3] It begins by making a distinction between the world outside and the mind inside. Each member of this outside-inside pair is supposed to be independent (in principle) of the other; to use the terminology of AI, each is supposed to be *prespecifiable.* Once this distinction is drawn, the demand that outside and inside be put into correspondence immediately arises. To meet the demand one supposes that inside the mind there is a model of the outside world. Thus the spatial metaphor of inside and outside becomes elaborated into the metaphor of the mind as a container (of representations), and in this way one arrives at the thesis that cognition is the mental *re*presentation of the outside world.

In recent years there has been a major shift away from this metaphoric system and its pragmatic implications among a growing number of cognitive scientists. In each of the disciplines that make up cognitive science, the change in orientation involves trying to replace conceptual metaphors and empirical procedures that assign things to the mind or to the world taken separately with metaphors and procedures that take the mind and the world to be mutually constitutive. This alternative orientation does not yet have a single accepted name, but the two most prevalent terms are *embodiment* and *situated action.* In our book, *The Embodied Mind,* Varela, Rosch, and I proposed the term *enactive* as a name for this alternative orientation. The conviction that motivates the enactive approach is that cognition is not the representation of an independent world by an independent mind, but is rather the enactment of a world and a mind on the basis of a history of embodied action. I would like to summarize briefly our idea of enactive cognitive science as a background for my discussion here.

Our intention in formulating the enactive approach is to avoid reified versions of the inner-versus-outer metaphor by studying cognition not as representation but as *embodied action.* By using the term *embodied,* we mean to highlight two points: first, that cognition depends upon the kinds of experience that come from having a body with various perceptuomotor capacities and, second, that these capacities are embedded in and constituted by their biological, psychological, and sociocultural contexts. By using the term *action* we mean to emphasize that sensory and motor processes, perception and action, are fundamentally inseparable in all cognition.

Within this context of embodied action, the enactive approach makes two general proposals, one about perception and the other about cognition. The first is that perception consists in perceptually guided activity. Perception and action have evolved together, coupled to each other: perceptual systems serve to guide activity and motor systems serve to orient perception. Whereas representationism begins by asking how the independent outside world is to be "recovered" in the form of an internal representation, the enactive approach begins by asking how perceptuomotor processes enable the perceiving animal to explore its environment. The key idea is to embed perceptual processes in the sensorimotor behavioral repertoires of the perceiver and in the structure of the perceiver's environment. In visual perception, for example, this means that the reference point shifts from a perceiver-independent outside world that must be internally represented, to the visuomotor activity of the animal embedded in its environment.

Perception, then, or better perceiving, is not something that happens inside the mind or brain. It is a kind of activity performed by an embodied and situated agent. The character of the activity depends mainly on two things: first, on the kinds of neural networks that couple the sensory and motor processes in the animal and, second, on the environmental context of situated activity. Corresponding to these two factors are two logically distinct domains of description and explanation. The first is the organization proper to the organism, for example, its neurophysiological organization. The second is the organism as a unity in its situated activity. Hence, in the *neurophysiological* domain, the perceptual guidance of activity can be seen to be subserved by patterns of activity in the sensori-neuronal-motor linkages; whereas in the *ecological* domain, it can be seen as recurrent patterns of perceptuomotor interaction with the world.

The second proposal about cognition is that cognitive processes emerge from these recurrent patterns of perceptuomotor activity. The process of emergence can be understood in at least four senses: a phenomenological sense, a developmental sense, a structural sense, and an evolutionary sense. To summarize the research in these areas is impossible here, so I will simply provide a few pointers. The idea that cognitive processes emerge phenomenologically from bodily activity is a major theme in existential phenomenology, particularly in the writings of Merleau-Ponty.[4] The idea that cognitive processes emerge developmentally in the individual (as well as evolutionarily in the species) from perceptuomotor activity is a central theme in Piaget's genetic epistemology.[5] The idea that cognitive processes are structurally emergent from embodied activity is the central thesis of Lakoff and Johnson's experientialist and embodied program in cognitive semantics and the philosophy of language.[6] Finally, in AI the attempt to model how abstract reasoning could emerge from routine situated activity is central to the so-called nouvelle AI of Brooks, Chapman, and Agre, as well as others.[7]

The last element in the enactive approach that needs to be mentioned is that we take very seriously the lived or experiential dimensions of perception and cognition. Cognitive science, like all science, is a human practice, but it is distinctive because in it we turn back upon ourselves to make our own cognition our scientific theme. Cognitive science is thus an inherently circular project. Representationism tries to avoid or neutralize this circularity, but from the enactive standpoint it is fundamental, and so the issue can never be how to avoid the circularity, but rather how to situate oneself properly within it. Our central contention in *The Embodied Mind* is that an honest recognition of the circularity demands that we not lose sight of lived human experience in the scientific study of mind.

The term *embodiment* as we use it, then, points both to the body as a lived experiential reality and to the body as the milieu of biological and cognitive processes. Our position is that in the task of self-understanding we must draw from both these domains, the phenomenological and the cognitive scientific. Given their own commitments to embodiment, phenomenology and cognitive science must take account of each other.

We try to take this commitment to embodiment yet another step in *The Embodied Mind*. In addition to bringing cognitive science and phenomenology into a kind of "mutual accomodation" or "reflective equilibrium,"[8] we wish to foster what we call a *circulation* between cognitive science and human experience. By this we mean circulating back and forth between the science and experience so that cognitive science enlarges its horizon to encompass the developmental possiblities inherent in human experience, and human experience enlarges its developmental horizon to encompass the insights gained from cognitive science.

This is the reason why we draw from Asian traditions of philosophy and psychology, in particular from Buddhism. Western phenomenology and cognitive science have been mainly concerned with understanding what the mind-body relation is as a matter of ontology, not with the ways in which the mind-body relation can manifest itself in lived experience as a matter of developmental possibility. In contrast, Asian philosophical and psychological traditions tend to be rooted in practices that work directly with the mind-body relation in actual experience. In general it is fair to say that embodiment is understood to be inherently developmental in the Asian traditions: the mind-body relation is not taken to be a constant given, but is seen to admit of many modalities within lived experience itself.[9] In particular, mind as embodied action is not only a given condition (something ontological); it is also something to be cultivated and perfected (something valuational).[10]

The main example that we discuss in *The Embodied Mind* is the Buddhist practice of cultivating mindfulness. As a result, it is possible to see our project as being primarily concerned with building a bridge between Buddhism and cognitive science. In fact, this reading would be appropriate to the structure and tone of our book, but unfortunately so as I now think. Although this sort of bridge-building is certainly interesting and important, it is not my main concern. What motivates me is the conviction that it is possible to improve human life through the kind of self-understanding that cognitive science and phenomenology together can provide. Asian traditions in general, not just Buddhism, have important contributions to make to this endeavor, and this is one reason why I am interested in them. I now think, however, that some of the Buddhist-inspired treatments of consciousness in our book are unacceptable as they stand. I will come back to this matter later after having had a look at some recent discussions of consciousness and embodiment in cognitive science.

Dennett and Cartesian Materialism

In cognitive science, the recent interest in consciousness is due in large part to Daniel C. Dennett's recent book, *Consciousness Explained.*[11] In this book, Dennett presents his position as an alternative to what he calls "Cartesian materialism." Cartesian materialism occurs when one discards Descartes's dualism, but retains the idea that there is a central place in the brain that is the site of consciousness. Dennett dubs such a hypothetical place "the Cartesian theater."[12] Although most cognitive scientists would reject the idea of a Cartesian theater, Dennett shows that Cartesian materialist assumptions persist nonetheless, for example, in discussions of the temporal representation of conscious events. My concern here will not be with Dennett's arguments against

Cartesian materialism, but rather with what he thinks follows from denying Cartesian materialism, particularly as it affects the topic of embodiment.

Dennett thinks that rejecting Cartesian materialism implies a number of things. First, there is no single definitive stream of consciousness. The reasoning here is that if there were a central integrative area for consciousness in the brain, then the order in which signals arrive at this area would determine the temporal order of experience—the stream of consciousness—down to a millisecond timescale. But if there is no such place, then there is no way to determine exactly when I become conscious of something. Dennett writes

> [S]ince you are nothing over and above the various subagencies and processes in your nervous system that compose you, the following sort of question is always a trap: "Exactly when did I (as opposed to various parts of my brain) become informed (aware, conscious) of some event?" Conscious experience . . . is a succession of states *constituted* by various processes occurring in the brain and not something over and above these processes that is *caused* by them.[13]

For Dennett, consciousness is constituted by a succession of brain states. Since the states are distributed all over the brain, rather than being centrally integrated, he thinks that there is no single definitive narrative that is the actual stream of consciousness: at any point in time there are only "multiple drafts" of narrative-fragments, which, over longer periods of time, yield something that is approximately like a stream or narrative.

Second, Dennett argues that the so-called unity and continuity of consciousness are an illusion. The multiple drafts process generates the illusion of unity—of a central subject of consciousness—and of continuity over time, but the processes that constitute consciousness are actually decentralized throughout the brain and are discrete rather than continuous.

Finally, Dennett argues that there is no such thing as "actual phenomenology." By this he means that there is nothing to my conscious experience over and above the *judgements* I make about how things seem to me. And the "I" who seems to be the subject of these judgements is an illusion too: the term "judgement" as Dennett uses it mainly refers to discriminations or content-determinations made by distributed and discontinuous brain processes. Dennett's point is that there are no presentations ("real seemings" as he calls them) that brain-judgements are about: for something to seem a certain way to me is just for there to be some process in the brain that discriminates or represents or judges it to be that way.

Although Dennett presents his "multiple drafts" model of consciousness as an alternative to Cartesian materialism, the model nevertheless has some distinctly Cartesian features, especially when compared to more embodied conceptions. To see this, it will be useful to remind ourselves of what Descartes himself said.

Descartes presents two different conceptions of the mind-body relation in his writings. The first I will call his *localizationist* conception. According to this conception, the brain is privileged over the rest of the body in relation to the immaterial mind because the brain is the site of the mind-body interaction. Moreover, within the brain there is a central faculty of sensory integration, and the anatomical site of this faculty is the pineal gland. Thus Descartes writes

> the mind is not immediately affected by all parts of the body, but only by the brain, or perhaps just by one small part of the brain, namely the part which is said to contain the "common sense" [pineal gland]. Every time this part of the brain is in a given state, it presents the same signals to the mind, even though the other parts of the body may be in a different condition at the time.[14]

Cartesian materialism is the modern materialist version of this sort of localizationism. But Descartes has another conception of the mind-body relation, one which I will call his *proto-embodiment* conception. Shortly before the passage just quoted he writes:

> There is nothing my nature teaches me more vividly than that I have a body, and that when I feel pain there is something wrong with the body, and that when I am hungry or thirsty the body needs food and drink and so on. . . . Nature also teaches me, by these sensations of pain, hunger, thirst, and so on, that I am not merely present in my body as a sailor [French: as a pilot] in a ship, but that I am very closely joined and, as it were, intermingled with it, so that I and the body form a unit. If this were not so, I, who am nothing but a thinking thing, would not feel pain when the body was hurt, but would receive the damage purely by the intellect, just as a sailor perceives by sight if anything in his ship is broken.[15]

Notice the difference between these two conceptions of the mind-body relation. Descartes presents the localizationist conception when he is considering the mind-body relation from the third-person perspective of the anatomist. But the proto-embodiment conception he presents when he is looking at the mind and the body from the first-person perspective of his own experience as an embodied being. In particular, he is trying to account for consciousness as bodily feeling (sentience) and for the fact that I do not simply understand, or judge, or intellectually discern that I am, say, in pain—as a pilot judges by sight that his ship is broken—but that I *feel* pain. The facts of embodied experience demand a conception of mind-body *unity,* one which is considerably different from the localizationist conception of a mind-body *connection* at a particular privileged site in the brain. Descartes himself recognizes this demand for psychophysical unity, for in his "Replies to the Sixth Set of Objections" to the *Meditations* he writes: "the mind [has] to be coextensive with the body—the whole mind in the whole body and the whole mind in any of its parts."[16]

I think that Dennett is still in the grip of a certain sort of localizationist conception. The reason is that he thinks "You are nothing over and above . . . your nervous system" and that the brain is the seat of consciousness. But this is wrong: You are not just your nervous system: you are an embodied organism. Although the brain is without doubt the principal organ of mind, the mind does not reside in the brain *per se*: it resides in the embodied organism embedded in the world. It is the organism that is the proper subject of consciousness, not the brain.

The point is not a trivial one: there are important reasons for not collapsing the difference in level between the organism and its brain. Consider, for example, Dennett's denial of "actual phenomenology" in relation to the qualitative content of perceptual experience. For Dennett, qualitative content is at bottom a matter of judgement: perceptual experience has no qualitative content over and above the content of the perceptual judgements we are disposed to make. As he puts it in his book *Consciousness Explained:* "There is no such phenomenon as really seeming—over and above the phenomenon of judging in one way or another that something is the case."[17] Dennett's assumption, however, is that the only way the perceptual experience of the *subject* could be "presentational," rather than judgemental, is if there were some "Witness" or "Audience" in an inner Cartesian theater in the subject's *brain*. In other words, Dennett takes the idea of non-judgemental, experiential content to imply Cartesian materialism; consequently, denying Cartesian materialism rules out presentational content. But the inference does not follow. First, there is no reason to assume that the presentational character of perceptual experience at the *subject level* is either logically or empirically incompatible with decentralized and discrete processes at the *brain level*. When one claims, as phenomenological psychologists and philosophers do, that perceptual experience is not entirely judgemental, one is describing perceptual experience at the subject level, not at the level of the subject's brain. Cartesian materialism, on the other hand, is a theory of the brain's organization—to invoke a distinction that Dennett himself often makes, it is a "subpersonal" rather than a "personal" level theory—and so denying the theory has no immediate bearing on the subject-level character of perceptual experience. Second, there is nothing that is given or presented to the brain in the subject-level sense. What the brain does is to modulate its own activity in reponse to internally and externally generated influence. Hence it is a mistake to look inside the brain, rather than to the whole embodied perceiving-acting animal, for the subject of perceptual experience.

This line of argument is important both for the philosophy of mind and for cognitive science. In the philosophy of mind it is relevant to the debate about "qualia," the supposedly purely phenomenal properties of mental states. Dennett rightly attacks this notion of qualia, but he does so on behalf of the idea that qualitative content is exhaustively constituted by judgement and discriminative dispositions. But the reason why perceptual experience has qualitative content is not that there are purely phenomenal properties of experience ("qualia" as they are typically understood in Anglo-American philosophy of mind). Nor is it because qualitative content is exhaustively constituted by judgement. Rather, the reason is that perception is always *embodied*. It is embodiment, rather than judgement, that invests quality with intentional content and intentional content with quality. As Merleau-Ponty puts it in a discussion of visual perception in his *Phenomenology of Perception:*

> Vision is already inhabited by a meaning (*sens*) which gives it a function in the spectacle of the world and in our existence. The pure *quale* would be

given to us only if the world were a spectacle and one's own body a mechanism with which some impartial mind made itself acquainted. Sense experience, on the other hand, invests the quality with vital value, grasping it first in its meaning for us, for that heavy mass which is our body, whence it comes about that it always involves a reference to the body. . . . Sense experience is that vital communication with the world which makes it present as a familiar setting of our life.[18]

It would be a mistake to suppose that this reference to the body is a merely contingent feature of perceptual experience. Building on the tenets of Gestalt psychology, Merleau-Ponty argues that the figure-ground structure is essential to any perception.[19] So too a tacit awareness of the body is essential to the figure-ground structure of perceptual experience. To perceive an object is precisely not to perceive oneself as subject; thus, the perceptual subject, not only stands out against an external background, but is also situated within an implicit bodily space. In Merleau-Ponty's words: "one's own body is the third term, always tacitly understood, in the figure-background structure, and every figure stands out against the double horizon of external and bodily space."[20]

In cognitive science, emphasizing embodiment brings us back to the enactive approach. Once again, in this approach we treat perception as the perceptually guided activity of the animal, rather than the reconstruction of the environment from an image or proximal array. As J. J. Gibson put it describing his own "ecological approach": "In my theory, perception is not supposed to occur in the brain but to arise in the retino-neuro-muscular system as an activity of the whole system. . . . It is an exploratory circular process, not a one-way delivery of messages to the brain."[21] And: "Perceiving is an achievement of an individual, not an experience in the theatre of consciousness . . . perception is not a mental act. Neither is it a bodily act. Perceiving is a psychosomatic act, not of mind or of body, but of a living observer."[22]

These ideas are not exclusively Gibsonian. A good example in vision research of the enactive approach is the research program in computational vision known as "active" or "animate vision."[23] In animate vision, the key issue is not how the world can be reconstructed from images, but rather how visual processes enable the animal to explore its environment. Visual processing algorithms are seen to be embedded in the body—in the sensorimotor behavioral repertoires of the whole perceiver—rather than being simply in the head.

Coming back to Dennett, he is more Cartesian than he recognizes: he considers perception to be a form of judgement; he thinks that consciousness is constituted largely by language; and he comes very close to withholding consciousness from most nonhuman animals. All of these are familiar Cartesian themes. Dennett also adheres to a version (albeit a sophisticated materialist one) of the Cartesian localizationist conception: although he does not think that there is a consciousness center in the brain, he does think that the brain is the proper site of consciousness, rather than the embodied animal embedded in its environment. The irony here is that Descartes himself glimpsed the problem with the localizationist idea: it does not do justice to consciousness as embodied experience. Localizing consciousness in the brain, rather than the person as a whole, amounts to conceiving of the mind-brain as a pilot and the body as a ship.

It can hardly be surprising, then, that Dennett's multiple drafts model has no bodily dimension. Dennett says that, "Human consciousness . . . can best be understood as the operation of a *'von Neumanesque'* virtual machine *implemented* in the *parallel architecture* of a brain that was not designed for any such activities."[24] The idea, roughly, is that human consciousness is like a sequential program implemented in the parallel hardware of the brain.

I have two objections to this idea. First, Dennett treats consciousness as if it were largely an attentional process.[25] But although *attention* might arguably proceed sequentially in a way roughly analogous to the sequence of state-transitions in a Turing machine, this sort of sequential structure is not appropriate to every kind of awareness. As William James and the phenomenologists have argued, embodied awareness should be seen as a field having a foreground-background structure. Attention operates within the "horizon" of this field. Consider in this light how Alan Turing arrived at his mathematical formalization of an algorithm or effective procedure as a function computable by a Turing machine.[26] He was thinking, self-consciously, introspectively, and with a remarkably heightened degree of attention, about how he as a mathematician went about solving problems. It was out of his own mathematical stream of consciousness—as modified and rigorously structured by attention—that he distilled the sequence of *attentional* steps he went through in mathematical problem-solving. Hence Dennett's von Neumanesque or Turingesque virtual machine might be an acceptable model of attention, but not of consciousness in its widest sense as the field of awareness.

My second objection to Dennett's idea of consciousness as a serial virtual machine is that it neglects in particular the embodied dimension of awareness. Dennett never considers how consciousness includes the proprioceptive awareness of the body and the interoceptive awareness of visceral and musculoskeletal structures. Although his multiple drafts constitute a serial virtual machine that is "installed" or "implemented" in the hardware of the brain, the drafts have no essential somatic base.[27]

Damasio and the Embodied Brain

The immediately preceding criticism of Dennett has also been voiced by the neursoscientist Antonio R. Damasio.[28] In his recent book *Descartes' Error,*[29] Damasio has tried to present a more embodied perspective on the mind-brain-body relation, one which is directly relevant to the concerns we raised in *The Embodied Mind,* and so I would like now to consider it.

Damasio argues for a point long recognized by phenomenological philosophers and psychologists: "The mind is embodied, in the full sense of the term, not just embrained."[30] The case that he makes for the embodiment of mind is a neuroscientific one: he argues that "the body, as represented in the brain, may constitute the indispensable frame of reference for the neural processes that we experience as the mind."[31] The aspect of Damasio's perspective on embodiment on which I wish to focus is his idea that the body is the basic reference point for emotion and feeling.

Damasio draws a distinction in his use of the term *emotion* and the term *feeling*. He uses "emotion" to refer to a collection of changes going on in the organism; "feeling," on the other hand, refers to the experience of those changes. Feeling is thus a kind of experience *of* the body in both senses of the genitive: feeling belongs to the body and the intentional object of feeling is in part internal bodily change (emotion). Damasio makes a further distinction between what he calls "primary emotion" and "secondary emotion." Primary emotions are the changes that occur in the body as a result of sensorimotor and perceptual activity. Feelings are the experiences of these changes in connection to what incited them. Secondary emotions are additional bodily changes that arise on the basis of feelings, and they too can be felt: this sort of experience is higher-order feeling.

In the formation of feelings and secondary emotions, images play a central role. First, sensory systems categorize and detect things in the world. This sensory process brings about various bodily changes and responses in the organism. In some animals, these changes can themselves be experienced; they can be felt. In this sort of feeling, images are being formed of the bodily changes (primary emotions) in connection with the type of situation that incites them. But these images can in turn incite further bodily changes: these are the secondary emotions. Finally, secondary emotions too can sometimes be experienced; they can sometimes be felt. Damasio believes that the cognitive-evaluative component in emotion and feeling enters at the level of secondary emotion and has to do with the ability to form an image of the connection between a primary emotion and a type of situation.

From this brief description it is clear that embodiment plays a central role in Damasio's thinking. He writes:

> That process of continuous monitoring, that experience of what your body is doing *while* thoughts and specific contents roll by, is the essence of what I call a feeling. If an emotion is a collection of changes in body state connected to particular mental images that have activated a specific brain system, *the essence of feeling an emotion is the experience of such changes in juxtaposition to the mental images that initiated the cycle.* In other words, a feeling depends on the juxtaposition of an image of the body proper to an image of something else, such as the visual image of a face or the auditory image of a melody.[32]

Damasio's most interesting idea, however, concerns those feelings that do *not* originate from emotion in his sense, but rather from "background" body states. He calls this sort of feeling "background feeling." The idea is that background feelings correspond to the bodily state between the episodic changes of emotion. Or, as he puts it: "The background feeling is our image of the body landscape when it is not shaken by emotion."[33] Background feeling is thus integral to our sense of self.

Damasio's dicussion of background feeling parallels phenomenological discussions, in particular Merleau-Ponty's discussion of the body-image or corporeal schema in his *Phenomenology of Perception,* though Damasio does not seem to be aware of the parallel. Just as Damasio considers background feeling in relation to our "body states *now*" in the present and in relation to "what our bodies *tend to be like*," so too Merleau-Ponty distinguishs between the two layers of "the body at this moment" and the "habit body." Damasio and Merleau-Ponty both consider pathological disruptions of the background body sense, such as the phantom limb experience and anosognosia. For Damasio, the neural representations of the body involved in background feeling provide the biological ground for an unreflective bodily sense of self; for Merleau-Ponty there is a prepersonal depth to the intentionality of the body-image.

These parallels show how Damasio's neurological perspective can do far more justice to the aspects of embodiment that concerned Merleau-Ponty than could the neuropsychology of his own time. Nevertheless, I think that Damasio has still not gone far enough in his thinking about embodiment.

My main criticism concerns his use of the notion of an image. As we have seen, this notion is central to Damasio's thinking about emotion and feeling: "a feeling depends on the juxtaposition of an image of the body proper to an image of something else..." Now Damasio thinks that being able to form and manipulate images is the mark of having a mind. As he puts it: "Brains can have many intervening steps in the circuits mediating between stimulus and response, and still have no mind, if they do not meet an essential condition: the ability to display images internally and to order those images in a process called thought."[34] But what does it mean to "display" an image internally? Talk of "display" sounds suspiciously homuncular. To answer this question we need to know what Damasio understands an image to be in neural terms. For Damasio images are specific patterns of topographically organized activity in early sensory cortices. And to display an image is for a certain topographic activity pattern to be reactivated. In other words, images correspond to activities in specific populations of neurons, and imagetic display corresponds to reactivating the very same group of neurons. I think this is unnecessarily localizationist. To equate having a mind with having a brain that can reactivate *topographically* defined neural activity is to collapse two different domains—the domain of organism behavior, and cognition and the domain of brain topography. As Merleau-Ponty argued in his very first book, *The Structure of Behavior,* if we look at the brain at a purely topographical level, then behavior cannot be said to be contained within the brain; behavior is "related to the brain only as a functional entity."[35] What this means is that the relevant level for linking brain to behavior is not topographic, but rather *topological*: the proper components of brain activity relevant to an understanding of feeling can be distributed processes that are related nonspatially (where "space" is understood in an anatomical sense), instead of being spatially localizable parts that are topographically related. And far from being an arcane assumption of Merleau-Ponty's early writings, this "topological" idea is a working hypothesis among certain neuroscientists and neural network modelers.[36]

Once again, the matter at stake here is whether we can do justice to both spheres—the neuroscientific and the phenomenological. Localizationist assumptions hamper the endeavor because they superimpose the embodied organism onto its brain, an imposition that I have argued is illegitimate. Although Damasio's localizationism is not particularly obtrusive, it is unnecessary and does not sit well with his other important contributions to the neuroscientific study of embodiment.

The Embodied Self

Earlier in my discussion I hinted that I no longer find our treatment of the self in *The Embodied Mind* to be satisfactory. Now that we have looked briefly at the idea of background feeling in Damasio and phenomenology, I am ready to take up this matter.

In Part II of *The Embodied Mind,* we argue that experience can be shown to be gappy or discontinuous and that experience can emerge without there being any central organizing self. The position that we develop parallels Dennett's idea that consciousness seems continuous but is really discontinuous. But there is an important difference between our argument and Dennett's: we appeal, not only to cognitive neuroscience, but also to the first-person experiential accessibility of certain sorts of disunity and discontinuity.

It is here that we draw on the experiential analysis of self in Buddhism. In a nutshell, the Buddhist attitude is that the stream of experience is "empty" of a single unified self and that the emptiness of such a self can be realized in an immediate personal way. One of the reasons we draw on Buddhism is that it provides a disciplined method by which the momentary arising of experience can be discerned through a kind of calm and mindful attention. This method is the basic Buddhist meditational practice known as mindfulness-awareness or calmness-insight meditation. Another reason for drawing on Buddhism is that it tries to provide a phenomenological account of how we come to have an affectively charged sense of an intrinsic self, despite the fact that no real self can be found that corresponds to this intentional construct. Finally, one of the key insights of Buddhism is that the proper understanding of the absence of a single unified self does not lead to nihilism, but rather to a sense of genuine freedom and other-directed engagement.

To show why I am no longer happy with our presentation of the experience of self, let me quote a few passages from our book:

> As the meditators develop some stability of mindfulness/awareness . . . they begin to have insight into what the mind, as it is experienced, is really like. Experiences, they notice, are impermanent. . . . Moment by moment new experiences happen and are gone. It is a rapidly shifting stream of momentary mental occurrences. Furthermore, the shiftiness includes the perceiver as much as the perceptions. There is no experiencer . . . who remains constant to receive experiences, no landing platform for experience.

> In our habitual and unreflective state, we impute continuity of consciousness to all of our experience. . . . But this apparent . . . continuity of consciousness masks the discontinuity of momentary consciousnesses related to one another by cause and effect.

An examination of experience with mindfulness/awareness reveals that one's experience is discontinuous—a moment of consciousness arises, appears to dwell for an instant, and then vanishes, to be replaced by the next moment. [37]

In essence, what I think is wrong in these passages is the idea that continuity is something that gets "imputed" to experience and that "masks" the deeper truth of discontinuity. This is at best a misleading way of speaking, for continuity does not need to be imputed, and discontinuity is not necessarily a deeper truth.[38]

Remember that the moment-to-moment discontinuity at issue is experientially accessible to a kind of awareness that has calm and mindful attention as its mode. But for one to be aware of this moment-to-moment arising as such means that the moments must themselves be experienced as arising in relation to a tacit and preobjective background. Hence the gaps between the momentary experiences that reveal this background are just as important as the discrete moments. In fact, there are many discussions of the awareness of such a preobjective background in Buddhism and the sense of spaciousness it provides. The point that I am making is, therefore, not a criticism of Buddhism, but of the tone of our presentation.

Second, one of the fundamental points of Western phenomenological writing, especially of writings concerned with temporality, is that certain sorts of unity and continuity are not imputed to experience; they are inherent in the very temporal structure of embodied awareness. This is one of the deepest and most difficult topics in Western phenomenology—I am thinking of Husserl's *Phenomenology of Internal Time Consciousness*, Heidegger's discussion of temporality and Dasein in *Being and Time*, and Merleau-Ponty's discussion of temporality and subjectivity in the penultimate chapter of his *Phenomenology of Perception* — and so I do not propose to take up the topic here. The point I wish to make now is simply that when we say that unity and continuity are "imputed" or "projected" onto experience and that this projection "masks" a more fundamental discontinuity and disunity, we are slipping into an objectivist way of thinking that is contrary to our own intentions and that devalues lived experience in the everyday world.

These issues were first brought to my attention several years ago in conversations with Hubert Dreyfus. In his recent review of *The Embodied Mind*,[39] Dreyfus argues that in our discussion of self we commit the anti-phenomenological mistake of "the exposure hypothesis." This mistake involves taking what one experiences in a "detached, inactive, disembodied stance" and reading it back into "involved, active everyday experience." Dreyfus accuses us of making this mistake when we draw on the experiences gained in Buddhist mindfulness-awareness meditation in investigating the phenomenology of self. Furthermore, Dreyfus accuses us of inconsistency: since mindfulness-awareness involves a *transformation* of awareness, we cannot use it to *discover* or *reveal* what experience was all along.

Since I think that we misemphasize the experience of discontinuity in mindfulness-awareness meditation, I agree that Dreyfus has a point. But Dreyfus is mistaken when he says that mindfulness-awareness is detached and inactive in comparison to active everyday experience and when he argues that we make the mistake of the "exposure hypothesis." The issues here are important because they take us to the heart of the phenomenology of embodiment and its relation to cognitive science.

First, Dreyfus thinks that Heidegger and Merleau-Ponty do not depart from everyday experience because they describe everyday skillful activity from within: for example, Heidegger describes writing at his desk while doing so and Merleau-Ponty describes everyday perception while perceiving. One of our points in *The Embodied Mind*, however, is that such "involvement" is theoretical because it is primarily a matter of thinking: Heidegger and Merleau-Ponty do attempt to be mindful of their activity, but they do so only by thinking about what they are doing as they do it.

Second, Dreyfus appears to believe that thinking about an activity while doing it does not alter in any way its phenomenological status. But this is certainly mistaken, as many phenomenologists have observed, both Western and Asian. Therefore, if Dreyfus is right that any practice that transforms experience cannot be used to discover what experience was all along, then the point applies to Heidegger and Merleau-Ponty as much as to Buddhism.

In fact the objection is not legitimate and rests on a philosophical mistake. The mistake is to suppose that there is some independent vantage point outside of experience from which to determine what counts as discovery and what counts as transformation. In other words, the mistake is an objectivist one. Experience is not objectifiable, however: any reflection upon experience is itself a form of experience that does not leave experience unchanged. Experience is inherently open-ended and developmental, and for this reason there is no inconsistency in supposing that transforming experience can make one aware of aspects of one's previous experience that were overlooked.

It is within this framework that mindfulness-awareness meditation needs to be understood. This discipline does not foster a detached and inactive attitude. Instead, it is based on the idea that there is a kind of "natural mindfulness" that is an already present condition but that requires practice to cultivate. The point of the practice is to overcome habits of mindlessnes, of being mindlessly involved in the world without even realizing that that is what one is doing. And the realization that one is habitually not acting in a fully present and mindful manner becomes existentially apparent as one develops mindfulness.[40] Mindfulness-awareness meditation is thus ultimately directed towards *mindful* active involvement in the world, rather than *mindless* involvement.

Unlike most Western phenomenology, which remains within the province of philosophy as theoretical reflection, Asian phenomenologies typically involve working with the body in a direct way. Mindfulness-awareness meditation is one example but there are many others, such as artistic cultivation in poetry, calligraphy, and painting, and martial arts such as Aikido and Tai Ji Quan. "The initial step in all these disciplines is that the mind . . . deliberately places the body into a special form or posture."[41]

Dreyfus thinks that taking this step, in the case of meditation at least, "disrupts" normal experience and so has no phenomenological validity for the everyday world. What Dreyfus means exactly by "normal experience" and the "everyday world" he never makes clear. (One wonders whether it amounts to the normal and everyday as seen by the late-twentieth-century philosophy professor at Berkeley.) In any case, Drefyus appears to assume that the everyday world is an unproblematic given and that any discipline or practice that changes one's mode of embodiment takes one out of the everyday world. This conception of the everyday world is naive and unacceptably restrictive.

The point of my argument is not to defend Buddhist mindfulness meditation *per se* (except to the extent that Dreyfus misrepresents it). Rather, it is to uphold the idea that phenomenology can be a source of insight into the inherently developmental nature of embodiment in the lived world. Dreyfus precludes this possibility when he restricts the phenomenology of embodiment to his impoverished conception of the everyday world.

In this paper, I have been concerned with how cognitive science increasingly encounters embodiment in its own scientific terrain. By making evident how the mind is immanent in the entire body of the organism, cognitive science is providing another metaphor for understanding the mind-body relation—the metaphor of the mindful body. This metaphor is neither dualistic nor reductionistic, and it naturally connects to the concerns of both Western and Asian phenomenologies: it conveys the immanence of the mind in the body while at the same time implying that the modes in which the mind is immanent are open to development and transformation.

Notes

Some portions of this paper were also presented at a Lindisfarne Association Conference on "The New Philosophies of Life and Mind," Crestone, Colorado, 8-15 August, 1993.

1   Francisco J. Varela, Evan Thompson, and Eleanor Rosch, *The Embodied Mind: Cognitive Science and Human Experience* (Cambridge: MIT Press, A Bradford Book, 1991), p. xv.

2   Mark Johnson, "Conceptual Metaphor and Embodied Structures of Meaning: A Reply to Kennedy and Vervaeke," *Philosophical Psychology* 6 (1993): 413-22, p. 418.

3   See P. Agre, "The Symbolic Worldview: Reply to Vera and Simon," *Cognitive Science* 17 (1993): 61-70. The discussion in this and the following paragraph is greatly indebted to this article.

4   Maurice Merleau-Ponty, *Phenomenology of Perception,* trans. Colin Smith (London: Routledge Press, 1962).

5   Jean Piaget and Barbel Inhelder, *The Psychology of the Child,* trans. Helen Weaver (New York: Basic Books, 1969); Jean Piaget, *Genetic Epistemology* (New York: Columbia University Press, 1970), and *Biology and Knowledge* (Edinburgh: Edinburgh University Press, 1971).

6   George Lakoff, *Women, Fire, and Dangerous Things: What Categories Reveal about the Mind* (Chicago: University of Chicago Press, 1987). Mark Johnson, *The*

Body in the Mind: The Bodily Basis of Imagination, Reason and Feeling (Chicago: University of Chicago Press, 1987).

7   P. Agre and D. Chapman, "What Are Plans for?" *Robotics and Autonomous Systems* 6 (1990): 17-34; D. Chapman and P. Agre, "Abstract Reasoning as Emergent from Concrete Activity" (presented to the Workshop on Planning and Reasoning about Actin, Portland, Ore., July 1986); R. Brooks, "Intelligence without Reason," *ISCAI* (1991).

8   As, for example, Owen Flanagan does using the work of William James; see his *Consciousness Reconsidered* (Cambridge: MIT Press, A Bradford Book, 1992).

9   See Yuasa Yasuo, *The Body: Toward an Eastern Mind-Body Theory,* trans. Nagatomo Shigenori and Thomas P. Kasulis (Albany: State University of New York Press, 1987).

10   See Drew Leder, *The Absent Body* (Chicago: University of Chicago Press, 1990), for an excellent discussion of "ontovaluational" atittudes towards the lived body, in particular of the difference between the Cartesian and neo-Confucian perspectives.

11   Daniel C. Dennett, *Consciousness Explained* (Boston: Little Brown, 1991).

12   Maurice Merleau-Ponty, in his first book, *The Structure of Behavior,* anticipates Dennett's idea of Cartesian materialism in neuroscience. Referring to the "pseudo-Cartesianism of scientists and psychologists," Merleau-Ponty writes: "Just as Descartes is obliged to reserve the mediation of the body and perception to the pineal gland as the seat of the common sense, so physiologists have had to give up designating fixed spatial and chromatic values in the periphery of the nervous system and to make those which in perception are distributed over the different points of the visual field depend on the assimilation of the corresponding excitations into variable associative circuits. Descartes' pineal gland plays the role of the association zone of modern physiologists." *The Structure of Behavior*, trans. Alden Fisher (Pittsburgh: Dusquesne University Press, 1963), p. 192.

13   Daniel C. Dennett and Marcel Kinsbourne, "Escape from the Cartesian Theater," Authors' Response to Open Peer Commentary on Daniel C. Dennett and Marcel Kinsbourne, "Time and the Observer: The Where and When of Consciousness in the Brain," *Behavioral and Brain Sciences* 15 (1992): 183-247, p. 236.

14   Rene Descartes, "Meditations on First Philosophy," in *Philosophical Writings of Descartes, Volume II,* trans. by John Cottingham, Robert Stoothoff, Dugald Murdoch (Cambridge: Cambridge University Press, 1984), pp. 59-60.

15   Ibid., p. 56.

16   Ibid., p. 298.

17   Dennett, *Consciousness Explained*, p. 364.

18   Merleau-Ponty, *Phenomenology of Perception,* pp. 52-53.

19   Ibid., p. 4.

20   Ibid., p. 101.

21   J. J. Gibson, "A Direct Theory of Visual Perception," in *The Psychology of Knowing* , ed J R. Royce and W. W. Rozeboom(New York: Gordon and Breach, 1972), pp. 217-18.

22   J. J. Gibson, *The Ecological Approach to Visual Perception* (Ithaca, N.Y.: Cornell University Press, 1979), pp. 239-40.

23   See D. H. Ballard, "Animate Vision," *Artificial Intelligence* 48 (1991): 57-86.

24   Dennett,*Consciousness Explained,* p. 210.

25   This tendency is particularly evident in his idea that consciousness is dependent on self-probing.

26 See Andrew Hodges, *Alan Turing: The Engima of Intelligence* (London: Unwin Hyman Limited, 1983).

27 It is for this reason that Dennett thinks he can imagine consciousness being "teleported" from one body to another. Consciousness is purely informational, for Dennett, and has only a contingent connection to embodiment: "If what you are is that organization of information that has structured your body's control system (or, to put it in its more usual provocative form, if what you are is the program that runs on your brain's computer), then you could in principle survive the death of your body as intact as a program can survive the destruction of the computer on which it was created and first run" (*Consciousness Explained,* p. 430). This strikes me as a very Cartesian and "intellectualist" (to use Merleau-Ponty's term) notion of consciousness: although the philosopher might find imaginable this idea of embodiment being only contingently linked to self-identity, I doubt that anyone whose sense of self is intimately tied to bodily skills (e.g., the actor, dancer, surgeon, athlete, or martial arts master) would be persuaded.

28 See his commentary on Dennett and Kinsbourne:Antonio R. Damasio, "The Selfless Consciousness," *Behavioral and Brain Sciences* 15 (1992): 208-9.

29 Antonio R. Damasio, *Descartes' Error: Emotion, Reason, and the Human Brain* (New York: Grosset/Putnam, 1994).

30 Ibid., p. 118.

31 Ibid., p. xvi.

32 Ibid., p. 145.

33 Ibid., pp. 150-51.

34 Ibid., p. 89.

35 Merleau-Ponty, *The Structure of Behavior,* p. 72.

36 For example, see Humberto R. Maturana and Francisco J. Varela, *Autopoiesis and Cognition: The Realization of the Living,* Boston Studies in the Philosophy of Science, vol. 43 (Dordrecht: D. Reidl, 1980); Stephen Grossberg, "How Does the Brain Build a Cognitive Code?" *Psychological Review* 87 (1980): 1-55, and "Competitive Learning: From Interactive Activation to Adaptive Resonance," *Cognitive Science* 11 (1987): 23-63; W. Singer, "Synchronization of Cortical Activity and Its Putative Role in Information Processing," *Annual Review of Physiology* 55 (1993): 349-74. My thinking about the topographic-topological distinction has also been very influenced by Francisco J. Varela, "Resonant Cell Assemblies: A New Approach to Cognitive Functions and Neuronal Synchrony," unpublished MS.

37 Varela, Thompson, and Rush, *The Embodied Mind,* pp. 60-61, 69, 73, respectively.

38 It is important to understand that the issue here is a phenomenological one about experienced continuity and discontinuity. In other words, the issue does not concern discontinuity at the level of brain processes (though we do discuss that too), as it does for Dennett. Dennett's point is that brain-level processes are discontinuous: they involve discrete discriminatory states. He thinks it follows from this point that experience is not really qualitatively and temporally continuous; it only seems so. But again this sort of inference rests on collapsing the distinction between the organism as the proper subject of experience and the organism's brain.

39 Hubert L. Dreyfus, review of *The Embodied Mind,* by Francisco J. Varela, Evan Thompson, and Eleanor Rosch, *Mind* (1993).

40 Dreyfus thinks that saying this begs the question about the exposure hypothesis. No question is begged, however, for the reasons given in the preceding paragraph.

41 Thomas P. Kasulis, editor's introduction to *The Body*, by Yuasa Yasuo, p. 5.

9
Science and Things
On Scientific Method as Embodied Access to the World

Michael O'Donovan-Anderson

When Descartes watched his block of wax, and with it all of the qualities to which he supposed he owed his objective knowledge, melt in the heat of the fire, dissipating its affects into unreality, he could only attribute his continuing assurance that the same wax was still being presented to him—having merely shed one apparent guise for another—to a direct apperception of the waxness which remained, uniting shifting appearances and attesting to the thing-in-itself which, although ever hidden from the senses, was nevertheless present to the unencumbered understanding.

It is not clear whether the properly trained intellect is to have immediate and privileged access into essence upon sensual encounter with an object or whether it takes witness of that singularly startling transformation of one object-form into another to grant initial insight into the reality underlying the merely perceived. (For surely the discovery that water and ice are but individual object-forms of the same thing was no less than that—a dis-covery, unveiling the structural underpinning of the sensible order.) But irrespective of the details thought to be involved in apperceptive access to reality, the episode is an important one: for it is this conception of the epistemic position of the knowing subject, and his attitude toward the sensible, which most centrally characterizes both the ambition and the success of modern science.

I say this not because science has remained true to Descartes's epistemic method (Galileo and Bacon must be credited with the development of our scientific methodology), but because it is in modern science that the search for essence, for the underlying structures of reality hidden beyond the veil of sense, comes to historical fruition. It is of more than passing interest, and perhaps of great import, that the contemporary symbol of scientific success is our ability to reach beyond the extension of the senses—important because it underlies the understanding (or perpetuates the illusion) that it is by and through the "extra-sensory" perceptions provided by laboratory technology that we come to know the essences of things in a way that is true to the intention, if not the details, of Descartes's apperceptive method—interesting, even ironic, because it is precisely the scientific methodology that permits the practical success of Cartesianism, the substitution of retroductive inference for apperception, which now raises questions about the epistemic reliability of scientific discovery.

Hume's famous line represents well the tone of the critique: "For my part, whenever I look most intimately into what I call *myself*, I always stumble on some particular perception or other. . . . I can never catch *myself* at any time without a perception, and never observe anything but the perception" (*Treatise*, I, IV, IV). In our everyday experience of the world, we constantly receive, perceive, and otherwise encounter (what we take to be) the effects of real objects on our senses, but the object itself we never attain. It is on the relation between these sensible object-properties and the objects themselves, and on our epistemic warrant to move from one to the other, that philosophers of science (at least those involved in the realism debate) will most fundamentally differ. The Humean empiricist, for instance, will deny warrant for the move from appearance to underlying reality and is likely to advocate a bundle theory of objecthood, whereby an object is said to exist simply as a psychologically connected set of properties. A standard form of scientific realism, on the other hand, holds that the validity of the inference from appearance to underlying cause is justified by the very success enjoyed in the application of the retroduced model to novel situations and phenomena.[1] Indeed, with respect to certain types of predictive applications, as for instance regarding such time-dependent theoretical values as fertility, it is very difficult to explain the "fit" between actual and predicted phenomena without recourse to a literal interpretation of the theory at hand. Nevertheless, it is left open for the Humean to insist that inference of any kind, no matter how practically useful, may never itself ground claims of truth.

And so it is in this very general quandary that science finds itself: searching for the justification of its own success, and yet constrained in that search by the uncertainty of the inductions with which, it seems, the credit ought to rest. This stalemate, I shall argue, is the result of two related philosophical mistakes. The first is the understanding that the most fundamental disclosure of objecthood occurs in the realm of sensible properties, that what an object most essentially is can be expressed with reference to, or defined in terms of, its affective properties. And the second, built upon this idea that objective reality is to be accessed via (inference from) the sensible, is the focus of the realist debate on scientific *theories*, such that the existence of the objects inferentially (retroductively) discovered comes to rest on the reliability of theoretical inference and the truth of the discovering theory.

I take it that just as it was a mistake for philosophers to take themselves as representative subjects for epistemological inquiry, with the result that they report as "knowing" what is in fact theorizing about knowing, so it is also a mistake to take scientific theory, and theorizers, as representative of the epistemic activity of science. Any defense of realism must therefore begin by taking seriously Ian Hacking's insistence that scientific knowledge is the result of interaction with, not theorizing about, (the entities of) the world. Although retroductive theory has an extremely important role to play in determining the shape and direction of scientific research, we should not make a mistake analogous to confusing the contexts of discovery and of confirmation by confusing the genesis of a research program with the activity it embodies. And according to Hacking, at least, it is the interactional activity of science which grounds the knowledge it produces. This way of thinking has two major consequences: (1) understanding scientific method primarily as a way of controlling our interactions with the world (i.e., as a maximization of the efficiency of our usual epistemic methods, where this interaction is itself a mode of epistemic access and not merely a means of increasing our sensory data) and (2) taking the reality of scientific entities to be determinable independently of the truth of theories. Specifically, I shall argue that we should accept as real all those things for which we have interactional evidence of a type similar to our decidedly nontheoretical evidence for the reality of tables, chairs, and the other furniture of the middle-sized sensible world. Not incidentally, in recognition of the philosophical mistakes cited above, I shall be working under the understanding that knowledge of the identity and existence[2] of everyday objects is not rooted primarily in knowing their affective properties, but rather in knowing their place in an interlocking web of causal-functional relations, and likewise that everyday realism is based not on inference from the visible to the real, but on a co-responding interaction with the world. I shall not leave this assumption unsupported.

Coping with the World

Interpreting one's environment is perhaps the commonest of experiences. We enter a room, spy our favorite chair, and gratefully settle in. All this occurs, it seems, with neither conscious inference nor the overt participation of reason, which for all those who enjoy the undisturbed relaxation associated with comfortably sinking into a bit of furniture is a lucky thing. For inferential reason, we are told, is ill equipped to provide us with the certainty which this activity (no doubt) requires. And although in the unreflective rush of everyday existence one can scarcely afford the luxury of thorough deliberation, making understandable one's failure to note the constant workings of reason, freedom from the concerns of living clears the mind of such practical preoccupation and pragmatic prejudice. It is only in the cloistered environment of the philosopher that the true, inferential basis of our everyday judgements can be revealed, and with it the startling evidence of the ultimate inadequacy of such inferential reason to its appointed task. For no inference from mere appearance may unfailingly lead to the objects behind our impressions. Confidence in the reality of the objects which underlie those appearances may not, therefore, be legitimately grounded in the reliability of inferential reasoning. Thus, we can account for the confidence of the everyman only by assuming he is unreflective.

That this skeptical conclusion is only possible in the rarefied atmosphere of theoretical contemplation is universally accepted. The significance of this fact, however, is open to debate. Although it is surely true that everyday activity gives no cause for skeptical conclusions, we needn't trace this fact to a flawed application of inferential reasoning within that context; it hardly follows from the realization that no conscious inference from appearance to reality occurs in the context of everyday activity that the recognition of one's chair must therefore be based on a subconscious inferential methodology, while confidence in the support it will provide (due to its reality) results from a common, practical faith. On the contrary, it may be that such reasoning is simply not required for knowledge of the real. It is not that the inferential reasonings of the skeptic are flawed; they are simply inappropriate for their purported task of discovering reality—of knowing the existence and identity of entities.

On this point I take both Heidegger[3] and Ian Hacking[4] to be in agreement: Although the epistemologist or high-energy physicist may question the reality of certain entities, the existence of which are "theoretical" in so far as the context of inquiry calls on one to infer to them from observational evidence, neither the person who merely sits in her favorite chair nor the technician who skillfully utilizes her electron microscope will seriously entertain the possibility of the unreality of the entities with which she is dealing. But the important disanalogy here is not based on the failure of the latter pair (the technician and seated individual) to reflect on the groundings of their beliefs, but rather on the more general failure to note the primacy of bodily activity in defining our epistemic relation to the world. Certainty of the identity of things is not, nor need it be, grounded in the inferential move from property to underlying reality, for another option exists: that knowledge of the existence and identity of objects is grounded in, and disclosed through, the everyday contexts of activity, interaction, and use. As Heidegger writes: "The kind of dealing which is closest to us is as we have shown, not bare perceptual cognition, but rather that kind of concern which manipulates things and puts them to use; and this has its own kind of 'knowledge.'"[5]

We find ourselves returned to a basic epistemic question: how is it that we individuate, identify, and appropriately utilize the various objects of our world? This question suggests another, for to placate the skeptic we should like our way of knowing a thing to be related to its way of being a thing; the skeptical problem takes root in that gap between (what we took to be) our epistemic access to things and their reality, between properties and the underlying thing-in-itself. Thus: in what does the identity of a thing reside, or, as we might say, borrowing one of Heidegger's useful neologisms, what constitutes the thingness of the thing? It is perhaps easiest to approach these questions initially from the standpoint of the canonical answers, for troubles with these may yet suggest their own alternatives.

Traditional epistemology tells us that we approach the world in terms of definable occurrent properties. Every particular object, indeed, every identifiable class of objects, is characterized by some set of occurrent properties. As we move through the world, correct application of these properties, which in this context become criteria of identity, allow us to differentiate the objects of the world into their appropriate classes. Searle's cluster theory of reference, according to which a word refers to (picks out, or differentiates) an object in virtue of being associated with a particular set of properties and/or definite descriptions, a plurality of which apply to the referent, is a good example of the spirit and consequences of traditional epistemology. The object itself, of course, is not the set of properties (properties, after all, are properties *of* things), but that which unifies them, in which they inhere, or by which they are caused.

It is during the project of actually explicating the properties by which we know things that the inadequacy of the traditional picture of epistemology begins to reveal itself. What are we to say, for instance, about the set of properties by which we identify chairs? They are not all four-legged or made of the same material or squarish . . . in fact, the only property they are all likely to share is that they are *for sitting on*.[6] With the addition of this sort of predicate, we move immediately from the realm of observational reception of occurrent properties to an interactional, activity-based criterion of identification. But as long as we treat it as a simple property, on the same order as four-legged or blue, we cannot go far with the project of identification. For if we persist along traditional lines, such that "for sitting on" is understood as a definite, self-sufficient predicate drawing its meaning from the requirements of a particular form of human posture, then we may no longer restrict to chairs the range of objects to which this is applicable: tables, floors, window ledges, and the like are all suitable for sitting on. But they are not *for* sitting on.

Wittgenstein's critique of a rules-based epistemology is directly applicable here. We must understand such interactional predicates with the following in mind: (1) No criterion or set of rules can exhaustively define its own application; (2) the content of such criteria comes from their actual use and application (their functional place), not the set of rules which approximately describes that use. Thus we must understand such defining predicates as "for sitting on" as having an emphasis on the "for": that is, meaning those things which are actually utilized in a particular way. We can take this to be an indication that such predicates are representative of functional, rather than sensible, properties; alternately, that the meaning of such predicates can only be elucidated in terms of interaction. Either way the message is the same (if contentious): objects (artifacts, at least) are defined, characterized, and classified in terms of their function, and therefore with reference to our everyday interactions with them— hammers are things for hammering, glasses for drinking, lamps for illuminating. The interactively defined functions of things ground our epistemic genera in a way that sensible properties cannot. The "thingness" of the thing is revealed in contexts of use and physical interaction, and our knowledge of the thing is thereby rooted in these contexts. In our everyday lives the familiar—the well known—presents itself, not primarily in terms of sensible properties which call upon us to judge the nature of the still-hidden thing, but rather as being for some purpose, as having some particular function. The suggestion made by both Wittgenstein and Heidegger is that our basic encounter with things is characterized by the hermeneutic "as", presenting the purpose or equipmentality of the thing encountered (we know a chair *as* a thing for sitting)—and further that what it is to *be* a chair is to *be* a thing for sitting. This relation between epistemology and ontology is crucial: only if we maintain this relation—deny a gap between the realms and their results—can we avoid skepticism. Having given some reason to deny this gap in the case of our knowledge of artifacts, by noting the importance of bodily activity to that knowledge, the task we now face is to extend the analysis.

So let us pause to further illuminate the vital relation between epistemology and metaphysics. From Plato on, accounting for our modes of access to the world has always gone hand in hand with understanding the fundamental types of things which constitute that world; for a world composed of Transcendent Forms and physical reflections, we have the intellectual insight of the soul and the experiences of the body. For every thing (kind) worth knowing about, we need access—a way of knowing it. Not that there has always been a one-to-one correspondence between kinds of things and ways of knowing, but there has been surprising historical consistency on this point. Aristotle's framework is of particular relevance to the project undertaken here, for Aristotle distinguishes four ways (or kinds) of Being and, likewise, four ways of Becoming, from the cooperation of which arises each successive state of our eternally existing, ever changing world.[7] Together Primary Substances (material particulars), Secondary Substances (forms), Accidents (accidental properties), and Universals (types and genera of accidents) compose all the entities of the world. Aristotle situates his epistemic subject firmly within this single, composite realm of existence (unlike Plato, whose composite subject straddles two distinct ontic realms) and endows her not merely with the usual epistemic accoutrements (sensation and some form of Intuition), but also stresses her concrete involvement in the world as important to her ability to know it. For Aristotle the human being is both caused by, and is a cause in, the world—she is involved not merely as a being, but also as a participant in becoming. Because of the prominence Aristotle gives to a science of Becoming as necessary to complete knowledge of the world, the practical, causal involvements of the human are, for Aristotle, important for her role as knower. This emphasis on the importance of praxis is among the more important and unique aspects of Aristotle's philosophy, and it extends not just to ethics (where it must obviously be central) but to science and epistemology as well. One need only consider Aristotle's admission in the *Nicomachean Ethics* that practical activities can actually change one's perceptual relation to the world to see how deeply runs the importance of praxis to his philosophy.[8] Even his science understood itself to be as much practical and interactive as theoretical and (passively) observational.

This aspect of his work has its roots, I believe, in Aristotle's particular treatment of form as a metaphysical category. As is well known, Aristotle inherited from his teacher a strong belief that essence was to be found in form; to classify a thing by natural kind was precisely to classify it by form, and hence the importance of form as a category of Being. Less often emphasized is the role form plays as a category of Becoming and the importance of formal cause as a fundamental, or essential, explanation of events. But it is precisely because of the connection between these two metaphysical roles of form that praxis emerges, for Aristotle, as an important mode of our relation to the world.

For substances do not merely possess a characteristic way of Being (essence) in virtue of their form, but also a characteristic way of Becoming. For each kind of thing, and therefore each substance, there are certain natural potentials, brought to the substance by form which that substance will tend to actualize throughout its existence. These natural potentials range from the mundane tendency of physical objects to return to the earth to the complex development of living organisms from fetus to adult. Although of course fundamental explanations of motion are for Aristotle always teleological, it is only in virtue of form that substances possess a *telos*. From the point of view of physics, then, formal and final explanations are importantly interrelated; to know the essence (form) of a thing is to know its natural tendencies, to see where it fits into the network of nature's motions.

In an important reversal of Plato's order of knowledge, (a consequence of Aristotle's insistence that forms exist only in virtue of their inherence in matter, that is, insofar as matter and form together comprise substances), Aristotle maintains that the primary objects of knowledge are substances and that therefore form, rather than being available to immediate intuition, is an object of (scientific) discovery. It is, I believe, in this discovery of form that praxis plays its decisive role. For given the close ties between the essence (form) of substances and their natural tendencies—the principles of motion and rest contained in each subject in virtue of its form—one may come to know form by the discovery of these tendencies. And it is only in virtue of one's physical presence in the world and the capacity for causal interaction with substances which this entails that these natural tendencies, which exhibit themselves causally, may be discovered. It is my understanding that Aristotle's insistence on the metaphysical importance of Becoming (both to the nature of the world and to the essence of individual substances) led him to see the importance to knowledge of interactive investigation as a mode of epistemic access to the world.[9]

I have no wish to provide a detailed account of the role of praxis in Aristotle's epistemology or scientific method, but I would like to suggest that we can learn from his insight. We needn't maintain a strict natural teleology to acknowledge that natural kinds do have certain natural tendencies in virtue of their type, a certain stereotypical functional place in the world. This place is not defined in terms of appearance, but in terms of potentials for action and reaction; we might reasonably expect that knowing or discovering the object(s) occupying this place, then, would be more a task of doing than looking.[10]

In this context knowing the real ceases to be tied to the truth or reliability of a given inference or method of retroduction. We know the hammer is real, that we have had an authentic hammer encounter, if and when we hammer with it or discover that the thing is available for that use. Likewise while we sit in our chair, its reality presents itself to us in that very act. Here the skeptical problem ceases to make what little sense it may have made: once we see that knowledge cannot be reduced to sensation, it follows that the question How do you know there really is a chair in which you sit? cannot be reduced to How can you be sure that the chair-sense-data are really presenting a chair-thing? (and it is only the latter question which is the door to skepticism, for insofar as there can be no evidence for a chair-in-itself independent of the senses, the only available answer is that one cannot be so assured). Thus, once we instead take bodily activity and interaction to constitute a legitimate mode of epistemic access to the world, a mode of access which compliments but is not reducible to sensation, then the skeptic ought to lose his grip on epistemological inquiry.[11]

Science and Interaction

At this point the path I wish to follow in discussing scientific realism should be fairly apparent. I take the emphasis on the reliability of retroduction to be indicative of the traditional epistemological mistake, that access to the objects of the world is restricted to inference from detectable phenomena. Although the retroductive method is extremely important to the scientific search for the construction and constitution of the universe, it is not adequate to ground an understanding of being. For in abstracting from the interactive contexts in which being is revealed, the theoretical attitude discovers only possible entities, hypothetical things whose presence could explain the observed, but whose own reality remains uncertain and ungrounded. It is only after the move from theoretical inquiry to experimental interaction that the being of a thing can be revealed. The discussion of scientific entities is, however, an entirely more subtle enterprise than the discussion of chairs, for the temptation to conflate the *is* of constitution with that of being becomes ever greater the deeper one delves into the constitutional roots of the universe. This, of course, is part of the scientific illusion that underlies the twin problems of skepticism and anti-realism. Once science—a science thought to be rooted in perception and inference—is believed to constitute our exclusive mode of access to the "reality" behind the appearances, the theoretical inquiry into constitution becomes increasingly substituted for an understanding of being, until the former eclipses the latter in our understanding of the real. For *essence* can only *mean* "underlying reality" in this artificially restricted context. Thus the question of what a chair "really is" comes to require answers like quarks, muons, gluons, and such; and insofar as the constitutional *is* has replaced the *is* of being as the primary sense of real, certainty of existence becomes tied to inductive reliability—the existence of the chair becomes as questionable and theoretical as the merely hypothetical things which are said to constitute it. We must work to separate these two questions; for as we have seen above, the real, in the sense required by the scientific realist, is disclosed, not through an attitude of contemplative inference from sensible evidence, but rather through the contexts of use and interaction. Only interactive access to objects can reveal the causal interrelations and functional niche which defines the thing as such.

Thus the suggestion I would like to make regarding a more fruitful approach to the issue of scientific realism is twofold. First, we should carefully rethink the centrality accorded to theory and retroductive method in the canonical epistemology of science. Although the usual understanding of the scientific method, that the scientist retroduces to the underlying structures of the universe the existence of which would explain a given set of observational regularities, is certainly correct, it does not necessarily follow that our epistemic relation to the world is characterized by a belief in (the reliability of which depends on the truth of) the retroduced theories. Not only does this place the realist in the uncomfortable position of solving (or at least ignoring) the problem of induction, but because the vast majority of scientific theories are to some degree incorrect, the realist is stuck defending some notion of approximate truth. I take it that neither task is particularly desirable, and I believe both can be avoided by being more precise about the role of experimentation in scientific epistemology. In particular, although research programs are certainly theoretically driven, their results needn't be theoretically dependent, for the epistemic activity of science, especially with respect to the discovery of, and certainty about, the entities which constitute our universe, is concentrated in posttheoretical experimentation.

It must be remembered, however, that this experimentation is not itself characterized by inference from the observed, but is based on an interactive model of investigation which, if successful, will confirm the existence of the entity in question. This is a markedly different task from confirming a theory, and maintaining this distinction can be useful to the scientific realist. For this brings up the second part of my twofold suggestion, that the strongest argument for scientific realism is to be made by extending the umbrella of everyday realism to include those entities which have become sufficiently available to interaction that knowledge of their identity and existence is grounded in the same manner as that of the familiar objects of our everyday world. We needn't tie the successful progress of science to the truth of theories, for theoretical truth is not the ultimate grounding of existential claims. Instead we should focus our arguments for a realist acceptance of scientific entities directly on the process of experimental confirmation of the entities themselves.

Let us consider in more detail an actual, albeit simple, laboratory situation. Following Hacking's paradigm case of microscope use, we can imagine the following: Coming to a microscope for the first time, a student peers through the eyepiece. Seeing nothing (i.e., seeing only unbroken light), she *fiddles* with the focus knobs. After some movement, a pattern of dark and light, probably a very complicated pattern, emerges. The student *blinks* (washing her lenses), but the image remains, the student *wipes* the lenses of the scope, but the image remains; The student *moves* the specimen slide, and the image moves, too. Now the student takes a small probe and *moves* it under the scope onto the slide. (A large, very dark shape enters the view, at which point two things become apparent: first, that manipulating the image area actually alters the image and, second, that our visual representations and our motor space are linked in a very specific way which no longer applies in this new representational space. The probe visually moves in directions other than we expect. This takes some getting used to.) Taking the probe we *push* on the edge of the pattern, and a surprising thing happens: some of the pattern moves while some remains, or scatters in directions other than the direction of the exerted force. Repeated *manipulations* of this sort leave us with a pattern which is relatively stable and tends to react in predictable ways to the *interference* of the probe. To argue that the natural conclusion of this sequence, that we had identified an actual, microscopic individual, is an instance of "inference to the best explanation" ignores the fact that we were not in the position of investigating a visually clear phenomenon with interventions designed to produce more phenomena; the intervention helped *define* the visual phenomena, in terms of its reactions to the interventions, as corresponding to an individual.[12] As Hacking puts it, "we don't just peer, we interfere."[13]

Now let us imagine that what we had thereby individuated was a living cell. There are, of course, distinct parts to the cell, and we could follow the same steps above, perhaps with a higher power lens, to "visually" identify different internal structures of the cell. But what do these structures do? What are they for? What *kinds* of things make up a cell? To answer these questions, it is a sure bet that more interference and manipulation are required. We might notice, for example, that the cell tends to move away from bright light or moves more slowly in certain kinds of media, and we might suppose that some of the individual structures we identify within the cell may be responsible for these behaviors. This, of course, is a hypothesis, the testing of which requires very directed sorts of interventions: we might destroy a specific part of the cell (what we suppose to be its "eye") and determine if it is still antiphototropic. Likewise we might put a number of cells in what we know to be a nutrient-rich medium and, by destroying select parts of the cells, determine which parts are responsible for digestion or removing waste matter. As Hacking writes regarding genetic microscopy:

> I must repeat that just as in large scale vision, the actual images or micrographs are only one small part of the confidence in reality. In a recent lecture the molecular biologist G. S. Stent recalled that in the late forties *Life* magazine had a full color micrograph, labelled, excitedly, the first photograph of the gene (March 17 1947). Given the theory, or lack of theory, of the gene at that time, said Stent, the title did not make any sense. Only a greater understanding of what a gene is can bring the conviction of greater understanding of what the micrograph shows. We become convinced of the reality of bands and interbands on chromosomes not just because we see them, but because we formulate conceptions of what they do, what they are for. But in this respect too, microscopic and macroscopic vision is not different: a Laplander in the Congo won't see much in the bizarre new environment until he starts to get some idea what is in the jungle.[14]

In the above examples, supposition, hypothesis, and the production of visual phenomena have their place, but so too do interaction and manipulation. An indispensable part of having an "idea [of] what is in the jungle" or under the microscope, which allows one to see properly, is determining the functional place and interactive tendencies of the things one finds there. Sorts are discovered, defined, and seen in terms of their effective place in a web of interactions and processes, and we can only determine the characteristics of this place by intervening in, and sometimes disrupting, the natural processes themselves.

The epistemic importance of interaction and intervention is taken one step further in Hacking's paradigm case of electron microscopy. What rightly strikes Hacking as remarkable here is, not the amount of interaction which occurs with the specimen to be explored, but the degree of confidence and comfort one must have in one's interactions with the electrons. For clearly one has entered into a relation with the electron that is far more intimate even than one's relation with the observed, poked, and prodded cells in light microscopy; a stream of electrons has taken the place, not of the specimen, but of the *probe*, the *tool* of interference and interaction wielded by the microscope operator. This, perhaps, is what is so striking about the famous IBM image, constructed by carefully placing individual atoms in the form of the company logo. Of course it indicates that we know a lot about the behavior of atoms, enough to get them to line up in an extremely unnatural way, but more than this it indicates a level of comfort with the technological tools of the laboratory, such that the phenomena of which they take advantage are no longer known in terms of any inferential knowledge-that, but in terms of an interactive knowledge-how. Just as our epistemic encounter with a hammer qua hammer is poorly described in terms of a sensing subject hypothesizing the properties of the sensed object and interacting with the object in the hopes of confirming the hypothesis (with whatever confidence eventually gained in our understanding of the hammer being ascribed to the continued confirmation of our phenomenal expectations), so, too, once the electron has been so thoroughly harnessed as to be used continually and successfully as a tool, it would be a mistake to continue to describe our epistemic relation with electrons in terms of inference and hypothesis; knowing is not just seeing, but also coping.[15] It is just one more version of this same mistake to treat our interactive comfort as a by-product of some long process of purely sensual information gathering, to treat our coping as if it were grounded in seeing; interaction is a mode of epistemic access, producing its own knowledge, from the first epistemic encounter. When a sort of object, once hypothetical, becomes available to us as a tool, this indicates that our interactive access to the things must have grown steadily, providing us with knowledge-what (understanding the characteristics of their causal-functional place) in virtue of, and simultaneously with, knowledge-how. In the successful scientific endeavor, hypothesis gives way slowly, not (just) to a catalog of observed phenomena, but to the slow inclusion of the entity in that extended web of functionally related entities with which we have learned to cope. This is why we should take the central symbol of the success of Western science to be not its extension of our senses but its extension of our *bodies*. Like Merleau-Ponty's blind man who can "see" (determine the physical layout of, and thus cope with, his environment) with his cane, we extend our interactive capabilities often without extending our sensual capabilities; the cane has no nerve endings but, as a tool of interaction and interference, can display for us the structure of the physical world.

One approaches the world by interacting with it, inserting oneself into the functional order, coming gradually to identify objects in terms of their place in the network of causal and equipmental contexts which we negotiate each day: chairs are for sitting, cups for drinking, and beds for sleeping. Likewise, interactions with the microscopic things of the world reveal for us their place in the extended causal networks with which scientists are familiar, and accepting their reality involves fitting them into that network which is ultimately continuous with the everyday. Thus as scientific entities become increasingly available to interaction, as the scientist moves beyond the possibility that he is dealing with an observational artifact and comes to understand, or perhaps to create, the functional role of the entity in the larger network of interlocking, causal interactions, then does the reality of that entity become apparent.   The suggestion is not that interactional information constitutes a more accurate representational schema than does sensation; the criteria of identity revealed through interaction are not "representational" at all: they do not depict objects, but characterize their functions.[16] These practical criteria nevertheless close the skeptical gap, for it is understood that such availability to interaction *constitutes* objecthood: it is a condition of being an object (a spatiotemporal particular) that it be available to material interaction.

The suggestions I have made here are simple, even if their consequences prove difficult to trace. First, I suggest that our primary epistemic relation to the world is not one in which an "external" world is present to us in the form of sensations from which we are meant to infer the structure of that world. Rather, we come to know our world through the activity of being in the world. Second, I have suggested that the world and its objects might usefully be characterized (metaphysically) in functional/ecological terms.   To accept both of these suggestions equips one to see beyond simple skepticisms, for on this model there need be no gap between knowledge and reality, whether in science or in everyday life.

Notes

1   In other words, we retroduce to an entity from the observed effects of that entity. (Retroduction is a form of induction whereby we postulate the existence of an entity as the cause of the observed effects). But the question arises: why claim existence for this unobserved entity? All we see are effects. In the interest of certainty, then, we should restrict our interpretations of science to observed correlations and physical laws: an instrumentalism which eschews existential claims. Such scientific idealism, like the epistemic and metaphysical idealisms of which it is a species, is unavoidable on the accepted assumptions of the debate. The task we face, then, is to challenge these assumptions.
2   There is an ambiguity here which it will be useful to note. To ask, as Descartes did, how we can continue to know the wax even after its properties have changed is to simultaneously ask two related questions: (1) How do we recognize it as wax (know its type-identity)? (2) How do we know that there is some particular instance of wax before us (know its existence)? Although I will be primarily interested in the first of these questions, it is not easily separated from the second; to make an identification is to assume there is something to identify. The particulars of my argument will be directed towards an answer to the first question, but a similar strategy can be employed in answering the second. (See my "Epistemology and Embodiment: Knowing the Boundaries of Material Particulars.")
3   See, of course, Martin Heidegger's *Being and Time*, trans. John Macquarrie and Edward Robinson (New York: Harper & Row, 1962), and "The Thing," in *Poetry, Language, Thought*, trans. Albert Hofstadter (New York: Harper & Row, 1971); but also Hubert Dreyfus, *Being-in-the-World* (Cambridge, MA: MIT Press, 1991); Charles

Guignon, *Heidegger and the Problem of Knowledge* (Indianapolis, IN: Hackett, 1983); and Mark Okrent, *Heidegger's Pragmatism* (Ithaca, NY: Cornell, 1988).
4   See, e.g., Ian Hacking, *Representing and Intervening* (Cambridge: Cambridge University Press, 1983).
5   Heidegger, *Being and Time*, p. 95.
6   Aristotle would add, with Wittgenstein, that they share a certain "look," a "family resemblance" uniting all objects of the given class. But the content and significance of this look is given by the function of the object, a place defined by its purpose in the interlocking nexus of causes and functions which constitutes the physical world. The function in terms of which the object is identified may be discovered, but not by observation alone.
7   In what follows, I will explain, but not defend, my reading of the significance of praxis in Aristotle's "epistemology." No doubt the reading deserves some defense, but I do not wish to mar the simplicity of this introduction given that the defensibility of my reading is a matter of complete indifference to its function as an illustration of the overall argument I am making.
8   See, for instance, Aristotle, Nicomachean Ethics 1114b: "But someone may say, 'Everyone aims at the apparent good, and does not control how it appears; on the contrary his character controls how the end appears to him.'" Character, of course, is acquired primarily through habit (practical activity).
   I think it is clear that for Aristotle's ethical system to work, perception—and with it the descriptions under which objects and events appear—must be sensitive to character and habituation. This is why he does not simply dismiss the objection as unfounded, but instead insists that actions will still "depend on the agent" insofar as character does.
9   I think we can fruitfully understand Aristotelian science as positing a kind of natural ecology, being the totality of these interacting natural tendencies. We are able to discover these tendencies precisely in virtue of our active presence in the world.
   In "Thought and Action in Aristotle," Elizabeth Anscombe develops doing as a way of knowing, as it appears in Aristotle's ethics. Beginning from considerations about deliberation, and its relation to the practical syllogism, she argues that for Aristotle deliberation is itself a kind of action—reason flows naturally into activity. It is a short step to posit the possibility of activity with its own (noncognitive) content, sufficiently robust to accept characterization in terms of truth and falsity, and it looks as though Anscombe has something of the sort in mind with her analysis of "practical truth": "It is practical truth when the judgements involved in the formation of the choice leading to the action are all true, but the practical truth is not the truth of those *judgements*. For it is clearly that 'truth in agreement with right desire' which is spoken of as the good working out of practical intelligence, that is brought about—i.e. is made true—by action. . . The notion of truth or falsehood in action would quite generally be countered with the objection that 'true' and 'false' are senseless predicates as applied to what is done. If I am right there is philosophy to the contrary in Aristotle." *From Parmenides to Wittgenstein,* (Minneapolis: University of Minnesota Press, 1990) p. 77.
10   Of course, things certainly have characteristic "looks," but the criterion of identity for such objects is not rooted in stereotypical appearance, but rather in functional/causal place, the myriad occupants of which place, being thereby of the same genera, often have similar affective, sensible properties.
11   As we know from the work of Richard Rorty, however, the skeptical problem re-

surfaces as soon as we interpret the "look" of the "thing for sitting" as a representation which may or may not correspond with reality. With this in mind, we can restate the problem being faced in this paper as such: we traditionally assess the truth of theoretical models in terms of their accuracy, that is, in terms of the appropriate correspondence of their depiction of the world to the world itself. But the demand for accuracy in this sense is fundamentally incoherent, for it is basic to any nonidealistic representational epistemology that representations are pictorial interpretations of the unrepresented world, and as such representations by definition fall short of that world. To use Kantian terms, it is part of the definition of the noumena that it is not available as such to representation; this is precisely what differentiates noumena from phenomena. To demand of phenomena that they accurately depict the state of the noumena is to demand the unreasonable. But insofar as this is true, there is always room for the skeptic: the gap between representation and reality is built into the schema.

But the ensuing dilemmas are based on a misappraisal of the significance and appropriate method of assessment of scientific theories. The ontological concepts of the theoretical model have practical content, and it is at this level that the appropriateness of a model to the world can be determined. Insofar as posited objects are available to manipulation of particular (perhaps predicted) sorts, the theoretical ontology is confirmed. Unlike in the case of representation, there is no gap for the skeptic: part of what it is to be an object (indeed, part of what it is for the world to be a world) is to be available to interaction and manipulation. What it is, then, to be a particular sort of object is to be available to a particular sort of interaction; it is in this sense, as I will claim later, that availability to manipulation and interaction constitutes objecthood.

12   The argument for the necessity of intervention to our individuation of material particulars is given in part IV of my *Content and Comportment* (forthcoming).

13   Ian Hacking, *Representing and Intervening*, p. 189.

14   Ibid., pp. 204-5.

15   Of course, it is no criticism of this model to adopt a bit of epistemic humility: we cannot know if or when we know *everything* about electrons, in either of the senses of "know." We may not be distinguishing between balpeen-electrons and carpenter's-electrons because we have not yet encountered them in the causal circumstances in which their functional-interactive differences become apparent. We can acknowledge our epistemic limitations, our finite grasp of the world, without despairing of the reliability and accuracy of our current know-how (and its requisite know-that). And insofar as interaction is a mode of epistemic *openness* to the world, the results of which can be attributed to the actual structure of the world, there is no reason to suppose that our continued interactions with the objects of the world, whether middle-sized or formerly hypothetical, will not lead us to a greater, more thorough, and increasingly appropriate understanding of the world and its objects.

16   Although, as I argue elsewhere, they do set the limits on representational depictions. See my *Content and Comportment,* esp. p. IV.

Index

action
  embodied, 128, 130
  in hysterical body, 34
  involuntary, 30, 33
  schema for, 27-29, 34
  skilled, 27-33
  "specific," 38*n*11
Adelman, Jane, 98, 101, 102
Adorno, Theodor, 102-21,124*n*25
aesthetics, defined, 113
Alexander, Samuel, 61
Altman, Stuart, 17
amputation, 49-50, 52, 57, 61
animism, 51
Anzaldua, Gloria, 67
aperture, 101
apparition, 52, 54-55, 58, 60
apperception, 17, 19, 145-46
Aristotle, 12, 19, 30, 150-51,
  156*n*6, 157*nn*8-10
Artaud, 69, 71-72
Atlantic Monthly, The, 47

Bailey, Allan, 50
Barker, Francis, 104
Barnett, Samuel, 18-19
Bataille, Georges, 98, 106*n*18,
  108*n*28
Becoming, 150-1
behavior, 4, 12, 15, 17, 19, 137
  of cells, 154

in Darwinian terms, 16
and hysteria, 34-36
in Nagelian terms, 18
neurotic, 51
rule-governed, 27-32
Being/being, 150-2, 156
Being and Time (Heidegger), 139
Beloved (Morrison), 77-88
Benjamin, Walter, 102, 104, 109*n*41
Berkeley, George, 61
Berlant, Lauren, 65
Berry, Wendell, 25
Bhabha, Homi, 67
blood, 99
body
  analytic, 67
  anatomy of, 15, 24, 82, 128
  Black, 65
  as bearer of content, 118
  boundaries, 57-59, 61, 64*n*54,
    96, 98
  in Cartesian Dualism, 1-3
  composition of limbs, 52
  as construction, 104
  cultural, 5, 31, 37, 60
  Darwinian, 11-19
  decay, 98, 108*nn*27-28
  density of, 34
  duplicate, 54-55
  female, 65-66
  gendered, 66

identity, 24, 78
related to body, 78
signs, 81
ghost stories, 51-52, 60-61
Gibson J. J., 134

Haber, W. B., 58
habitus, 30-31, 33-35, 40*n*25,
40*n*27, 41*n*41
Hacking, Ian, 146, 148, 153-54
Haldane, J. S., 12
Hamlet (Shakespeare)/Hamlet, 5-6,
93-105
Haraway, Donna, 67
Harlow, Henry, 17
Hebraic Scripture, 99
Heidegger, Martin, 13, 139-40, 148-
49
Henderson, Mae, 89*n*19
Hillman, David, 5-6, 89*n*14, 89*n*16
history, as story, 78
homosexuality, 100
Hughes, Langston, 69
Hume, David, 14, 146
Hunt, John, 105*n*3,105*n*5
Hurston, Z. N., 85
Husserl, Edmund, 14, 24, 139
Hwang, David, 89*n*13
hysteria, 26, 34-37, 42*n*43

Iago, 122*n*1, 125*n*38
idealism, 2
identity, 38*n*7, 65-74
bodily ego, 59
as constituted, 80
as construct, 81, 86
gender, 78
grounded in body, 27, 88
of object/thing,148-50, 153-55,
157*n*11
personal, 13, 48-49, 52, 143*n*27
sexual, 31
images

in emotion formation, 136-37
of women in advertisements, 80
imagination, 113
*Imperceptible Mutabilities in the
Third Kingdom* (Parks), 70-71
incest, 100-2, 109*n*37
inference/induction, 146-47, 152
from appearance, 148, 153
to best explanation, 153
innards, 6, 93, 97
as food, 98
See also entrails
interaction, experimental, 152-55
intimacy, 84
introspection, 95
Irigaray, Luce, 24

James, William, 55, 135
Janette, Michele, 5
Jaynes, Julian, 124*n*21
Johnson, Mark, 127
Johnstone, Albert A., 7*n*8
Jones, Ernest, 100
Joyce, James, 121

Kant, Immanuel, 28, 113, 114, 118,
122
Kaplan, Bernard, 115, 116
Katwan, Ron, 7*n*9
kinesis, 118-19
Kingston, Maxine Hong, 77-88
kneading, 84
knowledge, 2, 48, 148, 151, 156
scientific, 146-7
visceral, 93-105
Kohut, Heinz, 103
Kolb, Lawrence, 59

Laban, Rudolf, 119
Laban notation, 119
Lacan, Jacques, 26-27, 67, 97
language, 5, 15, 24, 134
aesthetic, 4, 113-122

About the Editor

Michael O'Donovan-Anderson holds a Ph.D. in philosophy from Yale University. He is the author of several articles in philosophy and political theory, and of the forthcoming monograph *Content and Comportment: On Embodiment and the Epistemic Availability of the World.* He has taught philosophy at Yale, Harvard, and Stonehill College and is currently a member of the scientific staff at Language Engineering Corporation, a language and computing think-tank and software development company in Belmont, Massachusetts.